JUDGMENT IN MANAGERIAL DECISION MAKING

FIFTH EDITION

MAX H. BAZERMAN

Jesse Isador Straus Professor
of Business Administration
Harvard Business School

JOHN WILEY & SONS

Acquisitions Editor	Jeff Marshall
Marketing Manager	Charity Robey
Senior Production Editor	Norine M. Pigliucci
Senior Designer	Dawn Stanley
Production Management Services	Suzanne Ingrao

This book was set in New Caledonia by Binghamton Valley Composition and printed and bound by Courier Westford. The cover was printed by Lehigh Press.

This book is printed on acid-free paper. ∞

Library of Congress Cataloging in Publication Data
Bazerman, Max H.
  Judgment in managerial decision making / Max H. Bazerman.—5th ed.
    p. cm.
  ISBN 0-471-39887-X (pbk. : alk. paper)
  1. Decision-making.   2. Judgment.   3. Management.   I. Title.
HD30.23.B38   2001
658.4'03—dc21   2001017850

Printed in the United States of America

10 9 8 7 6 5 4

Dedicated to Katie Shonk, who makes my writing clear.

PREFACE

Between 1981 and 1983, I served on the faculty of the Organizational Behavior Department at Boston University. At the time, I was working on several laboratory studies on decision biases in negotiation. The faculty at Boston University provided me with a number of excellent colleagues, and yet they knew very little about the emerging research on judgment. This lack of awareness in colleagues that I respected motivated me to write this book. I wanted to make the area of judgment a more central part of the management literature. I also wanted to present this information to managers, students, and researchers in an interesting manner that would improve their judgment capabilities.

Behavioral decision research has developed considerably over the past 25 years, and now provides considerable insights into managerial decision making. This book attempts to embed behavioral decision research into the organizational realm by examining judgment in a variety of managerial contexts. The first seven chapters of the book provide readers with an opportunity to examine their individual judgment. Beginning with Chapter 8, the book shifts to consider a variety of interpersonal contexts that affect judgment.

The audience for this book is anyone who is interested in improving his or her judgment and decision making. The first four editions were used in economics, psychology, and organizational behavior courses, and in a variety of executive programs as well. The book does not assume advanced knowledge of statistics, psychology, economics, or decision making. Rather, the book presents new research insights in an accessible form. For the psychology audience, the book offers a systematic framework for using psychological findings to improve judgment. For the economics audience, the book offers a critique of the classic economic model of decision making. For the consumer, management, and financial communities, this book creates opportunities to make better decisions.

In the first edition, I noted that many fine colleagues influenced my understanding of judgment: Joel Brockner, Ed Conlon, Pete Fader, Hank Farber, Toni Giuliano, Harry Katz, Tom Kochan, Leigh McAlister, Bob McKersie, Maggie Neale, Jeff Rubin, Bill Samuelson, and David Schoorman. Four people read the entire original manuscript and provided extremely helpful feedback and support during the three years of its creation: John Carroll, Marla Felcher, Tim Hall, and Roy Lewicki. Each helped in important ways as I was assembling my understanding of judgment.

In July 1985, just as I was finishing the first edition, I joined the Organization Behavior Department of the J. L. Kellogg Graduate School of Management at Northwestern University, which provided me with an exciting research and teaching environment for 15 years. While I recently moved to Harvard University, Northwestern will always remain an important institution to me. My continuing interactions with excellent colleagues at these schools and others have been the primary sources of ideas that have improved later editions of this book. These colleagues include Jon

Baron, Sally Blount, Jeanne Brett, Tina Diekmann, Linda Ginzel, Bob Gibbons, Andy Hoffman, Don Jacobs, Boaz Keysar, George Loewenstein, Beta Mannix, David Messick, Don Moore, Keith Murnighan, Al Roth, Holly Schroth, Pri Pradhan Shah, Harris Sondak, Ann Tenbrunsel, Leigh Thompson, Mike Tushman, Kathleen Valley, and Kimberly Wade-Benzoni. The book has also benefited over the course of its editions from valuable student feedback.

A dramatic improvement in this book occurred between the first and second editions as a result of the excellent critical review and editing of Sally Blount. I hired Sally (when she was a graduate student at Kellogg) to do a final reading of the book. Instead, she provided a detailed critique of each chapter, offered specific reorganizing suggestions, and drafted numerous changes that improved the book.

The third edition added a new chapter (now Chapter 6) on fairness, social comparison processes, and decision making. The fourth edition added a new chapter on motivational biases (now Chapter 4). The fifth edition now adds a new chapter that applies the book's main concepts to the domain of investing (Chapter 7). This new chapter benefited from very insightful input from three dedicated readers: Don Moore, Terry Odean, and Jason Zweig. Don is my excellent research colleague and friend. Terry has done much of the most exciting behavioral finance research in recent years. And Jason is the world's best journalist covering money issues. The area of behavioral finance has been one of the most exciting developments to emerge from the study of judgment errors. I hope that this new chapter is interesting and that it will save you lots of money. Of course, in addition to the new chapter, I have updated the entire book with new ideas, examples, and applications.

Finally, the book has benefited from fantastic editorial help. Claire Buisseret and Rachel Campagna have provided useful editorial input that has improved the clarity of this book. Katie Shonk has researched, edited, or rewritten most of my work over the last ten years, including this book. My most significant skill in the writing domain is to realize that Katie is a much better writer than I am, and to value her skill sufficiently to allow it to show in my work.

In sum, this book has been enriched by my interactions with an unusually large number of people. Perhaps my most important skills are my ability to persuade excellent people to work with me and my ability to appreciate their innovative ideas. I believe that these skills have helped to create a book that will improve the decision-making skills of its readers, and I hope that you agree.

Max H. Bazerman

CONTENTS

CHAPTER ONE

Introduction to Managerial Decision Making

Phar-Mor, Inc., the nation's largest discount drugstore chain, filed for bankruptcy court protection in 1992, following discovery of one of the largest business fraud and embezzlement schemes in U.S. history. Coopers and Lybrand, Phar-Mor's former auditors, failed to detect inventory inflation and other financial manipulations that resulted in $985 million of earnings overstatements over a three-year period.

A federal jury unanimously found Coopers and Lybrand liable to a group of investors on fraud charges. The successful plaintiffs contended that Gregory Finerty, the Coopers and Lybrand partner in charge of the Phar-Mor audit, was "hungry for business because he had been passed over for additional profit-sharing in 1988 for failing to sell enough of the firm's services" (*Pittsburgh Post-Gazette*, February 15, 1996). In 1989, Finerty began selling services to relatives and associates of Phar-Mor's president and CEO (who has been sentenced to prison and fined for his part in the fraud). Critics claim Finerty may have become too close to client management to maintain the professional skepticism necessary for the conduct of an independent audit.

The Phar-Mor case is just one of many in which auditors have been held accountable for certification of faulty financial statements. Investors in the Miniscribe Corporation maintained that auditors were at least partially responsible for the now-defunct company's falsified financial statements; at least one jury agreed, holding the auditors liable to investors for $200 million. In the wake of the U.S. savings–and–loan crisis, audit firms faced a barrage of lawsuits, paying hundreds of millions in judgments and out-of-court settlements for their involvement in the financial reporting process of savings–and–loan clients that eventually failed.

The auditing partners of Coopers and Lybrand, like partners of other firms held liable for such negligence, are very bright people. In addition, I believe that they are generally very honest people. So, how could a prominent auditing firm with a reputation for intelligence and integrity have overlooked such large misstatements in Phar-Mor's financial records? How could auditors have failed to see that so many of their savings-and-loan clients were on the brink of failure? Critics of the profession suggest that auditor neglect and corruption may be responsible. In fact, very rarely do audit failures result from deliberate collusion of the auditor with its client in the issuance of faulty financial statements. Instead, audit failures are the predictable result of systematic biases in judgment. This book provides the tools to help you avoid these errors. By eliminating biases from your decision-making patterns, you can become a better decision maker and protect yourself, your family, and your organization from avoidable mistakes.

This book (Chapter 4, specifically) will provide evidence that it is psychologically impossible for auditors to maintain their objectivity; cases of audit failure are inevitable, even from the most honest of firms. Psychological research shows that expecting objective judgment from an auditor hired by the auditee is unrealistic. Although deliberate misreporting can occur, bias more typically becomes an unconscious, unintentional factor at the stage where judgments are made. When people are called upon to make impartial judgments, those judgments are likely to be unconsciously and powerfully biased in a manner that is commensurate with the judge's self-interest. Psychologists call this the self-serving bias (Messick and Sentis, 1985). When presented with identical information, individual perceptions of a situation differ dramatically depending on one's role in the situation. Individuals first determine their preference for a certain outcome on the basis of self-interest and then justify this preference on the basis of fairness by changing the importance of attributes affecting what is fair. Thus, the problem is not typically a desire to be unfair, but our inability to interpret information in an unbiased manner (Diekmann, Samuels, Ross, and Bazerman, 1997). The self-serving bias exists because people are imperfect information processors. One of the most important subjective influences on information processing is self-interest. People tend to confuse what is personally beneficial with what is fair or moral.

We have begun a new century with a vast amount of knowledge about how to use technology to integrate data and make routine decisions. However, computers cannot make decisions involving values and risk preferences. Here, human judgment is required. What advice was available to Coopers and Lybrand? The material in this book would have introduced the firm's partners to a number of cognitive biases that are predictable and likely to affect auditor judgment. Knowledge of these biases can be used to make more rational decisions. By identifying cognitive biases and suggesting strategies for overcoming them, this book gives managers the skills they need to improve their judgment.

Although most managerial decisions concern considerably less than $985 million, situations that require careful judgment arise continually in our daily lives. Such judgment is a major component of managerial work at all levels of the corporate world. Many managers accept judgment as innate: "Some people have it and others do not." This attitude can waste critical human resources in organizations. While decision-making skills may be partially innate, training can have a significant effect on the quality of managerial judgment.

THE ANATOMY OF A DECISION

Judgment refers to the cognitive aspects of the decision-making process. To fully understand judgment, we first need to identify the components of the decision-making process that require it. To get started, consider the following decision situations:

- You are finishing your MBA at a well-known school. Your credentials are quite good, and you expect to obtain job offers from a number of "dot com" start-ups. How are you going to select the right job?
- You are the director of the marketing division of a rapidly expanding consumer company. You need to hire a product manager for a new "secret" product that the company plans to introduce to the market in 15 months. How will you go about hiring the appropriate individual?
- As the owner of a venture capital firm, you have a number of proposals that meet your preliminary considerations but only a limited budget with which to fund new projects. Which projects will you fund?
- You are on the corporate acquisition staff of a large conglomerate that is interested in acquiring a small-to-moderate-sized firm in the oil industry. What firm, if any, will you advise the company to acquire?

What do these scenarios have in common? Each one proposes a problem, and each problem has a number of alternative solutions. Let us look at six steps you should take, either implicitly or explicitly, when applying a "rational" decision-making process to each scenario.

1. **Define the problem.**   The problem has been fairly well specified in each of the four scenarios. However, managers often act without a thorough understanding of the problem to be solved, leading them to solve the wrong problem. Accurate judgment is required to identify and define the problem. Managers often err by (a) defining the problem in terms of a proposed solution, (b) missing a bigger problem, or (c) diagnosing the problem in terms of its symptoms. Our goal should be to solve the problem, not just eliminate its temporary symptoms.

2. **Identify the criteria.**   Most decisions require the decision maker to accomplish more than one objective. When buying a car, you may want to maximize fuel economy, minimize cost, maximize comfort, and so on. The rational decision maker will identify all relevant criteria in the decision-making process.

3. **Weight the criteria.**   Different criteria will be of varying importance to a decision maker. Rational decision makers will know the relative value that they place on each of the criteria identified (for example, the relative importance of fuel economy versus cost versus comfort).

4. **Generate alternatives.**   The fourth step in the decision-making process requires identification of possible courses of action. Decision makers often spend an inappropriate amount of search time seeking alternatives, creating a barrier to effective decision making. An optimal search continues only until the cost of the search outweighs the value of the added information.

5. **Rate each alternative on each criterion.** How well will each of the alternative solutions achieve each of the defined criteria? This is often the most difficult stage of the decision-making process, as it typically requires us to forecast future events. The rational decision maker will be able to carefully assess the potential consequences of selecting each of the alternative solutions on each of the identified criteria.

6. **Compute the optimal decision.** Ideally, after all of the first five steps have been completed, the process of computing the optimal decision consists of (1) multiplying the ratings in step 5 by the weight of each criterion, (2) adding up the weighted ratings across all of the criteria for each alternative, and (3) choosing the solution with the highest sum of the weighted ratings.

The model of decision making just presented assumes that we follow these six steps in a fully "rational" manner. That is, decision makers are assumed to (1) perfectly define the problem, (2) identify all criteria, (3) accurately weigh all of the criteria according to their preferences, (4) know all relevant alternatives, (5) accurately assess each alternative based on each criterion, and (6) accurately calculate and choose the alternative with the highest perceived value.

There is nothing special about these six steps. Different researchers specify different steps—which typically overlap a great deal. For example, in a wonderful recent book on rational decision making, Hammond, Keeney, and Raiffa (1999) suggest eight steps: (1) work on the right problem, (2) specify your objectives, (3) create imaginative alternatives, (4) understand the consequences, (5) grapple with your tradeoffs, (6) clarify your uncertainties, (7) think hard about your risk tolerance, and (8) consider linked decisions. Both of these lists provide a useful order for thinking about what an optimal decision-making process might look like.

THE BOUNDS OF RATIONALITY

In this book, the term *rationality* refers to the decision-making process that is logically expected to lead to the optimal result, given an accurate assessment of the decision maker's values and risk preferences. The rational model is based on a set of assumptions that prescribe how a decision *should* be made rather than describing how a decision *is* made. In his Nobel Prize-winning work, Simon (1957; March and Simon, 1958) suggested that individual judgment is bounded in its rationality and that we can better understand decision making by explaining actual, rather than normative ("what should be done"), decision processes. While the bounded-rationality framework views individuals as attempting to make rational decisions, it acknowledges that decision makers often lack important information on the definition of the problem, the relevant criteria, and so on. Time and cost constraints limit the quantity and quality of available information. Furthermore, decision makers retain only a relatively small amount of information in their usable memory. Finally, limitations on intelligence and perceptions constrain the ability of decision makers to accurately "calculate" the optimal choice from the information that is available. Together, these limitations prevent decision makers from making the optimal decisions assumed by the rational model. The irrational decisions that result typically reflect a reliance on intuitive biases that overlook the full range of possible consequences. Decision makers will forego the best solution in favor of one that is acceptable or reasonable. That is, decision makers *satisfice*. Rather than examining all possible alternatives, they simply search until they find a solution that meets a certain acceptable level of performance.

The field of decision making can be loosely divided into two parts: the study of prescriptive models and the study of descriptive models. Prescriptive decision scientists develop methods for making optimal decisions. For example, they might suggest a mathematical model to help a decision maker act more rationally. Descriptive decision researchers consider the bounded ways in which decisions are actually made. Why use a descriptive approach when a prescriptive approach should lead to an optimal decision? My answer is that there is plenty of good advice available, and yet most people do not follow it. Why not? Because we fall victim to a variety of predictable errors that not only destroy our intuition, but also hinder our tendency to implement good advice. We need to understand these mistakes before moving on to wiser decision strategies.

Although the concepts of bounded rationality and satisficing are important in showing that judgment deviates from rationality, they do not tell us *how* judgment will be biased. These concepts help decision makers identify situations in which they may be acting on the basis of limited information, but they do not help diagnose the specific systematic, directional biases that affect our judgment. Fifteen years after the publication of Simon's work, Tversky and Kahneman (1974) continued what he had begun. They provided critical information about specific systematic biases that influence judgment. Their work, and work that followed, led to our modern understanding of judgment. Specifically, researchers have found that people rely on a number of simplifying strategies, or rules of thumb, in making decisions. These simplifying strategies are called *heuristics*. As the standard rules that implicitly direct our judgment, heuristics serve as a mechanism for coping with the complex environment surrounding our decisions. In general, heuristics are helpful, but their use can sometimes lead to severe errors. A central goal of this book is to identify and illustrate these heuristics and the biases that can result from them in the managerial setting. I will use examples of a variety of heuristics and biases to explain how people deviate from a fully rational decision process in individual and competitive situations.

Recently, Thaler (2000) has suggested that there are three categories of ways in which human beings are quasi-rational. One category is Simon's concept of bounded rationality, which was developed by Kahneman and Tversky. Second, Thaler suggests that we have bounded willpower. That is, we tend to give greater weight to present concerns than to future concerns, leading to a variety of ways in which our temporary motivations are inconsistent with long-term interests—for example, undersaving for retirement (this will be developed in Chapters 4 and 7). Finally, Thaler suggests that our self-interest is bounded; unlike the stereotypic economic actor, we care about the outcomes of others (this will be developed in Chapter 6). Overall, this book is consistent with Thaler's view of the quasi-rational decision maker, affected by bounded rationality, bounded willpower, and bounded self-interest.

INTRODUCTION TO JUDGMENTAL HEURISTICS

Consider the following example:

> While finishing an advanced degree in computer science, Marla Bannon put together a Web-based retailing concept that many of her colleagues consider to be one of the best ever developed. Although the product is great, Marla has far less skill in marketing her ideas, so she decides to hire a marketing MBA with experience in Web-based environments to formalize the business plan she will use to approach venture capitalists. Marla follows the heuristic of limiting her search to new MBAs from the top six management schools. How would you evaluate Bannon's strategy?

If we evaluate this strategy in terms of the degree to which it follows the rational model outlined earlier, Bannon's heuristic of limiting her search to six schools will be deficient, because her search will not be complete. Her heuristic may eliminate the best possible candidates from consideration if they do not attend one of the top schools. However, the heuristic also has some benefits. While it could eliminate the best choice, the expected time savings of focusing on only six schools may outweigh any potential loss resulting from Bannon's limited search strategy. For this reason, this job search heuristic could produce more good decisions than bad ones. In fact, economists would argue that individuals use heuristics such as this because the benefit of time saved often outweighs the costs of any potential reduction in the quality of the decision.

Heuristics provide time-pressured managers and other professionals with a simple way of dealing with a complex world, usually producing correct or partially correct judgments. In addition, it may be inevitable that humans will adopt some way of simplifying decisions. The only drawback of these heuristics is that individuals frequently are unaware that they rely on them. Unfortunately, the misapplication of heuristics to inappropriate situations leads people astray. When managers become aware of the potential adverse impact of using heuristics, they will be able to decide when and where to use them and, if it is to their advantage, eliminate certain heuristics from their cognitive repertoire.

People use a variety of types of heuristics. The poker player follows the heuristic "never play for an inside straight." The mortgage banker follows the heuristic "only spend 35 percent of your income on housing." Although an understanding of these specific heuristics is important to the poker player and mortgage banker, our concern in this book is with more general cognitive heuristics that affect virtually all individuals. Thus, the heuristics described next are not specific to particular individuals; rather, research has shown that they can be applied across the population. The three general heuristics that we will focus on are (1) the availability heuristic, (2) the representativeness heuristic, and (3) anchoring and adjustment.

The Availability Heuristic

People assess the frequency, probability, or likely causes of an event by the degree to which instances or occurrences of that event are readily "available" in memory

(Tversky and Kahneman, 1973). An event that evokes emotions and is vivid, easily imagined, and specific will be more available than an event that is unemotional in nature, bland, difficult to imagine, or vague. For example, a subordinate who works in close proximity to the manager's office will receive a more critical performance evaluation at year-end than a worker who sits down the hall, since the manager will be more aware of the nearby subordinate's errors. Similarly, a product manager will base her assessment of the probability of a new product's success on her recollection of the successes and failures of similar products in the recent past. Peter Lynch, the former director of Fidelity's Magellan Fund (one of the two largest mutual funds), argues in favor of buying stock in firms that are unavailable in the minds of most investors (for example, due to their blandness) because the more available the stock is, the more overvalued it will be. The availability heuristic can be a very useful managerial decision-making strategy, since instances of events of greater frequency are generally revealed more easily in our minds than less frequent events. Consequently, this heuristic will often lead to accurate judgment. This heuristic is fallible, however, because the availability of information is also affected by factors unrelated to the objective frequency of the judged event. These irrelevant factors can inappropriately influence an event's immediate perceptual salience, the vividness with which it is revealed, or the ease with which it is imagined.

The Representativeness Heuristic

When making a judgment about an individual (or object or event), people tend to look for traits an individual may have that correspond with previously formed stereotypes. "A botanist assigns a plant to one species rather than another by using this judgment strategy," wrote Nisbett and Ross (1980, p. 7). "The plant is categorized as belonging to the species that its principal features most nearly resemble." In this case, the degree to which the unknown plant is representative of a known species of plant is the best information available to the botanist. Managers also use the representativeness heuristic. They predict a person's performance based on an established category of persons that the focal individual represents for them. They predict the success of a new product based on the similarity of that product to past successful and unsuccessful product types. In some cases, the use of the heuristic is a good first-cut approximation. In other cases, it leads to behavior that many of us find irrational and morally reprehensible—like discrimination. A clear problem is that individuals tend to rely on such strategies even when information is insufficient and when better information exists with which to make an accurate judgment.

Anchoring and Adjustment

People make assessments by starting from an initial value and adjusting to yield a final decision. The initial value, or "anchor," may be suggested from historical precedent, from the way in which a problem is presented, or from random information. For example, managers make salary decisions by adjusting from an employee's past year's salary. In ambiguous situations, a trivial factor can have a profound effect on our decision if it serves as an anchor from which we make adjustments. Frequently, people will realize the unreasonableness of the anchor (for example, "the other firm was paying her only $22,000 a year"), yet their adjustment will often remain irrationally close to this anchor. Dawes (1988) points out that after having a good meal in a restaurant, we have an unrealistically high expectation for future meals at that restaurant as a result of anchoring. (The section on regression to the mean in Chapter 2 will clarify why you might more rationally reduce your expectations in the future.) The key conclusion is that, regardless of the basis of the initial value, adjustments from the initial value tend to be insufficient (Slovic and Lichtenstein, 1971; Tversky and Kahneman, 1974). Thus, different initial values can yield different decisions for the same problem.

AN OUTLINE OF THINGS TO COME

The main objective of this book is to improve the reader's judgment. How can the book help improve Marla Bannon's judgment? First, we must identify the errors in her intuitive judgment, making her aware of biases that are likely to affect her decision. This awareness will improve her current decision-making process and lead to a more beneficial outcome. However, Lewin (1947) suggests that in order for change to occur and last over time, the individual must do more than simply be aware of imperfections. For change to be successful, Lewin argues, it is necessary to (1) get the individual to "unfreeze" existing decision-making processes, (2) provide the content necessary for change, and (3) create the conditions that "refreeze" new processes, thus making the change part of the manager's standard repertoire. This book will attempt to unfreeze your present decision-making processes by demonstrating how your judgment systematically deviates from rationality. You will also be given tools to allow you to change your decision-making processes. Finally, the book will discuss methods that you can use to refreeze your thinking to ensure that the changes will last.

Nisbett and Ross (1980, pp. xi–xii) write:

> One of philosophy's oldest paradoxes is the apparent contradiction between the greatest triumphs and the dramatic failures of the human mind. The same organism that routinely solves inferential problems too subtle and complex for the mightiest computers often makes errors in the simplest of judgments about everyday events. The errors, moreover, often seem traceable to violations of the same inferential rules that underlie people's most impressive successes. . . . How can any creature skilled enough to build and maintain complex organizations, or sophisticated enough to appreciate the nuances of social intercourse, be foolish enough to mouth racist clichés or spill its lifeblood in pointless wars?

While Nisbett and Ross refer to the general population, the essence of their question defines a fascinating issue for the field of managerial effectiveness. This book views managers as intelligent employees who have been generally successful, but whose decisions are biased in ways that seriously compromise their potential. The reader will see how habit forces us into a set of hard-to-break heuristics, imposing constraints on our decision-making effectiveness.

Before individuals can change their decision-making processes, they must be convinced that elements of their cognitive repertoire could use improvement—that is, the unfreezing process must occur. The reader might ask, "Why should I change my existing decision-making processes when I've been so successful throughout my managerial career?" In response to this very appropriate question, I include a number of experiential decision-making items that encourage the reader to personally identify with the biases that are discussed. In presenting this material to MBA and executive students in a classroom setting, I have found that many individuals are initially offended by being "tricked" by an "ivory-tower" academic. It might be helpful to clarify at the outset that my intention is not to insult the reader, but to help identify and communicate biases that generally affect human judgment. Perhaps one reason for my personal interest in this material lies in my discomfort with the fact that many of these "evil" biases affect my own personal judgment.

Chapters 2 through 7 focus on individual decision making. In these chapters, little attention is given to the fact that many managerial decisions are made in conjunction with other individuals. Instead, the focus is simply on how individuals approach decisions. Chapters 8 and 9 reexamine judgment in the context of negotiation. Chapter 10 summarizes the book's arguments and focuses on how to incorporate the changes suggested throughout into the reader's decision-making processes. Specifically, the remaining chapters will focus on the following:

Chapter 2. This chapter identifies and illustrates a series of specific biases that affect the judgment of virtually all managers. These biases are caused by the three heuristics described in this chapter. Quiz items and short scenarios demonstrate these biases and emphasize their prevalence.

Chapter 3. Most management students are formally taught about the concept of risk in a microeconomics or statistics course. These courses typically treat risk from a prescriptive perspective, by suggesting rational methods for making decisions involving risk. This chapter expands on this approach by examining the psychological factors that explain how managers deviate from "rationality" in responding to uncertainty.

Chapter 4. Are there biases that are created by the self-serving motivations of individuals, rather than by purely cognitive mistakes? This chapter complements the presentation of cognitive biases in Chapters 1, 2, 3, and 5 with an overview of "motivated biases."

Chapter 5. There is much evidence that managerial decision makers who commit themselves to a particular course of action may make subsequent nonoptimal decisions in order to justify their previous commitment. This chapter examines the research evidence and psychological explanations for this behavior. We will see how escalation has a significant effect in a variety of managerial domains, including new product development, bank loans, and performance appraisal.

Chapter 6. When do people care about fairness? When will individuals accept nonoptimal outcomes in order to maintain fairness? This chapter examines how we think about fairness and explores inconsistencies in our assessments of fairness.

Chapter 7. Perhaps the research area that has been most influenced by decision research has been behavioral finance. In the last decade, we have learned a great deal about the mistakes that investors commonly make. This chapter will explore these mistakes and apply the messages of the book to help readers become wiser investors.

Chapter 8. This chapter outlines a framework to help the reader think about two-party negotiations. The focus is on how you can make decisions to maximize the joint gain available in a two-party decision-making situation, while simultaneously thinking about how to obtain as much of that joint gain as possible for yourself.

Chapter 9. This chapter looks at the judgmental mistakes we make in negotiations. The resulting framework shows how consumers, managers, salespersons, and society as a whole can benefit simultaneously by debiasing their negotiations.

Chapter 10. The final chapter evaluates five explicit strategies for improving judgment: (1) acquiring expertise, (2) debiasing, (3) taking an outside view, (4) using linear models, and (5) adjusting intuitive predictions. This chapter will teach you how to use the information in this book to create permanent improvements in your future decisions.

CHAPTER TWO

Common Biases

People make mistakes. More interestingly, people make a variety of systematic and predictable mistakes. The predictability of these mistakes means that once we identify them, we can learn to avoid them. As explained in Chapter 1, individuals develop rules of thumb, or heuristics, to reduce the information-processing demands of decision making. By providing managers with efficient ways of dealing with complex problems, heuristics produce good decisions a significant proportion of the time. However, heuristics also can lead managers to make systematically biased mistakes. Cognitive bias occurs in situations in which an individual inappropriately applies a heuristic when making a decision.

By highlighting a number of mistakes that even very smart people make on a regular basis, this chapter offers you the opportunity to audit your own decision-making process and identify the biases that affect you. Throughout the chapter, quiz items allow you to examine your problem-solving abilities and discover how your judgments compare to those of others. The quiz items illustrate 13 predictable biases that frequently lead managers to judgments that systematically deviate from rationality.

To begin, answer the following two problems:

Problem 1. The following 10 corporations were ranked by *Fortune* magazine to be among the largest 500 United States-based firms according to sales revenues for 1999:

Group A: Avis Rent a Car, TWA, Hershey Foods, Barnes and Noble, Hasbro

Group B: SBC Communications, McKesson, Ingram Micro, United Technologies, Utilicorp United

Which group of five organizations listed (A or B) had the larger total sales revenues?

Problem 2 (Adapted from Kahneman and Tversky, 1973). The best student in my introductory MBA class this past semester writes poetry and is rather shy and small in stature. What was the student's undergraduate major:

(A) Chinese studies or (B) Psychology?

If you answered A for each of the two problems, you may gain comfort in knowing that the majority of respondents choose A. If you answered B, you are in the minority. In this case, however, the minority represents the correct response. All corporations in group B were ranked in the Fortune 100, while none of the corporations in group A had sales as large. In fact, the total sales for group B was more than eight times the total sales for group A. In the second problem, the student described was actually a psychology major, but more important, selecting psychology as the student's major represents a more rational response given the limited information.

Problem 1 illustrates the availability heuristic discussed in Chapter 1. In this problem, group A consists of consumer firms, while group B consists of firms less well known to consumers. Because most of us are more familiar with consumer firms than conglomerates, we can more easily generate information in our minds about their size. If we were aware of our bias resulting from the availability heuristic, we would recognize our differential exposure to this information and adjust our judgments accordingly, or at least question them.

Problem 2 illustrates the representativeness heuristic. The reader who responds "Chinese studies" has probably overlooked relevant base-rate information—namely, the likely ratio of Chinese studies majors to psychology majors within the MBA student population. When asked to reconsider the problem in this context, most people acknowledge the relative scarcity of Chinese studies majors seeking MBAs, and change their response to "psychology." This example emphasizes that logical base-rate reasoning is often overwhelmed by qualitative judgments drawn from available descriptive information.

Problems 1 and 2 demonstrate how easy it is to draw faulty conclusions when we over-rely on cognitive heuristics. Throughout this chapter, additional quiz items are presented to further increase your awareness of the impact of heuristics on your decisions and to help you develop an appreciation for the systematic errors that emanate from overdependence on them. The 13 biases examined in this chapter are relevant to virtually all individuals. Each bias is related to at least one of the three judgmental heuristics introduced in Chapter 1, and an effort has been made to categorize them accordingly. However, the way our minds develop and use heuristics is not straightforward. Often, when we approach cognitive tasks, we use heuristics in tandem.

The goal of the chapter is to help you "unfreeze" your decision-making patterns by showing you how easily heuristics become biases when improperly applied. By working on numerous problems that demonstrate the failures of these heuristics, you will become more aware of the biases in your decision making. Once you are able to spot these biases, you will be able to improve the quality of your decisions.

Before reading further, please take a few minutes to respond to the problems presented in Table 2.1.

TABLE 2.1   Chapter Problems

Respond to the following problems before reading the chapter.

Problem 3: Which of the following lists was the cause of more premature deaths in the United States in 1999?

a. Tobacco use, obesity/inactivity, and alcohol   **b.** Cancer, heart disease, and auto accidents

Problem 4a: In four pages of a novel (about 2,000 words), how many words would you expect to find that have the form _ _ _ _ing (seven-letter words that end with "ing")? Indicate your best estimate by circling one of the following values:

$$0 \quad 1\text{–}2 \quad 3\text{–}4 \quad 5\text{–}7 \quad 8\text{–}10 \quad 11\text{–}15 \quad 16+$$

Problem 4b: In four pages of a novel (about 2,000 words), how many words would you expect to find that have the form _ _ _ _ _n_ (seven-letter words that have the letter "n" in the sixth position)? Indicate your best estimate by circling one of the following values:

$$0 \quad 1\text{–}2 \quad 3\text{–}4 \quad 5\text{–}7 \quad 8\text{–}10 \quad 11\text{–}15 \quad 16+$$

Problem 5: Mark is finishing his MBA at a prestigious university. He is very interested in the arts and at one time considered a career as a musician. Is he more likely to take a job:

(A) in arts management, or (B) with an Internet start-up?

Problem 6 (from Tversky and Kahneman, 1974): A certain town is served by two hospitals. In the larger hospital about 45 babies are born each day and in the smaller hospital about 15 babies are born each day. As you know, about 50 percent of all babies are boys. However, the exact percentage varies from day to day. Sometimes it may be higher than 50 percent, sometimes lower.

For a period of one year, each hospital recorded the days in which more than 60 percent of the babies born were boys. Which hospital do you think recorded more such days?

(A) The larger hospital.   (B) The smaller hospital.

(C) About the same (that is, within 5 percent of each other).

Problem 7: You have started buying stocks on the Internet, beginning with five different stocks. Each stock goes down soon after your purchase. As you prepare to make a sixth purchase, you reason that it should be more successful, since the last five were "lemons." After all, the odds favor making at least one successful pick in six decisions. This thinking is:

(A) correct   (B) incorrect.

Problem 8: You are the sales forecaster for a department store chain with nine locations. The chain depends on you for quality projections of future sales in order to make decisions on staffing, advertising, information system developments, purchasing, renovation, and the like. All stores are similar in size and merchandise selection. The main difference in their sales occurs because of location and random fluctuations. Sales for 2000 were as follows:

Store	2000	2002
1	$12,000,000	
2	11,500,000	
3	11,000,000	
4	10,500,000	
5	10,000,000	
6	9,500,000	
7	9,000,000	
8	8,500,000	
9	8,000,000	
TOTAL	$90,000,000	$99,000,000

(continued)

TABLE 2.1   (*continued*)

Your economic forecasting service has convinced you that the best estimate of total sales increases between 2000 and 2002 is 10 percent (to $99,000,000). Your task is to predict 2002 sales for each store. Since your manager believes strongly in the economic forecasting service, it is imperative that your total sales equal $99,000,000.

Problem 9:   Linda is 31 years old, single, outspoken, and very bright. She majored in philosophy. As a student, she was deeply concerned with issues of discrimination and social justice, and she participated in antinuclear demonstrations.

Rank order the following eight descriptions in terms of the probability (likelihood) that they describe Linda:

__ a.   Linda is a teacher in an elementary school.

__ b.   Linda works in a bookstore and takes yoga classes.

__ c.   Linda is active in the feminist movement.

__ d.   Linda is a psychiatric social worker.

__ e.   Linda is a member of the League of Women Voters.

__ f.   Linda is a bank teller.

__ g.   Linda is an insurance salesperson.

__ h.   Linda is a bank teller who is active in the feminist movement.

Problem 10:   A new Internet company recently made its initial public offering, becoming publicly traded. At its opening, the stock sold for $20/share. The company's closest competitor went public one year ago, also at a price of $20/share. The competitor's stock is now priced at $100/share. What will the new firm be worth one year from now?

$_____/share

Problem 11:   Which of the following appears most likely? Which appears second most likely?

a. Drawing a red marble from a bag containing 50 percent red marbles and 50 percent white marbles.

b. Drawing a red marble seven times in succession, with replacement (a selected marble is put back into the bag before the next marble is selected), from a bag containing 90 percent red marbles and 10 percent white marbles.

c. Drawing at least one red marble in seven tries, with replacement, from a bag containing 10 percent red marbles and 90 percent white marbles.

(*continued*)

BIASES EMANATING FROM THE AVAILABILITY HEURISTIC

Bias 1—Ease of Recall (based on vividness and recency)

> ***Problem 3.***   Which of the following lists was the cause of more premature deaths in the United States in 1999?
>
> (A)   Tobacco use, obesity/inactivity, and alcohol
>
> (B)   Cancer, heart disease, and auto accidents

Most people are highly influenced by the vividness of the diseases listed in group B, and choose this list as a result. In fact, list A provides the three leading causes of

TABLE 2.1 *(continued)*

Problem 12: Listed below are 10 uncertain quantities. Do not look up any information on these items. For each, write down your best estimate of the quantity. Next, put a lower and upper bound around your estimate, so that you are 98 percent confident that your range surrounds the actual quantity.

Estimate	*Lower*	*Upper*	
____	____	____	**a.** Wal-Mart's 1999 revenue
____	____	____	**b.** Kmart's 1999 revenue
____	____	____	**c.** Market value of General Motors as of March 14, 2000
____	____	____	**d.** Market value of Microsoft as of March 14, 2000
____	____	____	**e.** Market value of Cisco Systems as of March 14, 2000
____	____	____	**f.** Rank of Supervalu in the 1999 Fortune 500
____	____	____	**g.** Rank of Qualcomm in the 1999 Fortune 500
____	____	____	**h.** Total households in the United States, according to a 1994 Bureau of the Census poll
____	____	____	**i.** Number of species and subspecies of North American mammals extinct since 1600
____	____	____	**j.** Plastic waste generated in the United States in 1993 in tons

premature death in the United States (*Business Week*, 4/17/2000, p. 8). By contrast, auto accidents are only eighth on the list of premature killers, and cancer and heart disease are even farther down the list. The availability of vivid stories in the media biases our perception of the frequency of events. As a result, we may tend to underestimate the likelihood of premature death due to tobacco, alcohol, or overeating, causing us to miss opportunities to reduce these hazards through preventative measures such as school and workplace health programs.

Many life decisions are affected by the vividness of information. Although most people recognize that AIDS is a devastating disease, many individuals ignore clear data about how to avoid contracting AIDS. In the fall of 1991, however, sexual behavior in Dallas was dramatically affected by one vivid piece of data that may or may not have been true. In a chilling interview, a Dallas woman calling herself C. J. claimed she had AIDS and was trying to spread the disease out of revenge against the man who had infected her. After this vivid interview made the local news, attendance at Dallas AIDS seminars increased dramatically, AIDS became the main topic of Dallas talk shows, and requests for HIV tests surged city wide. Although C. J.'s possible actions were a legitimate cause for concern, it is clear that most of the health risks related to AIDS are not a result of one woman's actions. There are many more important reasons to be concerned about AIDS. However, C. J.'s vivid report had a more substantial effect on many people's behavior than the mountains of data available.

Tversky and Kahneman (1974) argue that when an individual judges the frequency with which an event occurs by the availability of its instances, an event whose instances are more easily recalled will appear to be more frequent than an event of equal frequency whose instances are less easily recalled. They cite evidence of this bias in a lab study in which individuals were read lists of names of well-known personalities of both genders. Different lists were presented to two groups. One group was read a list in which the women listed were relatively more famous than the listed men, but the list included more men's names overall. The other group was read a list in which the men listed were relatively more famous than the listed women, but the list included more women's names overall. After hearing their group's list, participants in both groups were asked if the list contained the names of more women or men. In both groups, participants incorrectly guessed that the gender that included the relatively more famous personalities was the more numerous. Participants apparently paid more attention to vivid household names than to less well-known figures, leading to inaccurate judgments.

While this example of vividness may seem fairly benign, it is not difficult to see how the availability bias could lead managers to make potentially destructive workplace decisions. The following came from the experience of one of my MBA students: As a purchasing agent, he had to select one of several possible suppliers. He chose the firm whose name was the most familiar to him. He later found out that the salience of the name resulted from recent adverse publicity concerning the firm's extortion of funds from client companies!

Managers conducting performance appraisals often fall victim to the availability heuristic. Working from memory, vivid instances of an employee's behavior (either positive or negative) will be most easily recalled from memory, will appear more numerous than commonplace incidents, and will therefore be weighted more heavily in the performance appraisal. The recency of events is also a factor: Managers give more weight to performance during the three months prior to the evaluation than to the previous nine months of the evaluation period.

Because of our susceptibility to vividness and recency, Kahneman and Tversky suggest that we are particularly prone to overestimating unlikely events. For instance, if we actually witness a burning house, our assessment of the probability of such accidents is likely to be greater than if we had merely read about the fire in the local newspaper; our direct observation of the event makes it more salient to us. Similarly, Slovic and Fischhoff (1977) discuss the implications of the misuse of the availability heuristic in debates about the perceived risks of nuclear power. They point out that any discussion of potential hazards, regardless of their likelihood, will increase the salience of these hazards and increase their perceived risks.

Bias 2—Retrievability (based on memory structures)

Problem 4a. In four pages of a novel (about 2,000 words), how many words would you expect to find that have the form _ _ _ _ing (seven-letter words that end with "ing")? Indicate your best estimate by circling one of the following values:

0   1–2   3–4   5–7   8–10   11–15   16+

Problem 4b. In four pages of a novel (about 2,000 words), how many words would you expect to find that have the form _ _ _ _ _n_ (seven-letter words that have the letter "n" in the sixth position)? Indicate your best estimate by circling one of the following values:

0   1–2   3–4   5–7   8–10   11–15   16+

Tversky and Kahneman (1983) found that most people respond with a higher number for Problem 4a than for Problem 4b. However, this response pattern must be incorrect. Since all words with seven letters that end in "ing" also have an "n" as their sixth letter, the frequency of words that end in "ing" cannot be larger than the number of words with "n" as the sixth letter. Tversky and Kahneman (1983) argue that "ing" words are more retrievable from memory because of the commonality of the "ing" suffix, whereas the search for words that have an "n" as the sixth letter does not easily generate this group of words.

Just as retrievability affects our vocabulary-search behavior, organizational modes affect information-search behavior within our work lives. We structure organizations to provide order, but this same structure can lead to confusion if the presumed order is not exactly as suggested. For example, many organizations have an information systems division that has generalized expertise in computer applications. Assume that you are a manager in a product division and need computer expertise. If that expertise exists within the information systems group, the organizational hierarchy will lead you to the correct resource. If, however, the information systems group lacks expertise in a specific application, but this expertise exists elsewhere in the organization, the hierarchy is likely to bias the effectiveness of your search. I am not arguing for the overthrow of organizational hierarchies; I am merely identifying the dysfunctional role of hierarchies in potentially biasing search behavior. If we are aware of the potential bias, we need not be affected by this limitation.

Retail store location is influenced by the way in which consumers search their minds when seeking a particular commodity. Why are multiple gas stations at the same intersection? Why do "upscale" retailers want to be in the same mall? Why are the biggest bookstores in a city often located within a few blocks of each other? An important reason for this pattern is that consumers learn the "location" for a particular type of product or store and organize their minds accordingly. To maximize traffic, the retailer needs to be in the location that consumers associate with this type of product or store.

Bias 3—Presumed Associations

People frequently fall victim to the availability bias in their assessment of the likelihood of two events occurring together. For example, consider your response to the following two questions: Is marijuana use related to delinquency? Are couples who get married under age 25 more likely to have bigger families? In assessing the marijuana question, most people typically try to remember several delinquent marijuana users and either assume or do not assume a correlation based on the availability of this mental data. However, a proper analysis would require you to recall *four* groups of people: marijuana users who are delinquents, marijuana users who are not delinquents, delinquents who do not use marijuana, and nondelinquents who do not use marijuana. The same analysis applies to the marriage question. Proper analysis would include four groups: couples who married young and have large families, couples who married young and have small families, couples who married older and have large families, and couples who married older and have small families.

Indeed, there are always at least four separate situations to consider when assessing the association between two dichotomous events. However, our everyday decision making commonly ignores this scientifically valid fact. Chapman and Chapman (1967) have noted that when the probability of two events co-occurring is judged by the availability of perceived co-occurring instances in our minds, we usually assign an inappropriately high probability that the two events will co-occur again. Thus, if we know a lot of marijuana users who are delinquents, we assume that marijuana use is related to delinquency. Similarly, if we know of a lot of couples who married young and have had large families, we assume that this trend is more prevalent than it may actually be. In testing for this bias, Chapman and Chapman provided participants with information about hypothetical psychiatric patients. The information included a written clinical diagnosis of a "patient" and a drawing of a person made by the "patient." The participants were asked to estimate the frequency with which each diagnosis (for example, suspiciousness or paranoia) was accompanied by various facial and body features in the drawings (for example, peculiar eyes). Throughout the study, participants markedly overestimated the frequency of pairs commonly associated together by social lore. For example, diagnoses of suspiciousness were overwhelmingly associated with peculiar eyes.

Summary A lifetime of experience has led us to believe that, in general, we recall frequent events more easily than infrequent events, and recall likely events more easily than unlikely events. In response to this learning, we have adopted the availability heuristic to help us estimate the likelihood of events. This simplifying heuristic often leads us to accurate, efficient judgments. However, as these first three biases (ease of recall, retrievability, and presumed associations) indicate, the misuse of the availability heuristic can lead to systematic errors in managerial judgment. We too easily assume that our available recollections are truly representative of the larger pool of events that exists outside our range of experience.

BIASES EMANATING FROM THE REPRESENTATIVENESS HEURISTIC

Bias 4—Insensitivity to Base Rates

Problem 5. Mark is finishing his MBA at a prestigious university. He is very interested in the arts and at one time considered a career as a musician. Is he more likely to take a job:

(A) in arts management, or (B) with an Internet start-up?

How did you decide on your answer? Odds are, you responded like most people. Using the representativeness heuristic discussed in Chapter 1, most people approach this problem by analyzing the degree to which Mark is representative of their image of individuals who take jobs in each of the two areas. Consequently, they usually conclude that Mark took the arts management job. However, as we discussed in our analysis of Problem 2 earlier in this chapter, this response overlooks relevant base-rate information. Reconsider the problem in light of the fact that a much larger number of MBAs take jobs with Internet start-ups than in arts management—relevant information that should enter into any reasonable prediction of Mark's career path. With this base-rate data, it is only reasonable to predict that he will be more likely to work for an Internet start-up.

Judgmental biases of this type frequently occur when individuals cognitively ask the wrong question. If you answered "arts management," you probably wondered, "How likely is it that a person working in the management of the arts would fit Mark's description?" In fact, the problem requires you to ask the question, "How likely is it that someone fitting Mark's description will choose arts management?" By itself, the representativeness heuristic incorrectly results in a similar answer to both questions, since this heuristic leads individuals to compare the resemblance of the personal description and the career path. However, when base-rate data are considered, they are irrelevant to the first question listed, but crucial to a reasonable prediction based on the second question. While a large percentage of individuals in arts management may fit Mark's description, there are undoubtedly a larger absolute number of management consultants fitting Mark's description because of the relative preponderance of MBAs in Internet start-ups.

Participants do use base-rate data correctly when no other information is provided (Kahneman and Tversky, 1972). In the absence of a personal description of Mark in Problem 5, people will choose "Internet start-up" based on the past frequency of this career path for MBAs. Thus, people understand the relevance of base-rate information, but tend to disregard such data when descriptive data are also available. Ignoring base rates has many unfortunate implications. Prospective entrepreneurs typically spend far too much time imagining their success and far too little time considering the base rate for business failures. Entrepreneurs think that the base rate for failure is not relevant to their situation, and many individuals lose their life savings as a result. Similarly, unnecessary emotional distress is caused in the divorce process because of the failure of couples to create prenuptial agreements that facilitate the peaceful resolution of a marriage. The suggestion of a prenuptial agreement is often viewed as a sign of bad faith. However, in far too many cases, the failure to create prenuptial agreements occurs when individuals approach marriage with the false belief that the very high base rate for divorce does not apply to them.

Bias 5—Insensitivity to Sample Size

Problem 6 (from Tversky and Kahneman, 1974). A certain town is served by two hospitals. In the larger hospital about 45 babies are born each day and in the smaller hospital about 15 babies are born each day. As you know, about 50 percent of all babies are boys. However, the exact percentage varies from day to day. Sometimes it may be higher than 50 percent, sometimes lower.

For a period of one year, each hospital recorded the days in which more than 60 percent of the babies born were boys. Which hospital do you think recorded more such days?

(A)   The larger hospital.

(B)   The smaller hospital.

(C)   About the same (that is, within 5 percent of each other).

Most individuals choose C, expecting the two hospitals to record a similar number of days in which 60 percent or more of the babies born are boys. People seem to have some basic idea of how unusual it is to have 60 percent of a random event occurring in a specific direction. By contrast, simple statistics tell us that it is much more likely to observe 60 percent of male babies in a smaller sample than in a larger sample. The interested reader can verify this fact with an introductory statistics book. However, anecdotally, this effect is easy to understand. Think about which is more likely: getting 6 heads in 10 flips of a coin or getting 6,000 heads in 10,000 flips of a coin. Our intuition correctly tells us that 6 out of 10 is not that unusual, but 6,000 in 10,000 is very unusual. Sampling theory tells us that the expected number of days in which more than 60 percent of the babies are boys is three times greater in the small hospital, since a large sample is less likely to deviate from the mean. However, most people judge the probability to be the same in each hospital, effectively ignoring sample size.

Although the importance of sample size is fundamental in statistics, Tversky and Kahneman (1974) argue that sample size is rarely a part of our intuition. Why not? When responding to problems dealing with sampling, people often use the representativeness heuristic. For instance, they think about how representative it would be for 60 percent of babies born to be boys in a random event. As a result, people ignore the issue of sample size, which is critical to an accurate assessment of the problem.

Consider the implications of this bias for advertising strategies. Market research experts understand that a sizable sample will be more accurate than a small one, but use consumers' bias to the advantage of their clients: "Four out of five dentists surveyed recommend sugarless gum for their patients who chew gum." Without mention of the exact number of dentists surveyed, the results are meaningless. If only 5 or 10 dentists were surveyed, the size of the sample would not be generalizable to the overall population of dentists.

Bias 6—Misconceptions of Chance

Problem 7.   You have started buying stocks on the Internet, beginning with five different stocks. Each stock goes down soon after your purchase. As you prepare to make a sixth purchase, you reason that it should be more successful, since the last five were "lemons." After all, the odds favor making at least one successful pick in six decisions. This thinking is:

(A)   correct.

(B)   incorrect.

Most people are comfortable with the preceding logic, or at least have used similar logic in the past. However, the logic in Problem 7 is incorrect. In fact, the performance of the first five stocks will not directly affect the performance of the sixth stock. Relying on their intuition and the representativeness heuristic, most individuals incorrectly conclude that a sixth poor performance is unlikely because the probability of getting six "lemons" in a row is extremely low. Unfortunately, this logic ignores the fact that we have already witnessed five "lemons" (in itself an unlikely occurrence), and the performance of the sixth stock is independent of the performance of the first five. Before you make similar mistakes in the stock market, be sure to read Chapter 7.

This question parallels research by Kahneman and Tversky (1972) showing that people expect a sequence of random events to "look" random. Specifically, participants routinely judged the sequence of coin flips H–T–H–T–T–H to be more likely than H–H–H–T–T–T, which does not "appear" random, and more likely than the sequence H–H–H–H–T–H, which does not represent the equal likelihood of heads and tails. Simple statistics, of course, tell us that each of these sequences is equally likely because of the independence of multiple random events.

Problem 7 moves beyond dealing with random events in recognizing our inappropriate tendency to assume that random and nonrandom events will balance out. Will the sixth stock perform well? Maybe! But your earlier failures are completely irrelevant to its potential for success.

The logic concerning misconceptions of chance provides a process explanation of the gambler's fallacy. After holding bad cards on ten hands of poker, the poker player believes he is "due" for a good hand. After winning $1,000 in the Pennsylvania State Lottery, a woman changes her regular number—after all, how likely is it that the same number will come up twice? Tversky and Kahneman (1974) note: "Chance is commonly viewed as a self-correcting process in which a deviation in one direction induces a deviation in the opposite direction to restore the equilibrium. In fact, deviations are not corrected as a chance process unfolds, they are merely diluted."

In the preceding examples, individuals expected probabilities to even out. In some situations, our minds misconstrue chance in exactly the opposite way. In sports such as basketball, we often think of a particular player as having a "hot hand" or "being on a good streak." If your favorite player has made his last four shots, is the probability of his making his next shot higher, lower, or the same as the probability of his making a shot without the preceding four hits? Most sports fans, sports commentators, and players believe that the answer is "higher." In fact, there are many biological, emotional, and physical reasons that this answer could be correct. However, it is wrong! In an extensive analysis of the shooting of the Philadelphia 76ers and the Boston Celtics, Gilovich, Vallone, and Tversky (1985) found that immediately prior shot performance did not change the likelihood of success on the upcoming shot. Out of all of the findings in this book, this is the effect that my managerial students have the hardest time accepting. We can all remember sequences of five hits in a row; streaks are part of our conception of chance in athletic competition. However, our minds do not think of a string of "four in a row" shots as a situation in which "he missed his fifth shot." As a result, we have a misconception of connectedness when, in fact, chance (or the player's normal probability of success) is really in effect.

The belief in the hot hand has interesting implications for how players compete. Passing the ball to the player who is "hot" is commonly endorsed as a good strategy. Similarly, the opposing team often will concentrate on guarding the "hot" player. Another player, who is less hot but is equally skilled, may have a better chance of scoring. Thus the belief in the "hot hand" is not just erroneous, but could also be costly if you make decisions under this illusion.

The mythical perception of a hot hand is not limited to basketball. Imagine that you receive a free copy of an investor newsletter that advises you to sell stock because the market will fall during the next six months. You ignore this newsletter, and then it happens to be correct. At the end of the six months, another free copy of this newsletter tells you the market will rise during the next six months. Again, you ignore the advice, and again the newsletter is correct. A third free copy of the newsletter advises you to buy stocks for the next six-month period. Once again, you ignore the newsletter, and once again it is correct. After these 18 months, you receive a direct-mail solicitation for this newsletter, pointing out that they have been giving you great free advice for the past 18 months. If you want this excellent advice in the future, you must pay a small subscription fee. Are you tempted to subscribe to this publication? Many people would be impressed by its consistent past performance and would sign up, expecting more sound advice.

Now consider what this advice may look like from the other side. Suppose a publisher creates eight financial newsletters, each managed by a different expert. In their first issues, each of the eight makes a six-month recommendation about the general direction of the market; four predict a rise in the market, and four predict a fall in the market. The four who predicted a fall in the market were correct, and the four who predicted a rise go out of business. Of the remaining four newsletters, two predict a rise for the second six-month period and two predict a fall. The market rises, and the two that predicted a fall in the second six-month period go out of business. Of the two remaining in business after 12 months, one predicts a rise in the market for the third six-month period, and the other predicts a fall. The market rises, and the newsletter that was correct all three times advertises this fact. It seems they have some important insight into financial markets. Yet, we can see that if there are many "experts" making predictions, some will be consistently correct simply by chance, though we will be biased to give credit to the one that got lucky.

Tversky and Kahneman's (1971) work also shows that misconceptions of chance are not limited to gamblers, sports fans, or laypersons. Research psychologists also fall victim to the "law of small numbers." They believe that sample events should be far more representative of the population from which they were drawn than simple statistics would dictate. Putting too much faith in the results of initial samples, scientists often grossly overestimate the replicability of empirical findings. The representativeness heuristic may be so well institutionalized in our decision processes that even scientific training and its emphasis on the proper use of statistics may not eliminate its biasing influence.

Bias 7—Regression to the Mean

Problem 8. You are the sales forecaster for a department store chain with nine locations. The chain depends on you for quality projections of future sales in order to make decisions on staffing, advertising, information system developments, purchasing, renovation, and the like. All stores are similar in size and merchandise selection. The main difference in their sales occurs because of location and random fluctuations. Sales for 2000 were as follows:

Store	2000	2002
1	$12,000,000	
2	11,500,000	
3	11,000,000	
4	10,500,000	
5	10,000,000	
6	9,500,000	
7	9,000,000	
8	8,500,000	
9	8,000,000	
TOTAL	$90,000,000	$99,000,000

Your economic forecasting service has convinced you that the best estimate of total sales increases between 2000 and 2002 is 10 percent (to $99,000,000). Your task is to predict 2002 sales for each store. Since your manager believes strongly in the economic forecasting service, it is imperative that your total sales equal $99,000,000.

Think about the processes you might use to answer this problem. Consider the following logical pattern of thought: "The overall increase in sales is predicted to be 10 percent ([$99,000,000 − $90,000,000]/$90,000,000). Lacking any other specific information on the stores, it makes sense simply to add 10 percent to each 2000 sales figure to predict 2002 sales. This means that I predict sales of $13,200,000 for store 1, sales of $12,650,000 for store 2, and so on." This logic, in fact, is the most common approach people use in response to this item.

Unfortunately, this logic is faulty. Why? Statistical analysis would dictate that we first assess the predicted relationship between 2000 and 2002 sales. This relationship, formally known as a correlation, can vary from total independence (that is, 2000 sales do not predict 2002 sales) to perfect correlation (2000 sales are a perfect predictor of 2002 sales). In the former case, the lack of a relationship between 2000 and 2002 sales would mean that 2000 sales would provide absolutely no information about 2002 sales, and your best estimates of 2002 sales would be equal to total sales divided by the number of stores ($99,000,000 ÷ 9 = $11,000,000). However, in the latter case of perfect predictability between 2000 and 2002 sales, our initial logic of simply extrapolating from 2000 performance by adding 10 percent to each store's performance would be completely accurate. Obviously, 2000 sales are likely to be partially predictive of 2002 sales—falling somewhere between independence and perfect correlation. Thus, the best prediction for store 1 should lie between $11,000,000 and $13,200,000, depending on how predictive you think 2000 sales will be of 2002 sales. The key point is that in virtually all such predictions, you should expect the naive $13,200,000 estimate to regress toward the overall mean ($11,000,000).

In a study of sales forecasting, Cox and Summers (1987) examined the judgments of professional retail buyers. They examined sales data, during a two-week period, from two department stores for six different apparel styles for a total of 12 different sales forecasts. The task was for professional buyers to forecast the sales in week 2 based on week 1 data. The sales from week 1, in fact, regressed to the mean in week 2. However, the forecasts of 31 professional buyers failed to reflect the tendency for regression to the mean.

Many effects regress to the mean. Brilliant students frequently have less successful siblings. Short parents tend to have taller children. Great rookies have mediocre second years (the "sophomore jinx"). Firms that achieve outstanding profits one year tend to perform less well the next year. In each case, individuals are often surprised when made aware of these predictable patterns of regression to the mean.

Why is the regression-to-the-mean concept, while statistically valid, counterintuitive? Kahneman and Tversky (1973) suggest that the representativeness heuristic accounts for this systematic bias in judgment. They argue that individuals typically assume that future outcomes (for example, 2002 sales) will be directly predictable from past outcomes (2000 sales). Thus, we tend to naively develop predictions based on the assumption of perfect correlation with past data.

In some unusual situations, individuals do intuitively expect a regression-to-the-mean effect. In 1998, when Mark McGwire hit 70 home runs, few expected him to repeat this performance the following year. When Wilt Chamberlain scored 100 points in a single game, most people did not expect him to score 100 points in his next game. When a historically 3.0 student got a 4.0 one semester, her parents did not expect a repeat performance the following semester. When a real estate agent sold five houses in one month (an abnormally high performance), his co-agents did not expect equally high sales from him the following month. Why is regression to the mean more intuitive in these cases? Because, when a performance is extreme, we know it cannot last. Thus, under very unusual circumstances, we expect performance to regress. However, we generally do not recognize the regression effect in less extreme cases.

Consider Kahneman and Tversky's (1973) classic example in which misconceptions about regression led to overestimation of the effectiveness of punishment and the underestimation of the power of reward. In a discussion about flight training, experienced instructors noted that praise for an exceptionally smooth landing was typically followed by a poorer landing on the next try, while harsh criticism after a rough landing was usually followed by an improvement on the next try. The instructors concluded that verbal rewards were detrimental to learning, while verbal punishments were beneficial. Obviously, the tendency of performance to regress to the mean can account for the results; verbal feedback may have had absolutely no effect. However, to the extent that the instructors were prone to biased decision making, they were liable to reach the false conclusion that punishment is more effective than positive reinforcement in shaping behavior.

What happens when managers fail to acknowledge the regression principle? Consider an employee who performs extremely well during one evaluation period. He (and his boss) may inappropriately expect similar performance in the next period. What happens when the employee's performance regresses toward the mean? He (and his boss) will begin to make excuses for not meeting expectations. Managers who fail to recognize the tendency of events to regress to the mean are likely to develop false assumptions about future results and, as a result, make inappropriate plans.

Bias 8—The Conjunction Fallacy

Problem 9.   Linda is 31 years old, single, outspoken, and very bright. She majored in philosophy. As a student, she was deeply concerned with issues of discrimination and social justice, and she participated in antinuclear demonstrations.

Rank order the following eight descriptions in terms of the probability (likelihood) that they describe Linda:

a.   Linda is a teacher in an elementary school.
b.   Linda works in a bookstore and takes yoga classes.
c.   Linda is active in the feminist movement.
d.   Linda is a psychiatric social worker.
e.   Linda is a member of the League of Women Voters.
f.   Linda is a bank teller.
g.   Linda is an insurance salesperson.
h.   Linda is a bank teller who is active in the feminist movement.

Examine your rank orderings of descriptions C, F, and H. Most people rank order C as more likely than H and H as more likely than F. Their rationale for this ordering is that C–H–F reflects the degree to which the descriptions represent the short profile of Linda. Tversky and Kahneman constructed Linda's profile to be representative of an active feminist and unrepresentative of a bank teller. Recall from the representativeness heuristic that people make judgments according to the degree to which a specific description corresponds to a broader category within their minds. Linda's profile is more representative of a feminist than of a feminist bank teller, and is more representative of a feminist bank teller than of a bank teller. Thus, the representativeness heuristic accurately predicts that most individuals will rank order the items C–H–F.

Although the representativeness heuristic accurately predicts how individuals will respond, it also leads to another common, systematic distortion of human judgment—the conjunction fallacy (Tversky and Kahneman, 1983). This is illustrated by a reexamination of the potential descriptions of Linda. One of the simplest and most fundamental qualitative laws of probability is that a subset (for example, being a bank teller and a feminist) cannot be more likely than a larger set that completely includes the subset (for example, being a bank teller). Statistically speaking, the broad set "Linda is a bank teller" must be rated at least as likely, if not more so, than the subset "Linda is a bank teller who is active in the feminist movement." After all, there is some chance (although it may be small) that Linda is a bank teller but not a feminist. Based on this logic, a rational assessment of the eight descriptions will result in F being ranked more likely than H.

Simple statistics demonstrate that a conjunction (a combination of two or more descriptors) cannot be more probable than any one of its descriptors. By contrast, the conjunction fallacy predicts that a conjunction will be judged more probable than a single component descriptor when the conjunction appears more representative than the component descriptor. Intuitively, thinking of Linda as a feminist bank teller "feels" more correct than thinking of her as only a bank teller.

The conjunction fallacy can also be triggered by a greater availability of the conjunction than of one of its unique descriptors (Yates and Carlson, 1986). That is, if the conjunction creates more intuitive matches with vivid events, acts, or people than a component of the conjunction, the conjunction is likely to be perceived falsely as more probable than the component. Participants in a study by Tversky and Kahneman (1983) judged the chances of a massive flood somewhere in North America, in 1989, in which 1,000 people drown, to be less likely than the chances of an earthquake in California, sometime in 1989, causing a flood in which more than 1,000 people drown. Yet, the latter possibility (California earthquake leading to flood) is a subset of the former; many other events could cause a flood in North America. Tversky and Kahneman (1983) have shown that the conjunction fallacy is likely to lead to deviations from rationality in judgments of sporting events, criminal behavior, international relations, and medical decisions. The obvious concern arising from the conjunction fallacy is that it leads us to poor predictions of future outcomes, causing us to be ill-prepared to cope with unanticipated events.

Finally, one might hope that groups would be less prone to representativeness errors than individuals. Unfortunately, this is not the case. Argote, Seabright, and Dyer (1986) found that groups not only exhibit the representativeness heuristic in the same directional pattern as individuals, but the biasing effect is even greater in groups than in individuals. Thus, the biases covered in this section may affect group decision making to an even greater degree than they affect individual decision making.

Summary We have examined five biases that emanate from the use of the representativeness heuristic: insensitivity to base rates, insensitivity to sample size, misconceptions of chance, regression to the mean, and the conjunction fallacy. Experience has taught us that the likelihood of a specific occurrence is related to the likelihood of a group of occurrences which that specific occurrence represents. Unfortunately, we tend to overuse this information in making decisions. The five biases we have just explored illustrate the systematic irrationalities that can occur in our judgments when we are unaware of this tendency.

BIASES EMANATING FROM ANCHORING AND ADJUSTMENT

Bias 9—Insufficient Anchor Adjustment

> ***Problem 10.*** A new Internet company recently made its initial public offering, becoming publicly traded. At its opening, the stock sold for $20/share. The company's closest competitor went public one year ago, also at a price of $20/share. The competitor's stock is now priced at $100/share. What will the new firm be worth one year from now?

Was your answer affected by the other firm's appreciation? Most people are influenced by this fairly irrelevant information. Reconsider how you would have responded if the other firm was now worth only $10/share. On average, individuals give higher estimates of the new firm's future value when the other firm is currently worth $100/share, rather than $10/share. Why? Studies have found that people develop estimates by starting from an initial anchor, based on whatever information is provided, and adjusting from there to yield a final answer. Slovic and Lichtenstein (1971) have provided conclusive evidence that individuals' adjustments away from anchors are usually not sufficient to negate the effects of the anchor. In all cases, answers are biased toward the initial anchor, even if it is irrelevant. Different starting points yield different answers.

Tversky and Kahneman (1974) have provided systematic, empirical evidence of the anchoring effect. In one study, participants were asked to estimate the percentage of African countries in the United Nations. For each participant, a random number (obtained by a spin of a roulette wheel, observed by the participant) was given as a starting point. From there, participants were asked to state whether the actual quantity was higher or lower than this random value and then develop their best estimate. It was found that the arbitrary values from the roulette wheel had a substantial impact on estimates. For example, for those who received 10 countries and 65 countries as starting points, median estimates were 25 and 45, respectively. Thus, even though the participants were aware that the anchor was random and unrelated to the judgment task, the anchor had a dramatic effect on their judgment. Interestingly, paying participants according to their accuracy did not reduce the magnitude of the anchoring effect.

Salary negotiations represent a very common context for observing anchoring in the managerial world. For example, pay increases often come in the form of a percentage increase. A firm may have an average increase of 8 percent, with increases for specific employees varying from 3 percent to 13 percent. While society has led us to accept such systems as equitable, I believe that such a system falls victim to anchoring and leads to substantial inequities. What happens if an employee has been substantially underpaid? The raise system described does not rectify past inequities, since a pay increase of 11 percent may leave that employee still underpaid. Conversely, the system would work in the employee's favor had she been overpaid. Employers often ask job applicants to reveal their current salaries. Why? Employers are searching for a value from which they can anchor an adjustment. If the employee is worth far more than his current salary, the anchoring and adjustment hypothesis predicts that the firm will make an offer below the employee's true value. Does an employee's current salary provide fully accurate information about his or her true worth? I think not. Thus, the use of such compensation systems accepts past inequities as an anchor and makes inadequate adjustments from that point. Furthermore, these findings suggest that when an employer is deciding what offer to make to a potential employee, any anchor that creeps into the discussion is likely to have an inappropriate effect on the eventual offer, even if the anchor is "ignored" as being ridiculous.

There are numerous examples of the anchoring-and-adjustment phenomenon in everyday life. For example:

- In education, children are tracked by a school system that may categorize them into a certain level of performance at an early age. For example, a child who is anchored in the C group may be expected to achieve a mediocre level of performance. Conversely, a child of similar abilities who is anchored in the A group may be perceived as being a better student than the student in group C merely because assignment to the A group confers high-performer status.
- We have all fallen victim to the first-impression syndrome when meeting someone for the first time. We often place so much emphasis on first impressions that we fail to adjust our opinion appropriately at a later date.

Joyce and Biddle (1981) have provided empirical support for the presence of the anchoring-and-adjustment effect among practicing auditors of Big Five accounting firms. Auditors participating in one condition were asked the following:

> It is well known that many cases of management fraud go undetected even when competent annual audits are performed. The reason, of course, is that Generally Accepted Auditing Standards are not designed specifically to detect executive-level management fraud. We are interested in obtaining an estimate from practicing auditors of the prevalence of executive-level management fraud as a first step in ascertaining the scope of the problem.
>
> 1. Based on your audit experience, is the incidence of significant executive-level management fraud more than 10 in each 1,000 firms (that is, 1 percent) audited by Big Five accounting firms?
>   a. Yes, more than 10 in each 1,000 Big Five clients have significant executive-level management fraud.

    b.   No, fewer than 10 in each 1,000 Big Five clients have significant executive-level management fraud.

  2. What is your estimate of the number of Big Five clients per 1,000 that have significant executive-level management fraud? (Fill in the blank below with the appropriate number.)

_____in each 1,000 Big Five clients have significant executive-level management fraud.

The second condition differed only in that participants were asked whether the fraud incidence was more or less than 200 in each 1,000 firms audited, rather than 10 in 1,000. Participants in the first condition estimated a fraud incidence of 16.52 per 1,000 on average, compared with an estimated fraud incidence of 43.11 per 1,000 in the second condition! Here, even professional auditors fell victim to anchoring and adjustment.

    The tendency to make insufficient adjustments is a direct result of the anchoring-and-adjustment heuristic described in the first chapter. Interestingly, Nisbett and Ross (1980) present an argument that suggests that the anchoring-and-adjustment bias itself dictates that it will be very difficult to get you to change your decision-making strategies as a result of reading this book. They argue that the heuristics we identify are currently serving as your cognitive anchors and are central to your judgment processes. Thus, any cognitive strategy that I suggest must be presented and understood in a manner that will force you to break your existing cognitive anchors. Based on the evidence in this section, this should be a difficult challenge—but one that is important enough to be worth the effort!

Bias 10—Conjunctive and Disjunctive Events Bias

    Problem 11.   Which of the following appears most likely? Which appears second most likely?
    a.   Drawing a red marble from a bag containing 50 percent red marbles and 50 percent white marbles.
    b.   Drawing a red marble seven times in succession, with replacement (a selected marble is put back into the bag before the next marble is selected), from a bag containing 90 percent red marbles and 10 percent white marbles.
    c.   Drawing at least one red marble in seven tries, with replacement, from a bag containing 10 percent red marbles and 90 percent white marbles.

The most common ordering of preferences is B–A–C. Interestingly, the correct order of likelihood is C (52 percent), A (50 percent), B (48 percent)—the exact opposite of the most common intuitive pattern! This result illustrates a general bias to overestimate the probability of conjunctive events, or events that must occur in conjunction with one another (Bar–Hillel, 1973), and to underestimate the probability of disjunctive events, or events that occur independently (Tversky and Kahneman, 1974). Thus, when multiple events all need to occur (Problem B), we overestimate the true likelihood, while if only one of many events needs to occur (Problem C), we underestimate the true likelihood.

Kahneman and Tversky (1974) explain these effects in terms of the anchoring-and-adjustment heuristic. They argue that the probability of any one event occurring (for example, drawing one red marble) provides a natural anchor for the judgment of the total probability. Since adjustment from an anchor is typically insufficient, the perceived likelihood of choice B stays inappropriately close to 90 percent, while the perceived probability of choice C stays inappropriately close to 10 percent.

How is each of these biases manifested in an applied context? The overestimation of conjunctive events is a powerful explanation of the timing problems that typically occur with projects that require multistage planning. Individuals, businesses, and governments frequently fall victim to the conjunctive-events bias in terms of timing and budgets. Home remodeling, new product ventures, and public works projects seldom finish on time or on budget. Consider the following real-life scenarios:

- After three years of study, doctoral students typically dramatically overestimate the likelihood of completing their dissertations within a year. This occurs even when they plan how long each component of the project will take. Why do they not finish in one year?

- A partner managed a consulting project in which five teams were each analyzing a different strategy for a client. The alternatives could not be compared until all teams completed their analysis. As the client's deadline approached, three of the five teams were behind schedule, but the partner assured the client that all five would be ready on time. In the end, the manager only presented three of the five alternatives to the client (two were still missing). Unimpressed, the client dropped the consulting firm. Whose fault was it that the project failed?

- The City of Boston undertook a massive construction project to move Interstate Highway 93 below ground as it passes through the city (The Big Dig). City officials developed a very clear budget based on each subcontractor's estimate. Nevertheless, as of mid–2000, the Big Dig was $1.9 billion over budget. What went wrong?

Why are we so optimistic in our assessments of a project's cost and time frame? Why are we so surprised when a seemingly unlikely setback occurs? Because of the human tendency to underestimate disjunctive events. "A complex system, such as a nuclear reactor or the human body, will malfunction if any of its essential components fails," argue Tversky and Kahneman. "Even when the likelihood of failure in each component is slight, the probability of an overall failure can be high if many components are involved." For this reason, complex projects from dissertations to highway digs often run into unexpected glitches. In his book "Normal Accidents," Perrow (1984) argues against the safety of advanced technologies such as nuclear reactors and DNA research. He fears that society significantly underestimates the potential for disaster because of our judgmental failure to recognize the multitude of things that can go wrong in these incredibly complex and interactive systems. This failure explains why, when an oil company like Exxon has a major spill off the Alaskan coast, it is perceived by the public as an unlikely, surprising event. However, when a company fails to double-line its tankers, or to monitor the alcohol intake of its captain, and so on, perhaps the likelihood of a "surprise" is higher than it appears.

An awareness of our underestimation of disjunctive events also has its positive side. Consider the following:

It's Monday evening (10:00 P.M.). Your boss calls to tell you that you must be at the Chicago office by 9:30 the next morning. You call all five airlines that have flights that get into Chicago by 9:00 A.M. Each has one flight, and all the flights are booked. When you ask the probability of getting on each of the flights if you show up at the airport in the morning, you are disappointed to hear probabilities of 30 percent, 25 percent, 15 percent, 20 percent, and 25 percent. Consequently, you do not expect to get to Chicago in time.

In this case, the disjunctive bias leads you to expect the worst. In fact, if the probabilities given by the airlines are unbiased and independent, you have a 73 percent chance of getting on one of the flights (assuming you can arrange to be at the right ticket counter at the right time)!

Bias 11—Overconfidence

Problem 12. Listed below are 10 uncertain quantities. Do not look up any information on these items. For each, write down your best estimate of the quantity. Next, put a lower and upper bound around your estimate, so that you are 98 percent confident that your range surrounds the actual quantity.

Estimate	*Lower*	*Upper*	
____	____	____	a. Wal-Mart's 1999 revenue
____	____	____	b. Kmart's 1999 revenue
____	____	____	c. Market value of General Motors as of March 14, 2000
____	____	____	d. Market value of Microsoft as of March 14, 2000
____	____	____	e. Market value of Cisco Systems as of March 14, 2000
____	____	____	f. Rank of Supervalu in the 1999 Fortune 500
____	____	____	g. Rank of Qualcomm in the 1999 Fortune 500
____	____	____	h. Total households in the United States, according to a 1994 Bureau of the Census poll
____	____	____	i. Number of species and subspecies of North American mammals extinct since 1600
____	____	____	j. Plastic waste generated in the United States in 1993 in tons

How many of your 10 ranges will actually surround the true quantities? If you set your ranges so that you were 98 percent confident, you should expect to correctly bound approximately 9.8, or 9 to 10, of the quantities. Let's look at the correct answers: (a) $166,809,000,000, (b) $35,935,000,000, (c) $63,838,500,000, (d)

$492,462,100,000, (e) $453,878,800,000, f) 99, (g) 409, (h) 97,000,000, (i) 22, (j) 19,300,000.

How many of your ranges actually surrounded the true quantities? If you surround 9–10, we can conclude that you were appropriately confident in your estimation ability. Most people only surround between 3 (30 percent) and 7 (70 percent), despite claiming a 98 percent confidence that each range will surround the true value. Why? Most of us are overconfident in our estimation abilities and do not acknowledge our true uncertainty.

In Alpert and Raiffa's (1969) initial demonstration of overconfidence based on 1,000 observations (100 participants on 10 items), 42.6 percent of quantities fell outside 90 percent confidence ranges. Since then, overconfidence has been identified as a common judgmental pattern and demonstrated in a wide variety of settings. For example, Fischhoff, Slovic, and Lichtenstein (1977) found that participants who assigned odds of 1,000:1 of being correct were correct only 81 to 88 percent of the time. For odds of 1,000,000:1, their answers were correct only 90 to 96 percent of the time! Hazard and Peterson (1973) identified overconfidence among members of the armed forces, while Cambridge and Shreckengost (1980) found extreme overconfidence among CIA agents.

The most well-established finding in the overconfidence literature is the tendency of people to be most overconfident of the correctness of their answers when asked to respond to questions of moderate to extreme difficulty (Fischhoff, Slovic, and Lichtenstein, 1977). That is, as participants' knowledge of a question decreases, they do not correspondingly decrease their level of confidence. However, participants typically demonstrate no overconfidence, and often some underconfidence, when asked questions with which they are familiar. Thus, we should be most alert to the potential for overconfidence when considering areas outside of our expertise.

Are groups as overconfident as individuals? Sniezek and Henry (1989) investigated the accuracy and confidence of group decisions about unknown situations. They found that, in general, groups make more accurate judgments than individuals about uncertain events. This is particularly true in groups in which there is a broad variance in individual judgments and a relatively high level of disagreement. However, groups are just as susceptible as individuals to unreasonably high levels of confidence in their judgments. Some 98 percent of participants believed that their group's judgments were in the top half of all group judgments with respect to accuracy. This finding suggests that overconfidence is a significant pitfall for groups as well as for individuals.

Theories about overconfidence have met with a great deal of controversy (see Lichtenstein, Fischhoff, and Phillips [1982] for an extensive discussion). Tversky and Kahneman (1974) explain overconfidence in terms of anchoring. Specifically, they argue that when individuals are asked to set a confidence range around an answer, their initial estimate serves as an anchor which biases their estimation of confidence intervals in both directions. As explained earlier, adjustments from an anchor are usually insufficient, resulting in an overly narrow confidence band. In their review of the literature, Lichtenstein, Fischhoff, and Phillips (1982) suggest two viable strategies for eliminating overconfidence. First, they have found that giving people feedback about their overconfident judgments has been moderately successful at reducing this bias. Second, Koriat, Lichtenstein, and Fischhoff (1980) found that asking people to explain why their answers might be wrong (or far off the mark) can decrease overconfidence by enabling them to recognize contradictions in their judgment.

Why should you be concerned about overconfidence? After all, it has probably given you the courage to attempt endeavors that have stretched your abilities. Unwarranted confidence can indeed be beneficial in some situations. However, consider the potential adverse effects of excess confidence in the following situations:

- You are a surgeon and are trying to persuade a patient's family to agree to a difficult operation. When the family asks you to estimate the likelihood that the patient will survive the operation, you respond, "95 percent." If the patient dies on the operating table, was he one of the unlucky 5 percent, or are you guilty of malpractice for an overconfident projection?

- You are the chief legal counsel for a firm that has been threatened with a multimillion dollar lawsuit. You are 98 percent confident that the firm will not lose in court. Is this degree of certainty sufficient for you to recommend rejecting an out-of-court settlement? Suppose you learn that if you lose the case, your firm will go bankrupt. Based on what you know now, are you still comfortable with your 98 percent estimate?

- You have developed a marketing plan for a new product. You are so confident in your plan that you have not developed any contingencies for early market failure. When the first stage of your plan falters, will you expedite changes in the marketing strategy, or will your overconfidence blind you to its flaws?

These examples demonstrate the serious problems that can result from the tendency to be overconfident. While confidence in your abilities is necessary for achievement in life, and can inspire respect and confidence in others, overconfidence can be a barrier to effective professional decision making.

Summary Whenever we try to estimate likelihoods (such as the probability of on-time project completion) or establish values (such as what salary to offer), we tend to seek out an initial anchor, which often weighs strongly in our decision-making processes. Our experience determining such figures has taught us that starting from somewhere is easier than starting from nowhere. However, as the last three biases (insufficient anchor adjustment, conjunctive and disjunctive events bias, and overconfidence) show, we frequently over-rely on these anchors and seldom question their validity or appropriateness in a particular situation. As with the other heuristics, we frequently fail even to realize that this heuristic has an impact on our judgment.

TWO MORE GENERAL BIASES

Bias 12—The Confirmation Trap

Imagine that the sequence of three numbers below follows a rule, and your task is to diagnose that rule (Wason, 1960). When you write down other sequences of three numbers, an instructor will tell you whether or not your sequence follows the rule.

2–4–6

What sequences would you write down? How would you know when you had enough evidence to guess the rule? Wason's study participants tended to offer fairly few sequences, and the sequences tended to be consistent with the rule that they eventually guessed. Common rules included, "numbers that go up by two," or "the difference between the first two numbers equals the difference between the last two numbers." In fact, Wason's rule was much broader: "any three ascending numbers." This solution requires participants to accumulate disconfirming, rather than confirming, evidence. For example, if you think the rule is "numbers that go up by two," you must try sequences that do not conform to this rule to find the actual rule. Trying the sequences 1–3–5, 10–12–14, 122–124–126, and so on, will only lead you into the confirmation trap. Similarly, if you think the rule is "the difference between the first two numbers equals the difference between the last two numbers," you must try sequences that do not conform to this rule to find the actual rule. Trying the sequences 1–2–3, 10–15–20, 122–126–130 again would only bring you feedback that strengthens your hypothesis. Only 6 out of 29 of Wason's participants found the correct rule on their first guess of the rule. Wason concluded that obtaining the correct solution necessitates "a willingness to attempt to falsify hypotheses, and thus to test those intuitive ideas that so often carry the feeling of certitude" (p. 139).

I have used this task hundreds of times in classes. My first volunteer typically guesses "numbers going up by two" and is quickly eliminated. My second volunteer is often just as quick with a wrong answer. Interestingly, at this stage, it is rare that I will have answered "no" to a sequence proposed by either volunteer. Why? Because people tend to seek confirmatory information, even when disconfirming information is more powerful and important.

Once you become aware of the confirmation trap, you are likely to find that it pervades your decision-making processes. When you make a tentative decision (to buy a new car, to hire a particular employee, to start research and development on a new product line), do you search for data that support your decision before making the final commitment? Most of us do. However, the existence of the confirmation trap implies that the search for challenging, or disconfirming, evidence will provide the most useful insights. For example, when you are seeking to confirm your decision to hire a particular employee, you will probably have no trouble finding positive information on the individual, such as recommendations from past employers. In fact, it may be more important for you to determine whether negative information on this individual, such as a criminal record, as well as positive information on another potential applicant, also exists. Now consider the last car you purchased. Imagine that, the day after you drove your new car home, your local newspaper printed two lists ranking cars by performance—one by fuel efficiency and one by crash test results. Which list would you pay more attention to? Most of us would pay more attention to whichever list confirms that we made a good purchase.

I recently watched my friend Dick Thaler engage a group of financial executives in the 2–4–6 task. After the basic demonstration, Thaler told the audience that he was forming two new consulting firms. One of them, called "Yes Person," would respond to any client's request for advice by telling them that all their ideas are great. In fact, to speed service and ensure satisfaction, Yes Person would allow the client to write the consulting report themselves if they liked. The other consulting firm, called "Devil's Advocate," would disapprove of any plans currently being considered by a client. Reports by Devil's Advocate would consist of a list of the top ten reasons a plan should not be undertaken.

Which consulting style would be more useful to the client? Thaler insisted to his audience that Devil's Advocate would provide a much more important service than Yes Person, and I agree. However, real-world consulting engagements often bear a closer resemblance to the Yes Person format than to that of Devil's Advocate, in part because consulting firms know that clients like to hear that their ideas are good. Our desire to confirm our initial ideas is so strong that we will pay people to back us up! When pressed, Thaler conceded that his two firms don't really exist, and could never succeed. After all, he pointed out, no firm would ever hire Devil's Advocate, and Yes Person already had too much competition from established consulting firms.

Bias 13—Hindsight and the Curse of Knowledge

Imagine yourself in the following scenarios:

- You are an avid football fan, and you are watching a critical game in which your team is behind 35–31. With three seconds left and the ball on the opponent's three-yard line, the quarterback calls a pass play into the corner of the endzone. When the play fails, you shout, "I *knew* that was a bad play."

- You are traveling by car in an unfamiliar area, and your spouse is driving. When you approach an unmarked fork in the road, your spouse decides to go to the right. Four miles and fifteen minutes later, it is clear that you are lost. You blurt out, "I knew you should have turned left at the fork."

- A manager who works for you hired a new supervisor last year. You were well aware of the choices he had at the time and allowed him to choose the new employee on his own. You have just received production data on every supervisor. The data on the new supervisor are terrible. You call in the manager and claim, "There was plenty of evidence that he was the wrong man for the job."

- As director of marketing in a consumer-goods organization, you have just presented the results of an extensive six-month study on current consumer preferences for the products manufactured by your company. At the conclusion of your presentation, a senior vice president responds, "I don't know why we spent so much time and money collecting these data. I could have told you what the results were going to be."

Do you recognize any of your own behaviors in these scenarios? Do you recognize someone else's remarks? Each scenario exemplifies "the hindsight bias" (Fischhoff, 1975). People typically are not very good at recalling or reconstructing the way an uncertain situation appeared to them before finding out the results of the decision. What play would *you* have called? Did you really know that your spouse should have turned left? Was there really evidence that the selected supervisor was a bad choice? Could the senior vice president really have predicted your study's results? While our intuition is occasionally accurate, we tend to overestimate what we knew beforehand based upon what we later learned. The hindsight bias occurs when people look back on their own judgments, as well as those of others.

Fischhoff (1975) examined the differences between hindsight and foresight in the context of judging the outcome of historical events. In one study, participants were divided into five groups and asked to read a passage about the war between the British and Gurka forces in 1814. One group was not told the result of the war. The remaining four groups of participants were told either that: (1) the British won, (2) the Gurkas won, (3) a military stalemate was reached with no peace settlement, or (4) a military stalemate was reached with a peace settlement. Obviously, only one group was told the truthful outcome—(1) in this case. Each participant was then asked what his or her subjective assessments of the probability of each outcome would have been without the benefit of knowing the reported outcome. Participants tended to believe that they would have judged the outcome that they were told happened as being most likely, even if they had not been told the outcome. Based on this and other varied examples, it becomes clear that knowledge of an outcome increases an individual's belief about the degree to which he or she would have predicted that outcome without the benefit of that knowledge.

Anchoring is often used to explain the hindsight bias. According to this view, knowledge of an event's outcome becomes an anchor by which individuals interpret their prior judgments of the event's likelihood. Since adjustments to anchors are known to be inadequate, hindsight knowledge can be expected to bias perceptions of what one thinks one knew in foresight. Furthermore, to the extent that various pieces of data about the event vary in support of the actual outcome, evidence that is consistent with the known outcome may become cognitively more salient and thus more available in memory (Slovic and Fischhoff, 1977). This tendency will lead an individual to justify a claimed foresight in view of "the facts provided." Finally, the relevance of a particular piece of data may later be judged important to the extent to which it is representative of the final observed outcome.

In the short run, hindsight has a number of advantages. For instance, it is flattering to believe that your judgment is far better than it actually is! In addition, hindsight allows us to criticize other people's apparent lack of foresight. However, the hindsight bias reduces our ability to learn from the past and to evaluate decisions objectively. In general, individuals should be judged by the process and logic of their decisions, not on their results. A decision maker who makes a high-quality decision that does not work out should be rewarded, not punished. Why? Because results are affected by a variety of factors outside the direct control of the decision maker. When we rely on hindsight offered by results, we will inappropriately evaluate the decision maker's logic, judging their outcomes rather than their methods.

Closely related to the hindsight bias is the "curse of knowledge," which argues that when assessing others' knowledge, people are unable to ignore knowledge that they have that others do not have (Camerer, Loewenstein, and Weber, 1989). Knowledge that is psychologically available is hard to forget when a person is imagining how much others know; sophistication stands in the way of a fair assessment. This "curse" explains the difficulty teachers often have adjusting their lessons according to what students already know, and the tendency of product designers to overestimate the average person's ability to master high-tech devices. Similarly, Hoch (1988) found that marketing experts (who are also consumers) are generally worse at predicting the beliefs, values, and tastes of other consumers than nonexpert consumers are. This results from the marketing experts acting as if the nonexpert consumer understood as much about the products as they did.

Have you ever given someone what you believed were very clear directions to your home, only to find that they got lost? Keysar (1992) argues that an individual often assumes that when she sends an ambiguous message (which is clear to her) to another individual, based on information that the receiver does not possess, her intent will be magically understood by the other party. Keysar had people read scenarios that provided them with privileged information about "David." They read that David had dinner at a particular restaurant based on a friend's recommendation. Half of the participants in the experiment learned that he really enjoyed his meal, and the other half learned that he disliked it very much. All of the participants read that David wrote his friend the following note: "About the restaurant, it was marvelous, just marvelous." The participants who knew that David enjoyed the restaurant had a strong tendency to believe that the friend would take the comment as sincere. In contrast, participants who knew that David disliked the restaurant had a strong tendency to believe that the friend would take the comment as sarcastic. This result occurred despite the fact that both groups of participants knew that the friend had access to the same note and no additional information about David's dining experience. A great deal of disappointment occurs as a result of the failure to communicate clearly in organizations. Part of this disappointment results from our false belief that people understand our ambiguous messages.

INTEGRATION AND COMMENTARY

Heuristics, or rules of thumb, are the cognitive tools we use to simplify decision making. The preceding pages have described 13 of the most common biases that result when we over-rely on these judgmental heuristics. These biases, along with

TABLE 2.2   **Summary of the 13 Biases Presented in Chapter 2**

Bias	Description
Biases Emanating from the Availability Heuristic	
1. Ease of recall	Individuals judge events that are more easily recalled from memory, based on vividness or recency, to be more numerous than events of equal frequency whose instances are less easily recalled.
2. Retrievability	Individuals are biased in their assessments of the frequency of events based on how their memory structures affect the search process.
3. Presumed associations	Individuals tend to overestimate the probability of two events co–occurring based on the number of similar associations they can easily recall, whether from experience or social influence.
Biases Emanating from the Representativeness Heuristic	
4. Insensitivity to base rates	When assessing the likelihood of events, individuals tend to ignore base rates if any other descriptive information is provided—even if it is irrelevant.
5. Insensitivity to sample size	When assessing the reliability of sample information, individuals frequently fail to appreciate the role of sample size.
6. Misconceptions of chance	Individuals expect that a sequence of data generated by a random process will look "random," even when the sequence is too short for those expectations to be statistically valid.
7. Regression to the mean	Individuals tend to ignore the fact that extreme events tend to regress to the mean on subsequent trials.

(continued)

their associated heuristics, are summarized in Table 2.2. Again, I must emphasize that more than one heuristic can operate on our decision-making processes at any given time. Overall, the use of heuristic "shortcuts" results far more often in adequate decisions than inadequate ones. The logic of heuristics is that, on average, any loss in decision quality will be outweighed by time saved. However, as I have demonstrated in this chapter, a blanket acceptance of heuristics is unwise. First, as illustrated by the quiz items, there are many instances in which the loss in decision quality far outweighs the time saved by heuristics. Second, the foregoing logic suggests that we have voluntarily accepted the quality tradeoffs associated with heuristics. In reality, we have not: Most of us are unaware of their existence and their ongoing impact

TABLE 2.2 *(continued)*

8. The conjunction fallacy	Individuals falsely judge that conjunctions (two events co-occurring) are more probable than a more global set of occurrences of which the conjunction is a subset.

Biases Emanating from Anchoring and Adjustment

9. Insufficient anchor adjustment	Individuals make estimates for values based upon an initial value (derived from past events, random assignment, or whatever information is available) and typically make insufficient adjustments from that anchor when establishing a final value.
10. Conjunctive and disjunctive events bias	Individuals exhibit a bias toward overestimating the probability of conjunctive events and underestimating the probability of disjunctive events.
11. Overconfidence	Individuals tend to be overconfident of the infallibility of their judgments when answering moderately to extremely difficult questions.

Two More General Biases

12. The confirmation trap	Individuals tend to seek confirmatory information for what they think is true and fail to search for disconfirmatory evidence.
13. Hindsight and the curse of knowledge	After finding out whether or not an event occurred, individuals tend to overestimate the degree to which they would have predicted the correct outcome. Furthermore, individuals fail to ignore information they possess that others do not when predicting others' behavior.

upon our decision making. Consequently, we fail to distinguish between situations in which they are beneficial and situations in which they are potentially harmful.

To emphasize the distinction between legitimate and illegitimate uses of heuristics, let's reconsider Problem 5. Participants tended to predict that Mark would be more likely to take a job in arts management, despite the fact that the contextual data overwhelmingly favored his choice of a position with an Internet start-up. In this case, the representativeness heuristic prevents us from appropriately incorporating relevant base-rate data. However, if the choice of "Internet start-up" were replaced with a less common career path for an MBA from a prestigious university (such as steel industry management), then the representativeness heuristic is likely to lead to an accurate prediction. In other words, when base-rate data are unavailable or irrelevant (that is, when the choices have the same base rate), the representativeness heuristic provides a reasonably good cognitive tool for matching Mark to his most likely career path. The key to improved judgment, therefore, lies in learning to distinguish between appropriate and inappropriate uses of heuristics. This chapter gives you the foundation you need to learn to make this distinction.

CHAPTER THREE

Judgment under Uncertainty

*I*n the last chapter, we examined how the inappropriate use of cognitive heuristics can lead to biased decision making. In this chapter, we will consider how subtle aspects in the presentation of information, referred to as framing, can significantly impact decision making—particularly when uncertainty is involved. Substantial evidence suggests that intuitions about risk routinely deviate from rationality because managers fail to appreciate the nature of uncertainty and the effects of framing. Yet, uncertainty is a fact of managerial life.

This chapter will help you make better decisions under uncertain conditions. The first part of the chapter includes a general discussion of perceptions of uncertainty, followed by a normative framework for approaching risk. The second part, the core of the chapter, identifies the systematic ways in which your risky judgment is likely to be biased.

AVOIDING UNCERTAINTY: A COMMON RESPONSE

Consider the following scenarios:

- During her search for a sales director, the president of a new Internet start-up interviews an experienced executive who describes his reputation for rewarding "results" and refusing to tolerate failure. Impressed by the applicant's tough talk, the president hires the applicant the next day, passing over several candidates who seemed less decisive.

- President Harry Truman claimed that America needed a "one-armed" economist. When asked why, Truman responded that he was tired of economists who said "on the one hand . . . but on the other hand . . ."

- When budget crises hit an organization, a common response is to cut out expenditures that are not expected to increase immediate productivity (such as management training). This administrative response reflects the belief that money should be allocated only to expenses that are sure to increase short-term profit and productivity.

What is the common element in these scenarios? In each case, the decision makers are grasping for certainty in an uncertain world. They want to know what *will* happen, not what *might* happen. Like these decision makers, most of us fail to accept that we often must make decisions in the face of uncertainty. Instead, we tend to wish away risk and believe that if we work hard enough, we can control outcomes. Observing that people tend to cope with uncertainty by ignoring it, Dawes (1988) argues that humans have a pathological need to "know now" in situations containing inherent uncertainty. He asserts that the need to do away with uncertainty frequently leads people to take too much credit for successes and too much blame for failures.

Despite the tendency to minimize the effects of uncertainty, people typically attempt to identify themselves and others according to degrees of risk aversion and risk seeking. Fischhoff, Slovic, and Lichtenstein (1981) have argued that risk taking is one of the first dimensions we think of in describing someone's personality. For instance, some people value risk-seeking behavior highly: "You won't get very far in life if you don't take risks."

In reality, most people are inconsistent in their approach to risk. When Slovic (1972) compared the scores of 82 people on nine different measures of risk taking, he found no evidence to suggest that a generalizable risk-taking trait exists. The correlations between the nine dimensions ranged from $-.34$ to $+.35$, with a mean of $+.006$. People who are aggressive in one situation may be conservative in another. A professional gambler may take a more careful approach toward his health. A conservative financial analyst may let "all hell break loose" on weekends. In addition, Slovic found that intelligence was not related to a general risk-taking level.

Managers are constantly faced with decisions that will lead to uncertain outcomes. Many of these risky decisions are crucial, involving jobs, safety, product reliability, and organizational existence. On a daily basis, managers face questions such as: How risky would it be to build one more nuclear power plant? How risky is it to expose assembly-line employees to the chemicals necessary to make animal flea collars?

At some point, our decisions are reduced to basic questions such as: What level of risk is acceptable? How much is safety worth? Some would answer, "No price is too great." Yet, if this is true, then society should devote all of its efforts to safety initiatives such as highway improvement and cures for cancer, to the exclusion of productivity. In all aspects of our lives, we must manage risk by trading off outcomes and costs. If we do not deal rationally with these choices, or only respond in a superficial manner, unfortunate inconsistencies occur. Fischhoff, Lichtenstein, and colleagues (1981) note:

> Our legal statutes are less tolerant of carcinogens in our food than in our drinking water or our air. In the United Kingdom, 2,500 times more money per life saved is spent on safety measures in the pharmaceutical industry than in agriculture (Sinclair, Marstand, and Newick, 1972).
>
> According to some calculations, U.S. society spends about $140,000 in highway construction to save one life and $5 million to save a person from death due to radiation exposure (Howard, Matheson, and Owen, 1978, p. 2).

As these examples demonstrate, perceptions of risk are often faulty, resulting in misdirected risk-reduction efforts by public and private decision makers (Fischhoff et al., 1981). The result is that we may be saving far fewer lives than we could for the same cost. We can protect ourselves from such errors by improving the judgments of managers in the private and public sectors.

The better understanding of risk offered by this chapter will enhance managers' ability to make and evaluate decisions in uncertain situations. Once you understand the nature of risky decisions, you will be more likely to evaluate them based on the quality of the decision process rather than on the capriciousness of their outcomes. Managers can make better decisions by accepting that uncertainty exists and by learning to think systematically in risky environments. After all, risk is not bad; it is simply unpredictable. Consider the insightful perspective of Dawes (1988, p. 267):

> Imagine a life without uncertainty. Imagine how dull life would be if variables assessed for admission to a professional school, graduate program, or executive training program really *did* predict with great accuracy who would succeed and who would fail. Life would be intolerable—no hope, no challenge.

A NORMATIVE BACKGROUND TO RISK

While this book is primarily descriptive, it is critical to consider some basic normative concepts regarding risk for two reasons. First, we know that individuals typically are neither rational nor consistent when making judgments under uncertainty. Thus, it is useful to outline a "rational" structure for approaching risky problems. Second, this normative structure provides a background for illustrating the systematic deviations from rationality that we are prone to when making decisions under uncertain conditions. (Readers with some background in statistics and economics may find this section to be a review, while others will find it essential for understanding the material that follows.)

Returning to Chapter 1, you will recall that a rational decision-making process includes: (1) specifying the problem, (2) identifying all factors, (3) weighting factors, (4) identifying all alternatives, (5) rating alternatives on each factor, and (6) choosing the optimal alternative. Up until this point, the rational model has not told us how to rate alternatives when the outcome of a particular factor or factors is uncertain, nor has it provided rules for determining the optimal alternative under uncertainty. These topics are central to a normative theory of preferences under risky conditions. To develop such a theory, we must begin with two concepts: *probability* and *expected value*.

Probability. The concept of probability conveys the likelihood that any particular outcome will occur. A probability of 1.0 represents certainty that an event will occur. A probability of zero represents certainty that an event will not occur. Any value in between represents uncertainty—the degree to which we believe that an event will occur. As discussed earlier, the outcomes of most events and decisions are uncertain. Through probability we can assign values to the likelihood that each potential outcome associated with an event or decision will occur. For example, assume that you flipped four quarters (A, B, C, D). The possible combinations of equally likely outcomes can be represented by the following 16 events:

Event	A	B	C	D	Event	A	B	C	D
1	T	T	T	T	9	T	H	H	T
2	T	T	T	H	10	H	T	H	T
3	T	T	H	T	11	H	H	T	T
4	T	H	T	T	12	H	H	H	T
5	H	T	T	T	13	H	H	T	H
6	T	T	H	H	14	H	T	H	H
7	T	H	T	H	15	T	H	H	H
8	H	T	T	H	16	H	H	H	H

By specifying all possible outcomes, we can observe the probability of various combinations of events. For example, the probability of two or more heads appearing is equal to 11/16 (including events 6 through 16). The probability of getting exactly two heads is 6/16 (including events 6 through 11).

While this presentation treats probability in a very simple way, probability can be very complex, both mathematically and psychologically. For example, it is much more difficult to assess the probability of a Democratic presidential candidate being elected in the year 2008 or the Nasdaq hitting 10,000 before the year 2020. Why? We are now forecasting the future, without being able to specify the likelihood of all possible outcomes. Unfortunately, most real-world decisions (excluding gambling, cards, and other games with a known range of outcomes) take this more complex form.

Expected Value. Calculating the expected value of any alternative involves weighting all potential outcomes associated with that alternative by their probabilities and summing them. For example, to calculate the expected number of heads resulting from four flips of a coin (the answer is obviously two), we would weight all possible combinations of the number of heads occurring in four flips of a coin by their likelihood of occurrence (see the combinations listed previously):

$$\text{Expected value} = 1/16(0) + 4/16(1) + 6/16(2) + 4/16(3) + 1/16(4) = 2$$

Again, the actual calculation of expected value becomes more complicated when we cannot specify the objective likelihood of all possible outcomes. For example, to assess the expected value of your salary 18 months from now, you must assess the likelihood of holding various positions and calculate the associated expected pay for each of the possible positions. As problems become more complex, such assessments can become very demanding, with a great potential for bias.

One simple rule for making decisions is always to select the alternative with the highest expected value. The argument for such an expected-value decision rule is that decisions made according to this rule will, in the aggregate, be optimal; that is, good and bad random errors will cancel out over time. This logic sounds rational, but consider the following scenarios:

- You can (a) receive $10,000,000 for sure (expected value = $10,000,000) or (b) flip a coin and receive $22,000,000 for heads but nothing for tails (expected value = $11,000,000). An expected-value decision rule would lead you to pick (b). What would you do?

- You are being sued for $50,000 and estimate that you have a 50 percent chance of losing the case (expected value = $25,000). However, the other side is willing to accept an out-of-court settlement of $24,000 (expected value = $24,000). An expected-value decision rule would lead you to settle out of court. Ignoring attorney's fees, court costs, aggravation, and so on, would you (a) fight the case, or (b) settle out of court?

Most people would choose (a) in both cases. This suggests that a number of situations exist in which people do not follow an expected-value rule. Understanding when and how people deviate from expected value brings the concept of risk into the problem.

Risk Considerations. The final prerequisite in our discussion of risk is the concept of a certainty equivalent. A certainty equivalent establishes the certain value that would make a decision maker indifferent between an uncertain event and that certain value. For example, if you had an opportunity to accept a 50 percent chance of obtaining $1,000,000, what would be the certain amount that would make you indifferent between the 50 percent chance of $1,000,000 and that amount? $100,000? $300,000? This is your certainty equivalent to a 50 percent chance of $1,000,000. For most people, this amount is far less than the expected value of the bet of $500,000.

An individual who has a certainty equivalent for an uncertain event that is equal to the expected value of the uncertain payoff is risk neutral. For example, if your certainty equivalent in the previous paragraph is $500,000, you are risk neutral concerning that choice; the benefit of a certain outcome is no more valuable to you than the benefit of an uncertain outcome with the same expected value. Thus, risk neutrality is synonymous with using an expected-value decision rule. An individual with a certainty equivalent for an uncertain event that is less than the expected value of that uncertain payoff is risk averse with regard to that decision. If your certainty equivalent in the foregoing problem is $400,000, then you are risk averse, since you are willing to take an expected value reduction of $100,000 to avoid the risk associated with the uncertain event. Although it is unlikely in this context, an individual with a certainty equivalent for an uncertain event that is more than the expected value for that uncertain payoff is risk seeking with regard to that decision. If your certainty equivalent is $550,000, you are risk seeking, since you are demanding extra expected value of $50,000 to forego the risk. Thus, you seek risk, holding the expected value constant.

The concepts of risk-averse and risk-seeking behavior will become crucial as we continue our discussion of judgment under uncertainty. When decision makers act in a risk-averse or risk-seeking manner, they make decisions that often exclude the maximizing of expected value. To explain departures from the expected-value decision rule, Daniel Bernoulli (1738) first suggested replacing the criterion of expected monetary value with the criterion of expected utility. Expected-utility theory suggests that each level of an outcome is associated with some degree of pleasure or net benefit, called *utility*. The expected utility of an uncertain choice is the weighted sum of the utilities of its outcomes, each multiplied by its probability. Although an expected-value approach to decision making would treat $1,000,000 as being worth twice as much as $500,000, a gain of $1,000,000 does not always create twice as much expected utility as a gain of $500,000. Most individuals do not obtain as much utility from the second $500,000 as they did from the first $500,000. Thus, under expected-utility theory, the decision maker is predicted to select the option with the highest expected utility, regardless of whether that choice has the highest expected value.

Furthermore, according to expected-utility theory, individuals identify outcomes in terms of their overall wealth and the additional wealth they would gain from each alternative outcome. That is, we view each choice within the context of the overall utility that we are currently experiencing and the effect that choice would have on our overall utility in the future. As we will see in the next section, Kahneman and Tversky's (1979) prospect theory refutes this aspect of expected-utility theory by arguing that individual decisions are often approached independently.

THE FRAMING OF INFORMATION

Consider the following problem (adapted from Bazerman [1983] and replicated by Miller and Fagley [1988]):

> **Problem 1.** A large car manufacturer has recently been hit with a number of economic difficulties, and it appears as if three plants need to be closed and 6,000 employees laid off. The vice president of production has been exploring alternative ways to avoid this crisis. She has developed two plans:
>
> *Plan A:* This plan will save one of the three plants and 2,000 jobs.
>
> *Plan B:* This plan has a one-third probability of saving all three plants and all 6,000 jobs, but has a two-thirds probability of saving no plants and no jobs.
>
> Which plan would you select?

There are a number of factors we might consider when evaluating these options. For example, what will be the impact of each action on the union? What will be the impact of each plan on the motivation and morale of the retained employees? How do the values of the vice president of production differ from those of the larger corporation? While all of these questions are important, a more fundamental question underlies the subjective situation and resulting decision. Reconsider this problem, replacing the choices just provided with the following choices:

Plan C: This plan will result in the loss of two of the three plants and 4,000 jobs.

Plan D: This plan has a two-thirds probability of resulting in the loss of all three plants and all 6,000 jobs, but has a one-third probability of losing no plants and no jobs.

Which plan would you select?

Close examination of the two sets of alternative plans finds them to be objectively the same. For example, saving one of the three plants and 2,000 of 6,000 jobs (Plan A) offers the same objective outcome as losing two of the three plants and 4,000 of 6,000 jobs (Plan C). Plans B and D are also objectively identical. However, informal empirical investigation demonstrates that most individuals (over 80 percent) choose Plan A in the first set and Plan D in the second set. While the two sets of choices are objectively identical, changing the description of the outcomes from jobs and plants saved to jobs and plants lost is sufficient to shift prototypic choice from risk-averse to risk-seeking behavior.

Individuals treat risks concerning perceived gains (for example, saving jobs and plants—Plans A and B) differently from risks concerning perceived losses (losing jobs and plants—Plans C and D). In an attempt to explain these common and systematic deviations from rationality, Kahneman and Tversky (1979) developed prospect theory, which suggests the following:

1.   People evaluate rewards and losses relative to a neutral reference point.

2.   People think about potential outcomes as gains (such as jobs and plants saved) or losses (jobs and plants lost) relative to this fixed, neutral reference point.

3.   People form their choices based on the resulting change in asset position as assessed by an S-shaped value function (see Figure 3.1).

On this graph, the X axis represents the nominal units gained or lost, and the Y axis represents the units of utility associated with varying levels of gain or loss. Overall, Figure 3.1 suggests that decision makers tend to avoid risk concerning gains and seek risk concerning losses. For example, the S-shaped value function implies that most individuals would choose a $10,000,000 sure gain over a 50 percent chance of getting a $20,000,000 gain, because the utility placed on $20,000,000 is not twice as great as the value placed on $10,000,000. However, most individuals would choose a 50 percent chance of a $20,000,000 loss over a sure loss of $10,000,000, since the negative value placed on $20,000,000 is not twice as great as the negative value placed on $10,000,000.

An important outcome of this theory is that the way in which the problem is "framed," or presented, can dramatically change the perceived neutral point of the question. In Problem 1, if the problem is framed in terms of losing jobs and plants (Plans C and D), the current position of having three plants open forms the neutral reference point. The choices that involve losses of plants and jobs are evaluated on

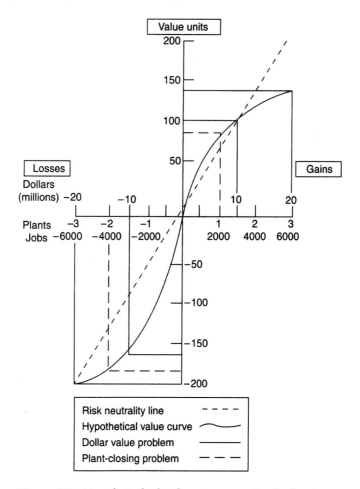

Figure 3.1 Hypothetical value function accounting for framing.

(*Source:* Adapted from Kahneman and Tversky [1979]. Reprinted by permission of the Econometric Society.)

the lower part of the curve in Figure 3.1, and risk-seeking behavior results. The negative value placed on the loss of three plants and 6,000 jobs is usually perceived as not being three times as negative as losing one plant and 2,000 jobs. However, if the problem is framed in terms of saving jobs and plants (Plans A and B), the potential disaster of losing everything becomes the neutral reference point. The choices are then evaluated on the upper part of the curve, and risk-averse behavior results. Figure 3.1 indicates that the gain placed on saving three plants and 6,000 jobs is frequently viewed as not being three times as great as saving one plant and 2,000 jobs.

Thus, one of the most important outcomes of prospect theory is that it identifies a systematic pattern of how the framing of the problem causes decision-making behavior to deviate from both expected-value and expected-utility theory. Both of these theories posit that the rational decision makers should be immune to the framing of choices. A second characteristic of our decision-making processes identified by prospect theory is that our response to loss is more extreme than our response to gain. According to Figure 3.1, the pain associated with losing X dollars is generally greater than the pleasure associated with winning the same amount. Tversky and Kahneman (1981) cite "people's reluctance to accept fair bets on a toss of a coin" as evidence of this effect.

Finally, prospect theory identifies a third way in which our decision-making processes deviate from expected-utility theory, which we discuss only briefly here. It concerns our treatment of probabilities. While expected-utility theory weights a risky option by its probability, prospect theory states that we tend to overweight the probability of low-probability events and underweight the probability of moderate- and high-probability events. Furthermore, underweighting is strongest for high-probability events. Thus, Kahneman and Tversky (1979) also incorporate systematic deviations from rationality in probability assessments as part of their decision model.

THE FRAMING OF RISKY DECISIONS

The preceding paragraphs have presented the logic of prospect theory and identified the ways in which its conclusions depart from the normative tenets of expected-utility theory. Broadly, these concepts include the impact of the framing of information on our decisions, our differential response to gains and losses, and our tendency to systematically misrepresent probabilities. Because of its descriptive power, prospect theory has inspired a great deal of excitement in the fields of decision theory, psychology, marketing, law, medicine, finance, organizational behavior, and economics over the past 20 years. The theory has been responsible for helping researchers develop a more thorough understanding of errors and inconsistencies in human judgment.

This section explores a variety of implications of prospect theory and research derived from it. Specifically, we will explore how your decisions are affected by the framing of choices, the role of anchors, pseudocertainty, the frame of insurance, evaluation of transactions, the value you place on your time, and how ownership creates a different frame for valuation.

The Framing of Choices

Tversky and Kahneman (1981) asked 150 subjects the following questions:

> **Problem 2.** Imagine that you face the following pair of concurrent decisions. First examine both decisions, and then indicate the options you prefer.

> **Decision *i***
> Choose between:
> **a.** A sure gain of $240
> **b.** A 25 percent chance to gain $1,000, and a 75 percent chance to gain nothing

Decision *ii*

Choose between:

c. A sure loss of $750

d. A 75 percent chance to lose $1,000, and a 25 percent chance to lose nothing

In decision *i*, 84 percent of the subjects chose (a) while only 16 percent chose (b). In decision *ii*, 87 percent of the subjects chose (d) while only 13 percent chose (c). The majority chose "a sure gain of $240" in decision *i* because of our tendency to be risk-averse concerning gains and positively framed questions. By contrast, the majority chose "a 75 percent chance to lose $1,000" in decision *ii* because of our tendency to be risk seeking concerning losses and negatively framed questions. In terms of Figure 3.1, the value associated with a gain of $240 is greater than 25 percent of the value associated with a gain of $1,000. Figure 3.1 also shows that the negative value associated with a loss of $750 is more than 75 percent of the negative value associated with a loss of $1,000. Combining the responses to the two problems, 73 percent of respondents chose (a) and (d), while only 3 percent chose (b) and (c).

Now consider the following problems presented by Tversky and Kahneman (1981) to 86 subjects (who were not previously exposed to Problem 2):

Problem 2a. Choose between:

e. A 25 percent chance to win $240, and a 75 percent chance to lose $760

f. A 25 percent chance to win $250, and a 75 percent chance to lose $750

Not surprisingly, all 86 subjects chose (f) over (e). In fact, (f) dominates (e) in all respects. Why is this problem interesting? When you combine (a) and (d) (the preferred choices) in Problem 2, (e) results, whereas when you combine choices (b) and (c) (the choices not preferred), (f) results.

Adding choices (a) and (d) = (e):

$$(100\%)(\$240) + [(75\%)(-\$1,000) + (25\%)(\$0)] = (25\%)(\$240) + (75\%)(-\$760)$$

Adding choices (b) and (c) = (f):

$$[(25\%)(\$1,000) + (75\%)(\$0)] + (100\%)(-\$750) = (25\%)(\$250) + (75\%)(-\$750)$$

The sum of the undesirable choices *dominates* the sum of the desirable choices! Thus, the framing of the combined problem in two parts results in a reversal of preferences. Prospect theory's preference curve (see Figure 3.1) accounts for this finding, but that does not imply that the choices are rational. In fact, this inconsistency violates the fundamental requirements for rational decision making: consistency and coherence.

Why should this finding interest managers? Many interconnected decisions in the real world, such as portfolio selection, budgeting, and funding for new projects, can be framed as separate or joint decisions. The findings suggest that the subdivision of decision making throughout an organization is likely to enhance the potential for inconsistency and nonrational choice, similar to that exhibited in Problem 2. Sales departments are encouraged to think in terms of the acquisition of corporate gains, while credit offices are encouraged to frame decisions in terms of avoiding corporate losses. To arrive at a coherent strategy for making judgments under uncertainty, individuals and organizations need to become more aware of this bias and develop procedures for identifying and integrating risky decisions across organizations.

By being risk averse some of the time and risk seeking at other times, we are likely to adopt a decision portfolio that is just as inferior as selecting the preceding choices (a) and (d). To override our intuitive tendency for our risk preferences to be highly affected by the problem frame, Kahneman and Lovallo (1993, see also Rabin and Thaler, 2000) have argued that we would generally be better off following an expected-value rule for most decisions. Deviations from risk neutrality in the real world should probably be reserved for critically important decisions, after careful consideration of the problem from multiple frames.

Anchors Matter

As previously suggested in our discussion of prospect theory, the typical decision maker evaluates outcomes relative to a neutral reference point. Consequently, the location of the reference point is critical to whether the decision is positively or negatively framed and affects the resulting risk preference of the decision maker. The plant-closing problem (Problem 1) illustrates the importance of reference points. In the positively framed case, the question is, How many plants (and jobs) can be saved? Saved from what? Saved from the possible loss of three plants. Thus, the loss of three plants is the neutral reference point. In contrast, in the negatively framed case, the question is, How many plants (and jobs) will be lost? Lost from what? Lost from the existing three operating plants. Here, three open plants is the neutral reference point. As we showed earlier, after shifting the reference point, most individuals move from evaluating the choice on the upper part of the curve (see Figure 3.1) to the lower part.

For another example of the importance of this reference point shift, consider the following scenario:

> **Problem 3.**   You were given 100 shares of stock in XYZ Corporation two years ago, when the value of the stock was $20 per share. Unfortunately, the stock has dropped to $10 per share during the two years that you have held the asset. The corporation is currently drilling for oil in an area that may turn out to be a big "hit." On the other hand, they may find nothing. Geological analysis suggests that if they hit, the stock is expected to go back up to $20 per share. If the well is dry, however, the value of the stock will fall to $0 per share. Do you want to sell your stock now for $10 per share?

What is your reference point in this problem? Is it the amount you can gain (the amount that you receive for the stock above $0 per share), or is it the amount you can lose (the amount that the stock has fallen from $20 per share when you sell it)? Figure 3.1 suggests that if you cognitively adopt $0 per share as your reference point, you will be risk averse and will take the sure "gain" by selling the stock now. If your reference point is $20 per share, however, you will be risk seeking and will hold onto the stock rather than accept a sure "loss."

How should this knowledge of the impact of reference points affect your decisions? First, when facing a risky decision, you should identify your reference point. Next, consider whether other reference points exist, and whether they are just as reasonable. If the answer is yes, think about your decision from multiple perspectives and examine any contradictions that emerge. At this point, you will be prepared to make your decision with a full awareness of the alternative frames in which the problem could be presented.

The framing of outcomes can affect not only your decisions, but your satisfaction with outcomes that you do not choose. Consider the following two outcomes (adapted from Thaler, 1985):

a. You receive a letter from the IRS saying that you made a minor arithmetic mistake in your tax return and must send them $100. You receive a similar letter the same day from your state tax authority saying you owe $50 for a similar mistake. There are no other repercussions from either mistake.

b. You receive a letter from the IRS saying that you made a minor arithmetic mistake in your tax return and must send them $150. There are no other repercussions from the mistake.

Which situation would be more upsetting? Most people are more upset by the two small losses than the one larger loss, despite the fact that the two sets of outcomes are equal. This emotional reaction is consistent with the nature of our reactions to losses, as well as with the preceding reference point arguments. The extra $50 loss is less bothersome from the point on the value function where you have already lost $100 than from the point where you have lost nothing.

Pseudocertainty

Prospect theory suggests that people underweight high-probability events but appropriately weight events that are certain. Thus, if an event has a probability of 1.0 or zero, we tend to accurately evaluate the event's probability. However, if the event has a probability of .99, we tend to respond as the expected-utility framework would expect us to respond to a probability of less than .99. As a result, Slovic, Lichtenstein, and Fischhoff (1982) observe that "any protective action that reduces the probability of harm from, say, .01 to zero will be valued more highly than an action that reduces the probability of the same harm from .02 to .01" (p. 24). In other words, people value the creation of certainty over an equally valued shift in the level of uncertainty.

Interestingly, the perception of certainty (that is, the perception that the probability of an event is zero or 1.0) can be easily manipulated. Slovic et al. (1982) consider the best way to advertise a disaster insurance policy that covers fire but not flood. The policy can be accurately advertised either as "full protection" against fire or as a reduction in the overall probability of loss from natural disasters. The logic of prospect theory presented in the previous paragraph predicts that the full-protection advertisement will make the policy most attractive to potential buyers. This is because the full-protection option reduces perceived uncertainty for loss from fire to zero, whereas the overall disaster policy reduces uncertainty some incremental amount to a value still above zero. The perceived certainty that results from the full-protection framing of this advertisement has been labeled "pseudocertainty" (Slovic et al., 1982).

Slovic et al. (1982) provided empirical evidence of the strength of the pseudo-certainty effect in the context of disease vaccination. Two forms of a questionnaire were created. Form 1 described a disease that was expected to afflict 20 percent of the population. Subjects in this condition were asked if they would receive a vaccine that protected half of the individuals vaccinated. Form 2 described two mutually exclusive and equally probable strains of the disease, each of which was expected to afflict 10 percent of the population. In this case, vaccination was said to give complete protection (certainty) against one strain and no protection against the other. Would you take the vaccine described in Form 1? What about the vaccine described in Form 2? In either case, the vaccine would objectively reduce one's overall risk from 20 percent to 10 percent. Slovic et al. found that Form 2 (pseudocertainty) was more appealing than Form 1 (probabilistic). Some 57 percent of subjects who were given Form 2 said that they would get the vaccination, compared to only 40 percent of the subjects who received Form 1.

In the following problems, Tversky and Kahneman (1981) simultaneously investigated the impact of certainty and pseudocertainty on judgmental choice:

Problem 4. Which of the following options do you prefer?
a. A sure win of $30
b. An 80 percent chance to win $45

Problem 5. Consider the following two-stage game. In the first stage, there is a 75 percent chance to end the game without winning anything, and a 25 percent chance to move into the second stage. If you reach the second stage you have a choice between
c. A sure win of $30
d. An 80 percent chance to win $45

Decide whether you prefer (c) or (d). Your choice must be made before the game starts—that is, before the outcome of the first stage is known.

Problem 6. Which of the following options do you prefer?
e. A 25 percent chance to win $30
f. A 20 percent chance to win $45

Tversky and Kahneman (1981) presented each of these problems to a different group of subjects. In Problem 4, 78 percent of the subjects chose (a) and 22 percent chose (b). In Problem 5, 74 percent of the subjects chose (c) and 26 percent chose (d). In Problem 6, 42 percent of the subjects chose (e) and 58 percent chose (f). Some interesting contrasts result. Consider Problem 5: By combining the first and second parts of the problem, it becomes evident that (c) offers a .25 chance to win $30 and (d) offers a .25 × .80 = .20 chance to win $45. This is the same choice offered in Problem 6! Yet the modal choice has shifted. In Problem 5, if you lose in the first stage, it does not matter what choice you made. If you win in the first stage,

Problem 5 reduces to Problem 4. Consequently, there seems to be no reason to respond differently to Problems 4 and 5. Since Problem 5 is equivalent to Problems 4 and 6, it can be inferred that Problems 4 and 6 should also be treated similarly. However, subjects responded similarly to Problems 4 and 5, but differently to Problem 6. Why this discrepancy in response to Problem 6?

The difference between Problems 4 and 6 illustrates a phenomenon that Tversky and Kahneman (1981) call the **certainty effect**: "A reduction of the probability of an outcome has more importance when the outcome was initially certain than when it was merely probable" (p. 455). The discrepancy, in response to objectively identical Problems 5 and 6, illustrates the **pseudocertainty effect** (Slovic et al., 1982; Tversky and Kahneman, 1981). The prospect of winning $30 is more attractive in Problem 5 than in Problem 6 because of the perceived certainty ("a sure win") associated with choice (c). However, this potential "certainty" is contingent upon reaching the second stage of the game, which still makes the outcome uncertain.

The certainty and pseudocertainty effects lead to judgmental inconsistencies. The certainty effect makes us more apt to be interested in reducing the likelihood of certain events than uncertain events. Under the pseudocertainty effect, we are more likely to favor options that assure us certainty than those that only reduce uncertainty. Rationally, any constant reduction of risk in an uncertain situation should have the same value for the decision maker. For example, reducing the risk of cancer from 20 percent to 10 percent should have the same value as a reduction from 10 percent to 0 percent. But prospect theory tells us that perceived certainty, or "pseudocertainty," has a special value to most people. Manipulations of pseudocertainty have important implications for the design of communications about medical treatments, personal insurance, corporate liability protection, and a variety of other forms of protection. The data suggest that individuals may buy insurance not only to protect against risk, but also to eliminate the worry caused by any amount of uncertainty (Tversky and Kahneman, 1981).

"Insurance Premium" Sounds Better than "Guaranteed Loss"

What is an insurance premium? It is a certain loss (the premium) that you accept in exchange for the reduction of a small probability of a large loss. Interestingly, Schoemaker and associates (Hershey and Schoemaker, 1980; Schoemaker and Kunreuther, 1979) and Slovic et al. (1982) have found that framing a sure loss as an insurance premium makes the loss more attractive—even when the objective amount of loss is the same. Slovic et al. (1982) asked study participants to pick between a sure loss (insurance premium) versus a risky option that had a small probability of a significant loss. For half of the participants, the risk-free option was called a certain loss. For the other half, the risk-free option was called an insurance premium. Study participants were much more likely to choose the risk-free loss when it was called an insurance premium than when it was called a certain loss.

This framing effect can be explained in a number of ways. Prospect theory would suggest that in the certain loss condition, people see the loss on the negative side of the chart (see Figure 3.1), and risk-seeking behavior results. By contrast, in the insurance condition, the reference point is more ambiguous, and risk-seeking behavior is less prevalent (Slovic et al., 1982).

Kahneman and Tversky (1979) and Hershey and Schoemaker (1980) also argue that "insurance" triggers social norms such as: "How can you not carry insurance?" and "All good citizens carry insurance." Buying insurance is something that most of us do without considering an alternative strategy. When was the last time you considered dropping your car insurance (assuming that you live in a state where it is legal to be uninsured)?

The framing of insurance and warranties may explain a very strange set of consumer decisions. After agreeing to buy a new automobile, consumers are typically offered the option of purchasing an extended warranty. The salesperson typically notes that, "For just a few dollars more per month, you'll never have to worry about repairs." Why do nearly half of new car buyers purchase extended warranties? It could be because they are a good deal. But this does not appear to be the case. Car dealers make a great deal of money on warranties. Documents in a recent lawsuit filed against Nissan show that the typical extended warranty cost $795. A mere $131 went toward covering repairs, $109 went to Nissan for administrative costs, and the remaining $555 was straight dealer profit. It seems that the vividness of a costly repair, coupled with a social norm favoring insurance and warranties, leads many consumers to make a risk-averse choice that they would probably not make if they considered their options more carefully. As we have seen, people are more likely to accept a certain loss if they view it as insurance rather than as a sure monetary loss. Consumers would be better off if they just said "no" to all extended warranties, put the money saved in the bank, and used it to pay for necessary repairs. Across their life span, they will be making a far better set of decisions.

What's It Worth to You?

The term **transactional utility** was introduced by Thaler (1985) and can be best seen in terms of the following scenario.
(Read this scenario twice—first with the words in parentheses and excluding the words in brackets, and second with the words in brackets and excluding the words in parentheses.)

> You are lying on the beach on a hot day. All you have to drink is ice water. For the last hour you have been thinking about how much you would enjoy a nice cold bottle of your favorite brand of beer. A companion gets up to go make a phone call and offers to bring back a beer from the only nearby place where beer is sold (a fancy resort hotel) [a small, rundown grocery store]. He says that the beer might be expensive and asks how much you are willing to pay for it. He says that he will buy the beer if it costs as much as or less than the price you state. But if it costs more than the price you state, he will not buy it. You trust your friend, and there is no possibility of bargaining with the (bartender) [store owner]. What price do you tell him?

Notice some of the features of this dual problem. First, in both the hotel and the grocery store versions, you get the same product. Second, there is no possible negotiation on price. Third, there will be no advantage to the resort hotel "atmosphere," since you are going to drink the beer on the beach. According to expected-utility theory, people should be willing to pay the same amount in both versions of the scenario. In fact, Thaler found that participants in an executive development program were willing to pay significantly more if the beer was purchased from the "fancy resort hotel." The results were medians of $2.65 for a beer bought at the resort and $1.50 for a beer bought at the store.

Why does this contradiction occur? Thaler suggests the reason is that while "paying $2.50 for a beer at a fancy hotel would be an expected annoyance, paying $2.50 at a grocery store would be an outrageous 'rip-off.' " This leads to the conclusion that something else matters besides the value you place on the commodity acquired. Did you ever buy something because it was "too good a deal to pass up," despite the fact that you had no need for the product? Thaler explains this phenomenon by suggesting that purchases are affected by both acquisition utility and transactional utility. **Acquisition utility** describes the value you place on a commodity (in this case, the beer). **Transactional utility** refers to the quality of the deal that you receive, evaluated in reference to "what the item should cost." Obviously, paying $2.50 for a beer at a grocery store leads to a greater negative transactional utility than paying $2.50 at the fancy resort hotel. One can argue that the inclusion of transactional utility in decision making is not rational, but it does describe our behavior.

How Much Is Your Time Worth?

So far, this chapter has dealt exclusively with decisions involving risk. An area that is clearly related to risk, yet conceptually different, is the way in which people make decisions about the value of their time.

> **Problem 7.**   Imagine that you are about to purchase a modem for $50. The computer salesperson informs you that the modem you wish to buy is on sale at the store's other branch, located a 20-minute drive away. What is the highest price that the modem could cost at the other store such that you would be willing to travel there for the discount?

> **Problem 8.**   Imagine that you are about to purchase a color television for $500. The television salesperson informs you that this television is on sale at the store's other branch, located a 20-minute drive from where you are now. What is the highest price that you would be willing to pay at the other store to make the discount worth the trip?

How much is 20 minutes of your time plus the cost of travel worth? The answer to this question, compared to the amount saved from the sale prices, should determine whether or not you will make the trip in each case. However, most people demand a greater discount in absolute dollars to make the television trip than to make the modem trip. Why? The issue of transactional utility enters into our assessments of the value of our time. Most people will be willing to travel the 20 minutes only to get a "very good deal." A $25 (5 percent) savings is not a big discount on the television, but it is an outstanding deal on the modem (you would be saving 50 percent). Normatively, however, the difference in percentage reduction is irrelevant. One should simply compare the savings obtained to the value of the time spent, and this value should remain consistent across decisions.

The Value We Place on What We Own

Imagine that you purchased a painting from an up-and-coming artist five years ago for $50. The artist has since become very famous, and the painting is now worth about $1,000. Imagine the minimum amount that you believe would lead you to sell this painting. Now, also think about how much you would be willing to pay for a similar-quality painting.

Most people would demand far more to sell the painting than the amount they would be willing to pay for a similar painting, or the amount that they would pay for that exact same painting if they did not own it. This pattern is called the **endowment effect** (Thaler, 1980).

In any exchange, a buyer must be willing to pay at least the minimum amount that a seller is willing to accept—otherwise no agreement takes place. Objectively, the valuation of a commodity should be based on its true value. However, the value that a seller places on a commodity often includes not only its intrinsic worth, but also value based on his or her attachment to the item.

In a very clever experiment, Kahneman, Knetsch, and Thaler (1990) placed mugs in front of one-third of the participants in their study. These "sellers" were told that they owned the mug and had the option of selling it if a price, to be determined later, was acceptable to them. They were then given a list of possible selling prices, ranging from $0.50 to $9.50 (in 50-cent increments), and were told to indicate for each possible price whether they would sell the mug for that amount or keep it.

Another third of the participants—the "buyers"—were told that they would be given a sum of money which they could keep or use to buy a mug. They were also asked their preferences between a mug and sums of money ranging from $0.50 to $9.50. The remaining third of the participants—the "choosers"—were given a questionnaire indicating that they would be given a choice between either a mug or a sum of money. They also marked their preferences between the mug and sums of money ranging from $0.50 to $9.50. All three groups were assured that their answers would not influence either the predetermined price of the mug or the amount of money to be received in lieu of the mug.

The results reveal a great deal about how our role in a buyer–seller relationship affects our value assessments. Sellers required a median value of $7.12 for the mug, the buyers $2.87, and the choosers $3.12. The buyers and choosers had very similar evaluations of the worth of the mug. In contrast, ownership made the mug much more valuable for the sellers; differences of 2:1 are common in such endowment experiments. The implication of this endowment effect is that people tend to overvalue what they own. The frame of ownership creates value that is inconsistent with a rational analysis of the worth that the commodity brings to the individual. This inconsistent valuation partially explains why so many home sellers set an inappropriately high value on their homes and find themselves without any bidders for extended periods of time. An understanding of the endowment effect is critical to making wise assessments of the value of your commodities.

INTEGRATION OF VARIOUS FRAMING EFFECTS

Prospect theory represents one of the most important advances in our understanding of decision making. The phenomena covered in this chapter demonstrate some of the key findings of that work—namely, the critical importance that the framing of information has on how we make decisions in uncertain situations. From the information presented, you should now be able to identify situations in which you tend to adopt a particular frame to the exclusion of other perspectives. If you can understand and apply this knowledge, the consistency and quality of your decisions will be greatly improved.

The analytical framework presented in this chapter can help you increase your awareness of the nature of uncertainty and risky decisions, identify systematic ways in which judgment deviates from rationality in uncertain conditions, and allow you to generalize these ideas to your professional and personal life. Most important, a key purpose of the chapter has been to create an awareness of the inherently probabilistic nature of most decisions. As Dawes (1988) reminds us:

> [T]here is much uncertainty in the world, and one of our most basic choices is whether we will accept that uncertainty as a fact or try to invent a stable world of our own. Such people's natural desire to reduce uncertainty, which may be basic to the whole cognitive enterprise of understanding the world, runs amok to the point that they come to believe uncertainty does not exist (p. 273).

Accepting your own inability to eliminate many sources of uncertainty can be a scary process. However, this shift in mindset is certain to pay off in the form of more informed decisions and greater satisfaction with results.

CHAPTER FOUR

Motivational Biases

The holiday season has come and gone, leaving you with seven extra pounds. In an attempt to lose weight, you decide to reduce the fat in your diet. Upon arriving at a party, you sit in front of a bowl of your favorite, high-fat treat (cashews, potato chips, caramel popcorn, etc.). One piece goes into your mouth, and soon the bowl is empty. You have consumed over 60 grams of fat. The next day you regret your decision and wonder how you could have ignored your resolution to lose weight so easily.

*T*he day after the party, it appears as if your eating was inconsistent with your long-term preferences. Yet the preceding chapters tell us little about the mistake that you made. So far, this book has focused almost exclusively on cognitive errors, or errors that have their root in how we process information. In contrast, many of the errors we make are the result of motivational biases. This chapter considers situations in which we make decisions that are inconsistent with our long-term interests, because of a temporary motivation to pursue some alternative goal. I view such decisions as biased when preoccupation with a temporary goal lowers the overall benefit to the decision maker and is inconsistent with what the individual would prefer for him- or herself when acting more reflectively.

This chapter focuses on four categories of motivational biases. The first section describes common tensions we all face between doing what we want to do and doing what we think we should do, as illustrated by the party dilemma above. The second section examines the effects of positive illusions, or the general tendency to view oneself and the world more positively than reality suggests. In the third section I discuss egocentrism, or the self-serving ways in which people interpret fairness. The fourth section explores how we make biased decisions in order to avoid regret. In each section, I will review evidence of underlying motivational biases and offer suggestions on how to better manage these biases to create more optimal decisions.

WHEN MOTIVATION AND COGNITION COLLIDE

In Homer's *The Odyssey*, Ulysses was confronted with a classic negotiation problem during his long voyage at sea. He knew that he would soon encounter the Sirens, mythical female "enchanters" who lured seafaring men to their island—and to their subsequent death—by singing sweetly to them from their flowering meadow. No man had ever been able to resist the Sirens, and their beach was "piled with bone-heaps of men now rotted away." Ulysses was advised to put wax in his men's ears to block out the tempting voices of the Sirens. To protect himself, Ulysses told his men to bind him with ropes to the ship's mast and ordered them in advance not to release him, no matter how much he begged, until after they sailed safely by the Sirens. This way, Ulysses would have the pleasure of listening to the Sirens without falling into their trap. As his ship sets sail, he warns his men: "If I supplicate you and implore you to set me free, then you must tie me fast with even more lashings." Ulysses' plan works, and he and his men survive their latest adventure.

This section explores the internal inconsistencies that exist when what we want to do clashes with what we think we should do. Ulysses faced competing preferences: He knew that he would want to go to the Sirens, but he also knew that succumbing to this desire would be a fatal mistake. Grappling with such internal contradictions is part of the human condition:

- Ulysses wanted to visit the Sirens, but knew that he should not because they would kill him.
- The alcoholic craves a drink, but knows that he should abstain because of the negative consequences that will inevitably result.
- The gambler wants to win big in Las Vegas, but knows that she should avoid all gambling because she has difficulty knowing when to stop.
- The author does not want to exercise regularly, but knows that he should to improve his cardiovascular health.

In our daily lives, we constantly make choices between what we want to do and what we should do. A job hunter might have to choose between an enjoyable, low-status position and one that he thinks he should take for financial or practical reasons. Consumers must often decide whether to buy the product they want or a product they think they should purchase for health, environmental, or budgetary reasons. People often want to engage in an action that will fulfill their short-term desires, while believing they should act differently to maximize their long-term goals (Bazerman, Tenbrunsel, and Wade-Benzoni, 1998).

Individuals have preferences that put them in disagreement with themselves. Schelling argues that each individual behaves like two people: "one who wants clear lungs and long life and another who adores tobacco, or one who wants a lean body and another who wants dessert" (1984, p. 58). Economists and other social scientists have struggled to understand this multiple-selves problem for at least 45 years (Strotz, 1956), while others have devoted substantial effort and religious rhetoric to denying its existence (Stigler and Becker, 1977). Taking a more extreme view than most, Elster (1979), a philosopher and political theorist, regards the multiple-selves phenomenon as a collective action problem involving a multitude of selves within one person. According to Elster's conceptualization, the key goal for an individual should be to keep the self from defecting on a cooperative choice that will be in the best interest of the collectivity of selves.

The multiple-selves problem has been used to account for a variety of dysfunctional clinical behaviors such as alcohol, drug, and spousal abuse (Ainslie, 1975), as well as common consumer and investment errors that stem from the inappropriately high discounting that people apply to the future (Loewenstein, 1996). In almost all of these cases, one of our "selves" is in favor of a decision that provides immediate benefit rather than an alternative that would provide greater future rewards. I argue that the psychological basis for these identified internal inconsistencies is in fact widespread, covering a variety of decisions that are limited neither to clinically dysfunctional populations nor to temporal problems.

Schelling (1980, 1984) connected the multiple-selves problem to a broad range of economic behaviors, including saving money in non-interest-bearing Christmas clubs, giving free loans to the government by overpaying taxes in order to get a refund, and gambling. Schelling also connects his arguments to a variety of social phenomena such as smoking, drinking, drugs, scratching, overeating, procrastinating, exercising, and sexual behavior. By distinguishing the long-term self from the short-term self, Schelling clarifies the magnitude of the multiple-selves problem in everyday behavior. A key conceptual contribution of this work is its specification of control tactics that the long-term thinker can use to manage the short-term thinker. It is clear that in Schelling's view, as in most economic writing on this problem, the long-term thinker knows more than the short-term thinker.

Thaler (1980) agrees with Schelling that the key to resolving our internal conflicts is to recognize them and create means of self-control. Thaler identifies two selves, the *planner* and the *doer*, and describes the actions that the planner can take to control the doer, particularly through the multitude of self-help programs that have emerged in contemporary society, including Alcoholics Anonymous, drug abuse centers, diet clubs, and smoking clinics. Shefrin and Thaler (1988) argue that effective control techniques include:

- *Changing the doer's preferences*. For example, the planner can seek out a type of exercise that the doer will enjoy.
- *Monitoring the doer's behavior*. Participating in a diet club's weekly "weigh-ins" can deter overeating.
- *Altering incentives*. Alcoholics can take the drug Antabuse, which will make them ill if they take a drink.
- *Altering rules*. Students might forbid themselves from turning on the television until they've finished their homework.

Loewenstein (1996) questions the use of a metaphor that we all know does not describe reality—the idea of two selves existing within the same person. Rather, he identifies the conditions under which visceral responses lead to an overemphasis on transient concerns. According to Loewenstein, manifestations of physiological states, such as cravings induced by withdrawal, drive states such as hunger, thirst, and sexual desire, and moods and emotions create inconsistencies between deliberation and action. Loewenstein (1996) also notes that in many professions, success is measured by one's ability to manipulate the transient concerns of other people. Automobile and electronics salespeople and real-estate agents often try to orient the customer toward a transient concern, for example, by encouraging you to imagine yourself driving your new BMW home for the first time. Con men play on transient feelings of greed, while police interrogators use hunger, thirst, and sleep deprivation to extract confessions. Cults indoctrinate new members through food deprivation, forced incontinence, and social pressures to conform, all of which cause transient concerns to overwhelm long-term self-interest (Loewenstein, 1996). By contrast, many states try to protect consumers from short-term impulses by legislating revocability periods for high-priced items (e.g., condominium share purchases). Loewenstein (1996) connects his ideas on transient concerns to behavioral decision research on vividness described in Chapter 2 (Tversky and Kahneman, 1974), which argues that decision makers overweight proximal (temporal, physical, or sensory) attributes.

Internal inconsistencies between transient concerns and long-term self-interest reflect natural tensions between what people want to do and what they think they should do. People often hold conflicting preferences, and the basis of this conflict is the difference between "want" and "should." The want/should distinction (Bazerman et al., 1998) is broadly compatible with Loewenstein's (1996) argument; the "want" self is similar to the visceral response, while the "should" self tends to be more long-term focused. Using the two-selves description metaphorically, we develop a model that describes the contexts in which "want" and "should" dominate. We argue that the "want" self will tend to dominate in real-world decisions in which one option is salient at a time. When we assess options one at a time, we tend to place greater weight on affective, visceral criteria. In contrast, the more reasoned, reflective "should" self will tend to dominate when we confront multiple options at the same time. Thus, when we are given the option of a short-term reward (a day off, drugs, etc.) with long-term costs, the want self is salient, and the option seems attractive. But, when we consider the short-term desire versus passing on that desire in an explicit comparison, the should self becomes stronger. This pattern can be illustrated by the should self who makes New Year's resolutions, and the want self who breaks those resolutions.

The important practical question arising from this research is: What advice can we give to internally inconsistent decision makers? Stigler and Becker (1977) would tell us to leave them alone, since their behavior will naturally follow a rational course of action. However, this recommendation fails the market test of good advice: Virtually no reasonable human being would prescribe it for someone they care about. As outlined earlier in this chapter, Schelling (1984) and Thaler (1980) would concentrate on controlling the destructive impulses of the short-term decision maker. Kahneman and Ritov (1994) would argue that a choice between options captures our long-term interests more effectively, implying that the transient, want criteria should be suppressed if possible. I certainly believe that the advice of Schelling, Thaler, and Kahneman and Ritov would do far more good than harm. However, complete reliance on their advice would assume that the should self always optimizes self-interest.

Loewenstein (1996) is much friendlier to the want self, noting that transient responses are often adaptive to natural environments. That is, visceral reactions may make individuals aware of issues that they care a great deal about, but that they may have suppressed because of a desire to be responsible, mature, or otherwise to conform to society. In contrast to the tactics of self-control advocated by Thaler and Schelling, Loewenstein argues, "Hunger signals the need for nutritional input, pain indicates the impingement of some type of potentially harmful environmental factors, and emotions serve a range of interrupting, prioritizing, and energizing functions." A natural extension of this argument is that if the individual takes the time to carefully consider what to do, an important opportunity could be lost. The feelings of regret that might follow are described in folk singer Christine Lavin's song "The Moment Slipped Away":

> *He works the ward at the Bellevue Hospital*
> *The mail delivery*
> *For two years every weekday mornin'*
> *He said hello to me*
> *We joke about the local team*
> *The weather of the day*
> *Though there were many other things*
> *I really wanted to say*
> *You see he wasn't like the rest of us*
> *It was a struggle for him to walk*
> *And you had to concentrate really hard*
> *Just to understand his talk*
> *I wanted to ask him,*
> *Where do you get the courage*
> *To come to work each day*
> *But I quit that job*
> *I moved along*
> *And the moment slipped away*

As Lavin conveys, at times the should self may be too conservative, risk averse, or timid to do the right thing. The want self may serve a valuable purpose by signaling the value of emotional criteria to the should self. How do we give voice to the want self with the goal of improving the decisions of the should self? I offer advice on this issue from two areas of rational thought: Raiffa's decision-analysis perspective and the steps of rational decision making outlined in Chapter 1, and a negotiation framework for providing rational advice to negotiators that I will present in greater detail in Chapter 8.

Decision Theory Advises the Multiple Selves

Howard Raiffa has made important contributions to the fields of decision making and negotiations. In his book *Decision Analysis* (1968), Raiffa offers prescriptive advice to decision makers, including recommendations for formalizing the identification and weighting of multiple criteria. In an apocryphal, ever-changing story, Raiffa was on the faculty at Columbia and received an offer from Harvard. According to the story, he visited his dean at Columbia, who was also his friend, and asked for help with his decision. Sarcastically, the dean, borrowing from Raiffa's writings, told Raiffa to identify the relevant criteria, weight each criterion, rate each school on each criterion, do the arithmetic, see which school had the best overall score, and go there. Supposedly, Raiffa's response was, "No, this is a serious decision."

While he enjoys this story, Raiffa says it simply isn't true. However, the story, which describes a potential tension between the want self (who would make the decision based on gut instinct) and the should self (who would accept the higher score from a formal decision-theoretic analysis), led Raiffa to clarify what he would do in a situation where conflict existed between the two selves. He advocates an approach that entails questioning each self to find out which one is making the error. Perhaps the should self can confront the want self with its limited perspective—for example, the danger of ignoring long-term implications of the decision. Alternatively, it could be that the want self can elucidate for the should self some of the more elusive feelings that have been neglected by its formal analysis. Raiffa suggests that this communication should take place until reconciliation occurs.

When the two selves are in disagreement about an important decision, I would argue that this conflict signals the need to think more carefully about the information provided by each of the two selves. The best choice might become more clear after the "umpire" self realizes that the want or should self was neglecting some part of the problem. This decision-theoretic approach to the multiple-selves problem would most likely favor the should self, but give voice, opportunity, and input to the want self.

Negotiation Research Advises the Multiple Selves

One likely result of following the decision-theoretic advice adapted from Raiffa (1968) is that the want self may rebel against the decision. For example, a diet or exercise regime could be sabotaged by an individual's failure to reconcile the want self to the should self's new agenda. By creating a rational negotiation between the two parties (the want self and the should self), my modification of Raiffa's advice grants the want self more autonomy and a stronger voice in the decision-making process. This suggestion is inspired by, but more optimistic than, Schelling's view that "the possibility of bargains and compromises is limited, if not precluded, by the absence of any internal mediator. It is hard for the different selves to negotiate if they cannot be simultaneously present. Not impossible, perhaps, but hard" (1984, p. 94). We can all think of instances in which our should self made a decision with the logic of self-interest only to be later overruled by the impulsive behavior of the want self.

I recommend the development of a rational negotiation strategy for dealing with the want self. By treating the want self as a negotiator who has the power to declare an impasse, and allowing the parties to negotiate, I aim to bypass both the domination of the should self in the decision-making stage and the want self in the implementation stage. One could easily argue that this is what occurs naturally. However, I would counter that, just as outcomes to disputes between two different individuals or groups are often suboptimal, outcomes to disputes within the self are similarly suboptimal. Once we empower the want self in the decision-making process, what criteria should we impose on the negotiation between selves? First, we should require the parties to reach an agreement, since the independent and conflicting actions of the two selves will be worse than the result of their negotiated agreement. Ongoing conflict would lead the should self to continue to make a variety of decisions that the want self sabotages. Second, the agreement should be Pareto efficient (Chapter 8); that is, there should be no other agreement that the want self and the should self both prefer over the created agreement. This agreement might be reached through "discussions" and compromises between the two selves about key issues—for example, how often the want self will get to eat ice cream, how many days a week the should self will exercise, and so on. By agreeing to reasonable times and limits, the want self is likely to be more willing to follow the agreement. Third, the should self must not push for an agreement that is outside the bargaining zone; that is, the terms must not be unacceptable to the want self, either currently or in the future. The should self must remember that there is no court of law for suing yourself for a contract violation—the want self can void the contract at any time.

Now that two different prescriptive perspectives have been proposed, we must decide when each should be used. Intuition tells us that the decision-theoretic perspective is preferable as long as the want self doesn't veto its use. However, if there is a danger that the want self will rebel against the decision, I believe that it is probably in the interest of the individual to switch to the negotiation model.

POSITIVE ILLUSIONS

Taylor (1989) argues that most people view themselves, the world, and the future in a considerably more positive light than is objectively likely or than reality can sustain. Taylor and Brown (1988) suggest that positive illusions enhance and protect self-esteem, increase personal contentment, help individuals to persist at difficult tasks, and facilitate coping with aversive and uncontrollable events. Taylor (1989) even argues that positive illusions are beneficial to physical and mental health.

Other research, however, shows that there are significant limits to beneficial self-enhancement. The extent to which people can maintain unrealistically positive beliefs about themselves may be constrained to some degree by the objectivity of these beliefs, their credibility, and the potential to disconfirm them (Allison, Messick, and Goethals, 1989). For example, it is easier for individuals to maintain the view that they are more honest than others than to maintain the belief that they are better tennis players or wittier cocktail party conversationalists. Allison et al. (1989) reason that it is harder to have optimistic illusions when they are inconsistent with easily available, objective data. In the same way, it may be easier for negotiators to maintain the belief that they are fairer than other negotiators than to believe that they are more skillful at reaching profitable agreements.

In this section, I highlight four of the most important positive illusions: (1) unrealistically positive views of the self, (2) unrealistic optimism, (3) the illusion of control, and (4) self-serving attributions. After reviewing these illusions, I explore their application to group behavior, negotiator behavior, and potential effects on society. Finally, I close the section with some commentary on the costs and benefits of positive illusions.

Unrealistically Positive Views of the Self

Individuals tend to perceive themselves as being better than others on a variety of desirable attributes (Messick, Bloom, Boldizer, and Samuelson, 1985), causing them to have unrealistically positive self-evaluations across a wide range of social contexts (Brown, 1986). For example, people have been found to perceive themselves as being superior to others across traits such as honesty, cooperativeness, rationality, driving skill, health, and intelligence (Babcock and Loewenstein, 1997; Kramer, 1994).

I have given my MBA students lists of a variety of attributes (decision making, negotiation, and driving ability; earning potential; likelihood of leading a long life, etc.), and asked them to assess where they stand in comparison to other members of the class. On a scale in which zero means that they believe themselves to be worse than all members, 25 percent indicates that they consider themselves better than one-fourth of the students, and so on, my students' average rating is between 60 and 70 percent. While this could be true in comparison to the overall population, the problem is that the same people doing the rating are also the comparison group. Since the correct mean must be 50 percent, many of my students are not as good negotiators, drivers, and so on, as they might think.

Unrealistic Optimism

Unrealistic optimism is a judgmental bias that leads people to believe that their futures will be better and brighter than those of other people (Kramer, 1994; Taylor, 1989). Taylor reports that students expect that they are far more likely to graduate at the top of the class, to get a good job, to obtain a high salary, to enjoy their first job, to get written up in the newspaper, and to give birth to a gifted child than reality suggests. They also assume that they are less likely than their classmates to have a drinking problem, to get fired, to get divorced, to become depressed, or to suffer physical problems. Similar patterns emerge for individuals in other age groups. Taylor notes that we persist in believing that we can accomplish more in a day than is humanly possible, and that we seem immune to the continual feedback that the world provides on our limitations. Brinthaupt, Moreland, and Levine (1991) find that prospective group members are unrealistically positive about the outcomes that they will obtain from group membership. Specifically, individuals expect to receive more rewards than the average group member, expect their own rewards to be higher than the average group member's, and expect that the costs they will incur as group members will be lower than average. Kramer (1991) found that 68 percent of the MBA students in a negotiation class predicted that their bargaining outcomes would fall in the upper 25 percent of the class. These students also expected that they would learn more than their classmates, achieve more unique results, and contribute more to the class experience. This optimism can easily lead to turning down the best job offer that you will receive, rejecting an offer on your house (when no better offer is coming), and a variety of other regrettable behaviors.

Illusion of Control

People falsely believe that they can control uncontrollable events (Crocker, 1982), and they overestimate the extent to which their actions can guarantee a certain outcome (Miller and Ross, 1975). Evidence suggests that experienced dice players believe that "soft" throws are more likely to result in lower numbers being rolled (Taylor, 1989). These gamblers also believe that silence by observers is relevant to their success. Langer (1975) found that people have a strong preference for choosing their own lottery card or numbers, even when this has no effect on improving the likelihood of winning. Many superstitious behaviors are the result of an illusion of control. Obviously, these illusions can have strongly adverse effects on gamblers and managerial risk-takers.

Self-serving Attributions

People interpret the causes of events in a biased manner. Specifically, we tend to take a disproportionately large share of the credit for collective successes and to accept too little responsibility for collective failures (Kramer, 1994). Kramer (1994) notes that John F. Kennedy was describing this effect when he said, "Victory has a thousand fathers, but defeat is an orphan" (Sorenson, 1965, p. 322). Similarly, when successful negotiators are asked to explain their results, they tend to give internal attributions—reasons related to their own decisions. When asked about a failure, however, they tend to cite external factors; they attribute the failure to an unfortunate situation in which they found themselves. Self-serving biases lead people to focus on the aspects of a problem that allow them to avoid blame, thus enabling them to project a positive self-image. Kramer (1994) argues that self-serving attributions lead individuals to overestimate their contribution to their organization. Self-serving attributions also lead people to overestimate their likelihood of success and to underestimate the time it will take to complete a project—a pervasive miscalculation in organizations. When organizational members are contaminated by self-serving attributions, they are more likely to be dissatisfied with their actual outcomes and to disappoint other members, including their bosses.

Positive Illusions in Groups and Society

Positive illusions are not limited to the individual. Kramer (1994) argues that people extend self-enhancement to the groups to which they belong. People tend to believe that members of their group are more honest, more cooperative, more trustworthy, more diligent, and more industrious than members of other groups (Brewer, 1986; Kramer, 1994). Thus, desirable behaviors on the part of in-group members are likely to be attributed to internal, dispositional causes, while similar behaviors by out-group members are likely to be attributed to transitory or situational causes (Brewer and Kramer, 1985).

Not only do we tend to generalize positive illusions to members of our group, but we also tend to invert this pattern in assessing opponents. Frequently, decision makers negatively distort information about their adversaries. Salovey and Rodin (1984) found that individuals tend to denigrate others who are more successful than they are. Kramer (1994) reports that less-successful MBA students disparaged the performance of more-successful students in a negotiation class. These less-successful students were more likely to attribute the success of other students to uncooperative and unethical bargaining tactics, to ascribe more negative motivations to successful negotiators, and to rate them as excessively competitive and self-interested. Similarly, both Diekmann (1997) and Tenbrunsel (1995) have found that while students rate themselves above the mean of their class on a variety of positive attributes, they rate their specific negotiation opponent below the mean on these attributes. Kramer (1994), basing his argument partially on Janis's (1962) analysis of political events, ties this pattern of behaviors to tragic mistakes made in the political arena. For example, Kramer suggests that the Nixon administration's mismanagement of the Watergate embarrassment was partially the result of Nixon, and others close to him, denigrating the competence and motivation of his critics.

Kramer, Newton, and Pommerenke (1993) argue that this pattern of opponent denigration can be dangerous in the context of negotiation. They maintain that ne- gotiators' willingness to reveal information about their own interests may be contin- gent upon their expectation that the other party will reciprocate such disclosures or, at the very least, not exploit them to their own advantage. As a consequence, indi- viduals' judgments regarding such attributes as the other party's cooperativeness, fairness, and trustworthiness might be expected to play an important role in their negotiations. With the combined effects of self-enhancement and the denigration of opponents, negotiators who see themselves as better than others may undermine their ability to appreciate or fully empathize with the perspective of the other party. This may help explain why negotiators are not very good at understanding the cog- nitions of the other party. Both parties to a negotiation may feel that they tried harder to reach agreement and offered more substantial concessions than the other party, and that it was only the opponent's recalcitrance that forestalled agreement.

Positive illusions may also lead to dysfunctional societal behaviors. In the envi- ronmental realm, positive illusions may cause people to believe that their behaviors and attitudes are more environmentally sensitive than those of most people. People may think they are doing their fair share of sacrificing and working toward the res- olution of environmental problems, but their self-assessments are likely to be inflated (Wade-Benzoni, Thompson, and Bazerman, 2001). Consistent with Allison et al. (1989), Wade-Benzoni et al. found self-assessment of environmental sensitivity to depend on how much ambiguity surrounds the self-assessment. Specifically, individ- uals maintain unrealistically positive beliefs about their degree of environmental sen- sitivity when their self-evaluation is difficult to disconfirm, but possess more realistic assessments of themselves when they are constrained by the objectivity of the eval- uation. For example, assessments of general beliefs such as one's awareness of, con- cern for, understanding of, and interest in environmental issues and problems are difficult to confirm or disconfirm. In contrast, assessments of how well one performs on specific activities such as recycling, donating money to environmental organizations, and using energy-saving lightbulbs can be checked against objective measures. If individuals define their environmental sensitivity in terms of general (not easily confirmable) behaviors instead of specific (objectively measurable) behaviors, their self-evaluations are likely to be inflated.

In Wade-Benzoni et al.'s (2001) study of environmental behaviors, a strong correlation exists between how subjects rate their actions regarding the environment and their judgments of the importance of that action to society. Presumably, positive illusions enable subjects to believe that they are doing well relative to others on important activities, though they may admit to doing less well on activities they consider to be less important. These biases may cause individuals to think that their positive contributions to environmental issues are more important than the contributions of others. For example, an individual who puts a lot of effort into recycling, but refuses to take public transportation, may justify this decision by convincing him- or herself that recycling is the most important way of addressing the environmental crisis. Because individuals have the liberty to judge what they already do (which may be what is most convenient for them) as more important than behaviors that may call for inconvenient lifestyle changes, they are able to maintain positive views of themselves with minimal lifestyle adjustment. Overall, this pattern of self-enhancement may provide people with an easy way out of engaging in more responsible societal behaviors.

Are Positive Illusions Good for You?

A common view among social psychologists is that positive illusions are adaptive (Taylor, 1989). These illusions are said to contribute to psychological well-being by protecting an individual's positive sense of self and the motivation to persist at difficult tasks (Taylor and Brown, 1988). In addition, Taylor and Brown argue that positive illusions increase personal commitment, help individuals persist at difficult tasks, and facilitate coping with aversive and uncontrollable events. Certainly, it is reasonable to argue that positive illusions help create entrepreneurs who are willing to discount risks. Positive illusions allow us to maintain cognitive consistency, belief in a just world, and perceived control (Greenwald, 1980). Seligman (1991) advocates the selection of salespeople based on the magnitude of their positive illusions—what he calls "learned optimism." He argues that unrealistically high levels of optimism bolster salesforce persistence.

I believe that each of these findings is true and that in some specific situations (e.g., severe health conditions), positive illusions may prove to be beneficial. In addition, positive illusions may help people cope with tragic events, particularly when they have few alternatives and are not facing any major decisions. However, I also believe that the story told by this literature is incomplete and therefore dangerous in most decision-making environments. Every day, people invest their life savings in new businesses that have little chance of success. Similarly, falsely assuming that they are irreplaceable, people make ultimatums to their employers and often end up losing their jobs. Positive illusions are hazardous when they cause people to continually fool themselves. Because positive illusions typically provide a short-term benefit with larger long-term costs, they can become a form of emotional procrastination. I believe that you cannot maintain these illusions without reducing the quality of your decisions.

My views are shared by a growing number of scholars who caution that positive illusions are likely to have a negative impact on learning and on the quality of decision making, personnel decisions, and responses to organizational crises ("the hole in the ozone layer isn't that big"), and can contribute to conflict and discontent (Brodt, 1990; Kramer, 1994; Kramer, Newton, and Pommerenke, 1991; Tyler and Hastie, 1991). Positive illusions lead organizational members to claim an inappropriately large proportion of the credit for positive outcomes, to overestimate their value to the organization, and to set objectives that have little chance of success (Kramer, 1994). Self-enhancing interpretations of negative outcomes also prevent organizational members from learning from their poor decisions.

EGOCENTRISM

- The West blames the Third World for burning the rain forests and for overpopulation. At the same time, the Third World blames the West for pollution caused by industrialization and excessive consumption.

- A *U.S. News and World Report* survey asked, "If someone sues you and you win the case, should he pay your legal costs?" Eighty-five percent of respondents answered "yes." However, only 44 percent answered "yes" to this question: "If you sue someone and lose the case, should you pay his costs?" (January 30, 1995, p. 52)

- The use of tall smokestacks to reduce local air pollution contributes to the regional problem of acid rain. The higher the air pollution, the farther it travels from its source (Gore, 1992). When Northeastern Canada is affected by acid rain, citizens blame the industrialization of the northeast and midwest United States. The United States denies responsibility, claiming acid rain may be caused by the local burning of coal.

Perceptions and expectations are biased in a self-serving manner called *egocentrism* (Babcock and Loewenstein, 1997; Diekmann, Samuels, Ross, and Bazerman, 1997). While closely related to the positive illusions described in the previous section, egocentrism focuses specifically on how people who are exposed to the same information interpret the information in a way that favors themselves. Egocentrism concerns interpretations of events rather than trait assessments of the self.

When presented with identical information, individuals perceive a situation in dramatically different ways, depending on their role in the situation. Specifically, individuals first determine their preference for a certain outcome on the basis of self-interest and then justify this preference on the basis of fairness by changing the importance of attributes affecting what is fair (Messick and Sentis, 1983). While people frequently have the goal of reaching a fair solution, their assessments of what is fair are often biased by self-interest. For example, it is common for all parties in a conflict to suggest viable, but self-serving, solutions, which they justify based on abstract fairness criteria. Egocentrism allows people to believe that it is honestly fair for them to have more of a given resource than an independent advisor would judge. The problem lies not in a desire to be unfair but in our failure to interpret information in an unbiased manner (Diekmann et al., 1997; Messick and Sentis, 1983).

When two people who have written a book together are asked to estimate their own contribution, the sum of the two percentage estimations is invariably more than 100 percent (Taylor, 1989). In fact, this is just what was found when husbands and wives were asked to estimate the percentage of the household chores that they performed (Ross and Sicoly, 1979). Harris (1946; retold by many other authors) even found evidence of egocentrism between co-winners of the 1923 Nobel Prize for the discovery of insulin. After receiving the prize, Banting, one of the winners, contended that his partner, Macleod, who was the head of the laboratory, was more of a hindrance than a help. In turn, in speeches describing the research that led to the discovery, Macleod managed to forget to mention that he had a partner.

Hastorf and Cantril (1954) asked student football fans from Princeton and Dartmouth to view a short film of a football game between the two schools. Although both sides watched the same film, each side thought the opposing team played less fairly and engaged in more aggressive and unsportsman-like conduct. The researchers observed that the two groups of students "saw a different game." Similarly, in a study of arms control negotiations, Sutton and Kramer (1990) found that both sides of the Cold War attributed failure to reach agreement to the rigidity of the other side. President Reagan told reporters, "We came to Iceland to advance the cause of peace . . . and although we put on the table the most far-reaching arms control proposal in history, the General Secretary rejected it." On the very same day, General Secretary Gorbachev stated: "I proposed an urgent meeting here because we had something to propose . . . the Americans came to this meeting empty handed." Kramer (1994) cites these leaders' memoirs as proof that these quotes are more than political representations; they also reflect the underlying egocentrism of the diplomatic process.

Diekmann (1997) created a simulation in which MBA students allocated resources across two divisions of a company. "Advantaged" allocation recipients viewed these allocations to be fairer than similar allocations that favored their rivals. Advantaged allocation recipients even considered favorable allocations to themselves to be fair when the degree of favorability exceeded the inequality that they would have created had they been the allocator. Thus, they pointed to the fact that someone else had made the allocation to justify the favorable inequality. Finally, egocentrism in assessing fairness was greater when the merits of the alternative recipients were ambiguous. This study suggests that justifiability plays a key role in egocentric determinations of fairness.

Diekmann (1997) shows that egocentrism is greater when the favorable outcome that individuals will receive can be attributed to the individual's group rather than to just the individual. Thus, people are more comfortable with their egocentrism if they can base their biased judgments on their department's or their family's needs, rather than on their own personal needs. As my colleague David Messick has noted, when a football coach quits one job for a better paying job, we do not hear the coach say, "I wanted more money." Rather, we are much more likely to hear him say, "I wanted to ensure the financial security of my family." In reality, these are very similar statements.

Returning to the auditing scandal that introduced Chapter 1, the evidence in this section supports the possibility that Coopers and Lybrand may not have been guilty of intentional manipulation or cover-up of Phar-Mor's financial wrongdoing. Rather, the auditing firm may have been guilty of the motivational bias of egocentrically interpreting and searching for data favorable to maintaining the client relationship. In late 2000, the Securities and Exchange Commission was considering changing the rules governing the relationship between auditors and their clients, and held a series of discussions on the matter. George Loewenstein and I argued to the SEC that when an auditing firm depends on a client for financial or consulting business, it is not psychologically possible for the auditor to maintain true independence of judgment (Bazerman, Morgan, and Loewenstein, 1997; Bazerman and Loewenstein, 2001).

THE ROLE OF REGRET AVOIDANCE IN DECISION MAKING

Imagine that you are at an out-of-town business meeting that runs late. As soon as you can break away, you head to the airport to catch the last flight home. If you miss the flight, which is scheduled to leave at 8:30 P.M., you will have to stay overnight and miss an important meeting the next day. You run into traffic and do not get to the airport until 8:52 P.M. You run to the gate, arriving there at 8:57 P.M. When you arrive, either:

A. You find out that the plane left on schedule at 8:30 P.M., or

B. You see the plane depart, having left the gate at 8:55 P.M.

Which is more upsetting, A or B? Most people would quickly agree that B is more upsetting. Yet, both possibilities create the same net outcome for you—you've missed your flight, and will have to spend the night. B simply highlights the counterfactual but infuriating thought that with any minor change in schedule, you could have made the flight (Kahneman and Miller, 1986; Kahneman and Tversky, 1982).

The impact of counterfactual thinking and feelings of regret have been central to the work of Medvec, Madey, and Gilovich (1995), who discovered the fascinating phenomenon that silver-medal winners at the Olympics are less happy with their achievement than bronze-medal winners. Obviously, any athlete would choose to win silver over bronze. However, when these researchers coded the initial reactions and the facial expressions of athletes as they received their medals, they found that the bronze-medal winners appeared to be happier. Medvec et al. (1995) concluded that while the bronze-medal winners are thrilled simply to be medalists, silver-medal winners regret what might have been—Olympic gold.

Kahneman and Tversky (1982) compared the regret associated with action versus inaction. One investor considers selling her stock, does not sell, and finds out she would have made more money had she sold. Another investor sells his stock and finds out he would have done better had he not sold. Both investors have lost out on the same amount of earnings; objectively, they should experience the same amount of regret. In fact, the second investor invariably feels worse than the first investor! Why? The second investor is more likely to compare his action to the status quo—doing nothing. People feel greater regret for acts of commission (what they did) than for acts of omission (what they did not do) (Spranca, Minsk, and Baron, 1991).

In the travel story, the Olympics story, and the investor story, regret results from uncontrollable emotions. More relevant to decision making is a set of findings showing that individuals distort their judgment in order to avoid regret. Kahneman and Miller (1986) posit that people will experience greater regret when they choose an action that deviates from the norm and that turns out poorly, because they can easily imagine the counterfactual outcome of a more conventional choice. Simonson (1992) found that consumers could be led to make the more conventional of two choices by asking them how they would feel if their decision turned out poorly. One example of a conventional choice is picking a better-known, higher-priced brand over a lesser-known, less-expensive brand. Consumers are more likely to select the more expensive brand if they first consider how they would feel if they found out later that they made the wrong decision (Simonson, 1992). In fact, Simonson cites Kodak's use of this strategy in an ad showing a consumer regretting buying a cheaper film.

The desire to avoid regret clearly affects individuals' decisions (Larrick, 1993). In the absence of feedback on what would have happened had they followed a different course of action, people are able to maintain positive illusions about the quality of their decisions and outcomes. When they expect to receive feedback regarding what they did and did not do, individuals recognize the possibility that they will receive unfavorable comparative information. Larrick (1993) provides evidence that decision makers will distort their decisions to avoid such negative feedback, and he identifies two ways in which they can do so. First, they can choose options that shield them from feedback on foregone alternatives. Second, when feedback on the decision not chosen is inevitable, they can make choices that are likely to compare favorably to foregone options.

Larrick and Boles (1995) examined choices made between a certain alternative and a risky alternative. Each participant played a recruit in a simulated negotiation with a prospective employer called Alpha. In both conditions, recruits knew that they would receive an offer from another firm, Beta; the amount of the bonus from Beta had an *expected* value of $10,000. In the first condition, participants would later find out the outcome of the risky choice, regardless of the outcome chosen. In the second condition, participants only found out the outcome of the risky choice if they selected that choice. Recruits who knew that reaching an agreement with Alpha would likely preclude finding out the details of Beta's offer were more willing to make concessions to get an agreement with Alpha than were recruits who knew they would find out Beta's offer regardless of their choice. Larrick and Boles argue that recruits who would not find out the details of Beta's offer if they reached an agreement with Alpha could settle for less and still assume that they made a wise decision—they would not receive contradictory evidence. However, when recruits would find out Beta's offer regardless of whether they reached agreement with Alpha, they had to worry about how their agreement with Alpha would compare to the foregone outcome with Beta. This led them to be less concessionary and to hold out for a better deal from Alpha.

Overall, the studies reviewed in this section highlight the effects that the motivation to avoid regret can have on decision making. While each of these results may seem intuitive, few decision makers would list "avoiding regret" as a criterion in their decision-making process. Awareness of this interesting pattern of effects should alert decision makers to the common pitfall of allowing a potentially harmful motivational bias to distort decisions. Yet, it is also reasonable to argue that regret-avoiding decisions can be equally biased, because they reflect a concern for later uncontrollable emotional reactions. And, if these emotional reactions are uncontrollable, it can be argued that a consideration of these responses may maximize the experienced outcomes of the decision maker.

SUMMARY

Departing from the first three cognition-oriented chapters, this chapter focuses on biases that emanate from motivational pressures within the individual. I have reviewed the motivational pressures of momentary desire, the need to view ourselves in a positive manner, the tendency to view events the way we would like to see them turn out, and the desire to avoid regret. Certainly, other motivational biases exist. This chapter simply serves to highlight the additive role of motivation, beyond the role of cognition reviewed earlier, in understanding unusual patterns in our decision processes. While it may be difficult to control emotional responses, it is certainly possible to improve our decisions through a fuller understanding of how emotions affect them.

CHAPTER FIVE

The Nonrational Escalation of Commitment

If at first you don't succeed, try, try, again.
Then quit. No use being a damn fool about it.

—W. C. Fields

*I*n the previous chapters, we examined single decisions and the ways in which judgmental and motivational biases and the framing of information can influence our responses to them. However, many critical managerial decisions concern a series of choices rather than an isolated decision. We are prone to a particular type of bias when approaching decisions serially—namely, a tendency to escalate commitment to our initial decision. I open this chapter with an explanation of the individual tendency to escalate behavior. In the second section, I demonstrate how a competitive environment increases the tendency to escalate. In the third section, I provide a taxonomy of explanations for the psychological tendency to escalate and offer recommendations for eliminating nonrational escalation behavior.

Consider the following examples:

1. You personally decided to hire a new manager to work for you. Although you had expected excellent achievement, early reports suggest that she is not performing as you had hoped. Should you fire her? Perhaps her current level of performance is becoming a financial drain. On the other hand, you have invested a fair amount in her training, and she may just be in the process of learning the ropes. You decide to invest in her a bit longer and provide additional resources to help her succeed. Two months later, her performance is still sub par. Although you have more reason to "cut your losses," you also have a greater investment in this employee. When should you give up on your "investment"?

2. You accept a position with a prestigious consulting firm, believing that the job offers an excellent career opportunity in a firm that you can grow with. Two years later, you have not progressed as rapidly as you had expected. Anxious to demonstrate your worth to the company, you decide to invest large amounts of unpaid overtime to get ahead. Still, you fail to get the

recognition you think you deserve. By now, you have been with the organization for several years and would lose numerous benefits, including a vested interest in the company's pension plan, if you decide to leave. You are in your late thirties and feel you have invested your best years with this company. Do you quit?

3. You are a bank loan officer. A seemingly good credit risk comes to you and asks for a $50,000 business start-up loan. After a careful review of the application, you personally make the decision to grant the loan. Six months later, the loan recipient shows up in your office and says: "I have bad news, and I have good news. The bad news is that the company is having problems. In fact, without additional help, we will definitely go under, and you will lose the $50,000. The good news is that I am quite confident that if you lend us an additional $50,000, we can turn the whole thing around." Do you lend him an additional $50,000?

Although each of these decisions represents a very different situation, they share a number of common elements. In each case, you have a decision to make as a result of a previous decision. You hired the employee. You took the job. You made the loan. In each case, you have invested a great deal of time, effort, and resources in your selected course of action, and now things are not working out in an optimal way.

We frequently face similar decisions of varying importance. Should you sink more money into that old wreck you call a car? How long should you stay on hold with an airline before hanging up? When an investment starts to fail, should you stick with it? If you think about your own career and life, you will see that situations of this type are common. Inertia frequently leads us to continue on our previously selected course of action, or we may feel we have "too much invested to quit." How do you know when to quit? At what point does continuing on the same course of action become irrational? And why, when such behavior becomes irrational, is it so common? These are the central questions of this chapter.

The key to making intelligent decisions in dynamic contexts such as those presented above is being able to discriminate between situations in which persistence will pay off and situations in which it will not. Although we are taught from an early age to "try, try again," the fact is that misdirected persistence can lead you to waste a great deal of time, energy, and money. However, directed persistence can lead to commensurate payoffs.

A variety of authors from different fields have presented ideas relevant to the three hypothetical situations described above, using a number of different terms (such as escalation, entrapment, and persistence) to describe commitment to a previously selected course of action. Without presenting the diversity of definitions used in the literature, this chapter defines nonrational escalation as the degree to which an individual escalates commitment to a previously selected course of action to a point beyond that which a rational model of decision making would prescribe.

Accountants and economists provide insight into how to handle these scenarios. Experts from these areas tell us that in such situations we need to recognize that the time and expenses already invested are "sunk costs." That is, these costs are historical, irrecoverable, and should not be considered in any future course of action. Our reference point for action should be our current state, and we should consider all alternative courses of action by evaluating only the future costs and benefits associated with each alternative. For example, if you are considering whether to quit a doctoral program, it is irrelevant whether it took you six months or four years to get to the point you are at now; the key decision involves the future costs of exiting versus the future benefits of continuing.

While accountants teach their students to recognize sunk costs in an accounting context, the decisions of managers trained in accounting suggest that the textbook advice to ignore sunk costs seldom translates to solving real-world problems. Why is it so hard for managers to absorb the sunk-cost concept in a lasting manner? One deficiency in the typical training of the sunk-cost concept is the lack of a descriptive identification of why we intuitively tend to include sunk costs in our calculations. To eliminate escalatory behavior, we need to identify the existing nonrational behavior within ourselves, "unfreeze" that behavior, and prepare for change.

The psychological perspective of the escalation problem is very different from that of the accountants and economists. Psychologists begin by describing what decision makers actually do, rather than prescribing what they should do. In general, psychologists (Brockner and Rubin, 1985) have demonstrated that decision makers who commit themselves to a particular course of action have a tendency to make subsequent decisions that continue that commitment beyond the level suggested by rationality. As a consequence, they often allocate resources in a way that justifies previous commitments, whether or not those initial commitments now appear valid. The following section examines the components of this behavior in more detail.

THE UNILATERAL ESCALATION PARADIGM

Put yourself in the bank loan officer's predicament again. My description of the escalation situation has probably biased you to assume that it would be "bad" for you to escalate your commitment to the first loan by granting another one. The fact is, it might be economically rational to continue your investment in the lender. After all, it is not always wise to quit at the first sign of failure. Many would argue that doing so is a sign of a serious psychological deficiency.

How do you separate the rational from the nonrational tendency to escalate? One body of knowledge suggests that you should try to determine the rational course of action, ignoring the fact that you personally made the initial loan commitment. A number of studies have attempted to separate the effect of being the person who made the initial commitment. These studies have investigated the difference between how two groups of decision makers make a second decision that follows an initial failure. One group has already made the initial decision, while the other group inherits the initial decision.

In Staw's initial study of this type (1976), one group of participants (labeled the high-responsibility participants) was asked to allocate research and development funds to one of two operating divisions of an organization. The participants were then told that, after three years, the investment had either proven to be successful or unsuccessful and that they were now faced with a second allocation decision concerning the same division. A second group (labeled the low-responsibility participants) was told that another financial officer of the firm had made a decision that had been either successful or unsuccessful (the same content information about success or failure was provided to this group as to the previous one) and that they were to make a second allocation of funds concerning that division. When the outcome of the previous decision was negative (an unsuccessful investment), the high-responsibility participants allocated significantly more funds to the original division in the second allocation than did the low-responsibility participants. In contrast, for successful initial decisions, the amount of money allocated in the second decision was roughly the same across participants. Given that the greater escalation of commitment occurred only for the participants who had made a previously unsuccessful decision, Staw concluded that the mechanism underlying escalation is self-justification. That is, once an individual makes an initial decision to embark on a course of action, negative feedback is dissonant with the initial decision. One way to eliminate this dissonance is to escalate commitment to the initial action in the belief that it will eventually lead to success.

We also know a fair amount about the conditions that tend to lead people to escalate commitment to a chosen course of action. Staw and Ross (1978) found that the tendency to escalate commitment was pronounced when the failure could be explained away with a causal account unrelated to the individual's initial decision (e.g., a shift in the economy). Bazerman, Giuliano, and Appelman (1984) found that groups are less likely than individuals to escalate commitment; however, groups that do, tend to do so to a greater degree than individuals. Apparently, the presence of multiple members increases the likelihood that the group will recognize the irrationality of escalating commitment to previous unsuccessful actions. If this realization does not occur, however, the group dynamic reinforces support for the initial decision and increases the level of rationalization to escalate commitment. Schoorman (1988) found that supervisors who participate in a hiring or promotion decision, and who agree with the eventual decision to hire or promote, positively bias that employee's subsequent performance appraisals. In addition, supervisors who participate in such a decision and disagree with the eventual decision to hire or promote bias subsequent performance appraisals for that employee in a negative direction.

Staw and Hoang (1995) found that National Basketball Association teams escalate their commitment to their draft choices. The sunk costs that teams incur are the use of draft choices and money to select and sign players. Staw and Hoang found that draft order had strong effects on playing time, likelihood of being traded, and survival in the league, even after controlling for the performance of players. Friedman's (1996) account of the decisions of mountain climbers to go for the peak provides chilling insight into the role of escalation in vivid life-and-death situations. Interestingly, Friedman presented his paper at a conference in memory of Jeffrey Z. Rubin, a noted escalation scholar and mountain climber who died in a 1995 climbing accident. Rubin's climbing partner had turned around prior to the fall, believing the weather conditions to be too dangerous.

Taken together, the foregoing evidence suggests that managers should beware of the difficulty of separating initial decisions from related future decisions. Our decisions will tend to be biased by our past actions, and we have a natural individual tendency to escalate commitment, particularly after receiving negative feedback.

THE COMPETITIVE ESCALATION PARADIGM

In the unilateral escalation paradigm just described, justifications for nonrational escalation lie within the individual; we escalate because of our own previous commitments. In the competitive escalation paradigm, additional competitive forces feed the escalatory process. This section examines the process of escalation in competitive situations.

Imagine that two companies, A and B, are the most important in a given industry, while Company C is their potential target, an important third player, a key supplier, or a key buyer. C is worth $1 billion as a stand-alone company and would be worth $1.2 billion if managed by A or B, as a result of the synergy in the possible combination of A and C or of B and C. Assume that if A were to acquire C, B would be at a catastrophic disadvantage and would lose $0.5 billion. It would be similarly destructive to A if B were to acquire C; A would also lose $0.5 billion. Finally, assume that if either A or B makes an offer on C, the other company will learn of the offer. *Question:* As the head of Company A, what do you do?

A typical response of executives to whom I have posed this problem is to offer C $1.1 billion, which if accepted, would create a $100 million benefit to A and C. However, this offer, once made, creates a problem for B: If B does not act, B loses $0.5 billion. So, rather than suffering a $0.5 billion loss, B offers $1.2 billion to break even. Now, A has a problem: If A does not act, A loses $0.5 billion. So, A offers $1.3 billion to limit their losses to $100 million, rather than suffering a $0.5 billion loss. The problem is now B's, and we can easily see the auction escalating to an amount around $1.7 billion, where both A and B end up losing $0.5 billion in this competition. Any party quitting below that amount would still suffer a $0.5 billion loss.

This story is consistent with the lack of profit obtained by buyers in the merger mania of the 1980s—in the aggregate, the synergy that was obtained in acquisitions went to the sellers. This story is also consistent with a classroom auction that I have run many times: Imagine yourself in a room with 30 other individuals. The person at the front of the room takes a $20 bill out of his or her pocket and announces the following:

> I am about to auction off this $20 bill. You are free to participate or just watch the bidding of others. People will be invited to call out bids in multiples of $1 until no further bidding occurs, at which point the highest bidder will pay the amount bid and win the $20. The only feature that distinguishes this auction from traditional auctions is a rule that the second-highest bidder must also pay the amount that he or she bid, although he or she will obviously not win the $20. For example, if Bill bid $3 and Jane bid $4, and bidding stopped, I would pay Jane $16 ($20 − $4) and Bill, the second-highest bidder, would pay me $3.

Would you be willing to bid $2 to start the auction? (Make this decision before reading further.)

I have run this auction with undergraduate students, graduate students, and executives. The pattern is always the same. The bidding starts out fast and furious until it reaches the $12 to $16 range. At this point, everyone except the two highest bidders drops out of the auction. The two bidders then begin to feel the trap. One bidder has bid $16, and the other has bid $17. The $16 bidder must either bid $18 or suffer a $16 loss. The uncertain option of bidding further (a choice that might produce a gain if the other person quits) seems more attractive than the current sure loss, so the $16 bidder bids $18. This continues until the bids are $19 and $20. Surprisingly, the decision to bid $21 is very similar to all previous decisions: You can accept a $19 loss or continue and reduce your loss if the other person quits. Of course, the rest of the group roars with laughter when the bidding goes over $20—which it almost always does. Obviously, the bidders are acting irrationally. But which bids are irrational?

Skeptical readers should try out the auction for themselves. The bidding typically ends between $20 and $70. However, my highest auction ended at $204, and I have had 13 auctions hit the $100 mark. In total, I have earned over $25,000 running these auctions in classes over the last 16 years. (Note: While I win this money fair and square, I do not keep it. The money has either been used to provide food and beverage for the class or immediately given to charity.)

Shubik (1971) introduced the dollar auction. I adjusted the auction from $1 to $20 for inflation and to sharpen the impact. Teger (1980) has used the paradigm extensively to investigate the question of why individuals escalate their commitment to a previously selected course of action. Teger argues that participants naively enter the auction not expecting the bidding to exceed $1 (or $20); "after all, who would bid more than a dollar for a dollar?" The potential gain, coupled with the possibility of "winning" the auction, is enough reason to enter the auction. Once an individual is in the auction, it takes only a few extra dollars to stay in the auction rather than accept a sure loss. This "reasoning," along with a strong need to justify the bidder's decision to enter the auction in the first place, is enough to keep most bidders bidding for an extended period of time.

Thoughtful examination of the dollar auction suggests that individuals who choose to bid are entering into a trap. While it is true that one more bid may inspire the other party to quit, if both bidders hold this belief, the result can be catastrophic. Yet, without knowing the expected bidding patterns of the opponent, we cannot conclude that continued bidding is clearly wrong. What is the right course of action? Successful decision makers must learn to identify traps, and the key to the problem lies in identifying the auction as a trap and never making even a very small bid. One strategy for identifying competitive traps is to try to consider the decision from the perspective of the other decision maker(s). In the dollar auction, this strategy would quickly tell you that the auction looks just as attractive to other bidders as it does to you. With this knowledge, you can accurately predict what will occur and stay out of the auction.

You can also develop strategies that discourage escalatory behavior by your competitors. In the $20 bill auction, one class member could organize the class to collude against me. That class member could arrange for one member to bid $1, everyone else to refrain from bidding, and the class could later divide the $19 profit—communication can be a very effective tool. The same is true of the earlier scenario involving companies A, B, and C. In 1995, the basic pattern of this story played out with American Airlines, United Airlines, and USAir. USAir, the nation's fifth largest airline, announced that it was for sale at the right price. Analysts quickly speculated that the two industry leaders, United and American Airlines, were likely to be interested. However, their analyses were limited to the expectation that the value of USAir was higher to United or American as an acquisition than as a stand-alone company. These analyses ignored information suggesting that United and American would be extremely motivated to avoid losing a bidding war, since the sale of USAir to American would be a major setback for United, and the sale of USAir to United would be a similarly damaging blow to American. As the head of American or United, what would you do?

American developed a strategy aimed at avoiding the escalatory war described above. Robert Crandall, the chairperson of American, wrote an open letter to his company's 118,000 employees that stated, "We continue to believe, as we always have, that the best way for American to increase its size and reach is by internal growth—not by consolidation. . . . So we will not be the first to make a bid for USAir. On the other hand, if United seeks to acquire USAir, we will be prepared to respond with a bid, or by other means as necessary, to protect American's competitive position" (*Chicago Tribune*, November 10, 1995, p. B1). Although the letter was addressed to American Airlines employees, it was obvious that the most important target of this message was United. The message was clear: Keep things as they are, or we will both end up in a money-losing battle. Crandall's letter was very effective in avoiding an escalatory war (no offers were made on USAir in 1995). Five years later, when United made a preemptive bid on USAir for 232 percent of the company's stand-alone value, both United and American stock prices fell sharply.

Also failing to learn from Crandall's successful strategy, in 1996, Norfolk Southern Railroad acquired Conrail at a price far in excess of Conrail's market value. Esty (1998) traces this overpayment to a bidding war between CSX Corporation and Norfolk Southern. Because both companies were aware that the loser of the bidding war would incur a loss of market value once the bidding got started, each had an incentive to continue bidding beyond the value of Conrail. As a result, Esty (1998) shows that Norfolk Southern lost value by overpaying, while CSX lost value by losing the bidding war. In takeover contests where the losing bidder faces a loss in market share or competitive position, the natural outcome can be overpayment for target firms. Bidders become indifferent between winning the auction by overpaying and losing the auction and suffering a loss in competitive position.

In both the $20 auction and in corporate bidding wars, bidders have typically failed to consider the decisions of the other party, and continue to bid to justify their initial strategy. Finally, the auction moves to very high levels of financial loss when the two parties forget their original objective of earning money and switch to the objective of beating the other party. As an auctioneer, this is when I do very well!

The competitive-escalation paradigm has much in common with Staw's unilateral paradigm. In both cases, the decision maker makes an initial decision that he or she feels a need to justify through future decisions, and reaches a point where he or she has "too much invested to quit." However, there is one major difference between the two paradigms. In the dollar auction, competition with the other party—that is, the desire to "win"—is added motivation to escalate commitment.

WHY DOES ESCALATION OCCUR?

Each of the previous sections has provided some clues about the conditions under which nonrational escalation of commitment occurs. The first step toward eliminating escalation from our behavioral repertoire is to identify the psychological factors that feed it. The existing literature clearly suggests that there are multiple reasons why escalation occurs. Building on findings presented in earlier chapters, this section provides a taxonomy of these reasons. The first three classes of explanations, including perceptual biases, judgmental biases, and impression management, are general to all of the examples of escalation presented. The fourth class of explanations, competitive irrationality, differentiates the unilateral escalation paradigm from the competitive escalation paradigm. After presenting each class of explanations for this phenomenon, I consider the implications for the elimination of escalation.

Perceptual Biases

Consider the case at the beginning of this chapter, in which you made the decision to hire the employee who subsequently performed below your expectations. Evidence presented earlier in this chapter suggests that your perception of the employee's performance may be biased by your initial decision. That is, you may notice information that supports your hiring decision, while ignoring information that stands against your initial decision. Similarly, in the bank loan case, after making the initial loan decision, you may have a greater tendency to notice positive information about the company than negative information about the company. This phenomenon can be predicted by the suggestion in Chapter 2 that we pay more attention to confirming than disconfirming information. Similarly, Staw (1980) suggests that administrators often protect their initial decisions by actively seeking out information that supports these decisions—for example, information that suggests an employee is performing well. Caldwell and O'Reilly (1982) empirically show that participants who freely choose a particular course of action will then filter information selectively to maintain commitment to that course of action.

The perceptual biases that result from our commitment to a particular course of action suggest a number of corrective procedures. As recommended in Chapter 2, when we are making a decision, we need to search vigilantly for disconfirming information to balance out the confirming information that we intuitively seek. This need is particularly pronounced in serial decisions, where we have a natural tendency toward escalation. In addition, establishing monitoring systems that help us check our perception before making subsequent judgments or decisions could prove useful. For instance, if an objective outsider could evaluate our openness to disconfirming information, our perceptual barrier to nonescalatory behavior could be reduced or eliminated.

Judgmental Biases

Once we have filtered the information that we will use to make a subsequent decision, we still have to make the decision. The central argument of this section is that any loss from an initial investment (such as bidding more than $20 in the competitive-escalation paradigm, or more than the initial research-and-development funding in Staw's unilateral escalation paradigm) will systematically distort judgment toward continuing the previously selected course of action. The logic of this prediction lies in the framing concepts developed in Chapter 3.

Recalling the central thesis of the framing concept, individuals tend to be risk averse to positively framed problems and risk seeking to negatively framed problems. As the bank loan officer described at the beginning of the chapter, you made an initial investment of $50,000 to a start-up venture. After a short period of time, you are faced with the decision of accepting a loss of that $50,000 or risking an added $50,000 in the hope that this added investment will eliminate the loss entirely. The risk-averse response is to accept the sure loss of $50,000, while the risk-seeking action is to try to recover the initial funds by allocating an additional $50,000. From Chapter 3, we know that most of us prefer a 50 percent chance of a loss of $100,000 over a sure loss of $50,000, even though these choices have the same expected value. Based on this systematic preference, we would expect most individuals to give the additional loan if the expected success of that added loan was at least 50 percent. Now reconsider the problem assuming that you did not make the initial investment. You are now likely to evaluate the potential benefit of the second loan from a different reference point. From this reference point, the decision is either to quit now with no gain or loss or to take a 50:50 chance of winning or losing $50,000. Most individuals would quit, choosing not to accept the gamble. Following this line of reasoning, high- and low-responsibility participants in Staw's paradigm may have simply been responding to the framing of the allocation problem (Bazerman, 1984).

Individuals should learn to assess the new decision from a neutral reference point that eliminates the extreme risk-seeking behavior observed among high-responsibility participants (that is, decision makers who have already committed funds or resources to a course of action). This reference-point shift can be accomplished by convincing the decision maker that the initial investment has proven to be a loss and that the second decision represents a new problem to be examined objectively. If this shift is not feasible, a new decision maker should step in to make the subsequent decision.

Impression Management

Returning to the hiring decision from the beginning of this chapter, even if your perception and judgment led you to the conclusion that the underachieving employee should be fired, you might not choose to fire her. Why not? Firing the employee would be tantamount to a public announcement that your earlier decision was a mistake. You might decide to keep the employee simply to "save face." Caldwell and O'Reilly's (1982) work shows that individuals not only selectively perceive information, but also selectively provide information to others. Specifically, individuals who make an initial commitment to a particular course of action are more likely to provide confirming, rather than disconfirming, information to others. Thus, managing the impressions of others serves as a third reason for escalating commitment.

In addition to not wanting to admit failure to others, we also try to appear consistent to others. Increasing our commitment to our previous actions is one sign of consistency. Staw and Ross (1980) suggest that our society perceives that administrators who are consistent in their actions are better leaders than those who switch from one line of behavior to another. As support for their position, they offer the following excerpts from the press's evaluation of Jimmy Carter:

> Carter has exacerbated many of the difficulties he has faced. His most damaging weakness in his first two years has been a frequent indecisiveness ("The State of Jimmy Carter," 1979).
>
> A President must, plainly, show himself to be a man made confident by the courage of his clear convictions. . . . The American people find it easy to forgive a leader's great mistakes, but not long meanderings (Hughes, 1978).

Indecision was also cited as the second most common reason for dissatisfaction with Carter in a Gallup poll taken after the president's first year in office (Staw, 1981). In his book *Profiles in Courage*, John F. Kennedy wrote that the most courageous decisions politicians must make are those favoring an action that they believe to be in the best interests of their constituency, yet that they know will be disfavored by that very same constituency. Staw and Ross's findings suggest that this conflict is particularly severe when an action consists of turning one's back on a previously supported course of action.

An interesting paradox results: Making the best decision for your organization means that you should focus on future costs and benefits, ignoring any previous commitments. Yet, empirical evidence shows that you are more likely to be rewarded for escalating commitment than for changing course (Ross and Staw, 1986). From an organizational standpoint, this suggests that we need to replace systems that encourage impression management with those that reward good decisions. To do this, managers must convey to all members of the organization that impression management at the expense of high-quality decisions will not be tolerated. Second, organizations should strive to make the employees' values closer to those of the organization by modifying reward systems. The organization wants managers to make smart organizational decisions; managers want to make decisions that will further their careers. When rewards are based on results, employees will hide a bad result by escalating commitment. When management determines rewards by looking at the decision process, not at the outcome, employees will be motivated to make the best possible decisions at different stages, whether or not their initial decisions have been judged to be correct (Staw and Ross, 1987).

Competitive Irrationality

The previous three explanations for escalation can be generalized to both the unilateral and competitive paradigms. Research on competitive irrationality, however, adds an additional insight that distinguishes between the two paradigms. Specifically, competitive irrationality refers to a situation in which two parties engage in an activity that is clearly irrational in terms of the expected outcomes to both sides, despite the fact that it is difficult to identify specific irrational actions by either party. Many people would argue that getting involved in the dollar auction is an irrational decision, and while this is a very reasonable perspective, the argument is not completely valid. If it makes sense for you not to play, then it does not make sense for anyone else to play. If no one else plays, then you can bid a small amount and get a bargain. This reasoning sounds logical, but once you make the initial bid, another individual inevitably bids, and the bind that I have already described emerges. I argued earlier that continuing to bid then depends on your estimation of the likelihood that the other party will quit. Obviously, the same reasoning applies to the other party. If it is possible for someone to get a very cheap $20 (for $1, for example), then it must be rational for one individual to be able to bid. Yet we know the pitfall that results when multiple individuals adopt this attitude. Thus, in many ways, competitive irrationality presents an unresolved paradox, other than as an explanation of escalation. The only recommendation that can be derived from the competitive irrationality explanation of escalation is that many situations may look like opportunities but prove to be traps unless the actions of others are fully considered.

INTEGRATION

This section has suggested four additive causes that contribute to our tendency to escalate commitment to a previously selected course of action. By referring to the four causes as additive, I am calling attention to the fact that they are rarely mutually exclusive. Each one can cause escalation independently, but they more often act together to increase a decision maker's nonrational tendency to continue a previous mistake. To reduce escalation, we must attack each cause at the individual and organizational levels. In doing so, we must remember that we are trying to counter nonrational commitment to a course of action. Continuing commitment may make sense in many contexts.

Overall, the findings on the tendency to escalate suggest that managers need to take an experimental approach to management (Campbell, 1969). That is, as a manager, you should make a decision and implement it, but be open to dropping your commitment and shifting to another course of action if the first plan does not work out. This means constantly reassessing the rationality of future commitments and learning to identify failures early.

CHAPTER SIX

Fairness in Decision Making

You are graduating from a good MBA program. Following your discussions with a number of firms, one of your preferred companies makes you an offer of $90,000 a year, stressing that the amount is not negotiable. You like the people. You like the job. You like the location. However, you find out that the same company is offering $95,000 to some graduating MBAs from similar quality schools. Will you accept the offer?

Hurricane Andrew hits southern Florida, leaving many people homeless. For many commodities such as building materials, demand is up and supply is down. This is a condition that leads economists to predict an increase in prices. In fact, in the aftermath of the hurricane, a small building-supply company more than doubles its prices on many items that are in high demand, such as lumber. Are the price increases fair? Are they rational?

*I*n the first story, many students are very bothered by the difference between their salary and the salary of others, even if they learn that the difference does not predict how the company will treat them in the future. In the second story, most people believe that it is not fair for the company to raise its prices. In addition, there are reasons to believe that raising prices may not be rational either.

Concerns about fairness are central to a complete understanding of decision making. Research on fairness has focused on either the distribution of scarce resources (Messick, 1991) or the fairness of the distribution procedures (Lind and Tyler, 1988). This chapter explores a new direction in the study of fairness. Although I believe that readers are entitled to develop their own sets of ethical and moral values, I hope to provide the opportunity to examine the consistency of their fairness judgments just as earlier chapters have encouraged them to explore other components of their judgment.

This book's focus on rationality and cognition may have led some readers to temporarily ignore fairness concerns. Yet, fairness concerns can play a critical role in decision making. To reach successful decisions, individuals must learn to understand and anticipate the effects of fairness. The central purpose of this chapter is to integrate these concerns into a judgment framework.

Clearly, we care about fairness; it affects our decisions and lives. We are all entitled to our own personal judgments about what we think is fair. As a result, most fairness research has avoided making evaluative statements about the rationality of fairness judgments. This silence has inhibited our understanding of how our cognitive processes create anger, jealousy, and inefficiency. If we are to reduce or eliminate our dysfunctional perceptions of fairness, we need to confront the limits to rationality in these perceptions.

Fairness considerations may account for some of the limitations of the explanatory power of economic models. Kahneman, Knetsch, and Thaler (1986) argue that fairness considerations inhibit employers from cutting wages during periods of high unemployment, despite changes in supply and demand, and explain the lack of price adjustment in the consumer domain. In this chapter, I examine three systematic ways in which fairness considerations lead our decisions to deviate from a simple rational action model. First, I describe situations in which individual judgment deviates from the expectations of supply and demand considerations. Second, I examine how people respond to ultimatums and why we may make choices inconsistent with our own economic self-interest. Third, I consider how social comparison processes lead to decisions that may clash with our underlying preferences.

WHEN DO WE ACCEPT THE ROLE OF SUPPLY AND DEMAND?

In a provocative set of experiments, Kahneman et al. (1986) demonstrated that fairness considerations can dominate economically rational choices in decision making. Consider the action of the hardware store owner in the following scenario:

> A hardware store has been selling snow shovels for $15. The morning after a large snowstorm, the store raises the price to $20.

Would you rate this action as fair or unfair? From an economic perspective, the price should go up. When demand increases relative to supply, an increase in price is expected. However, despite the economic rationality of raising the prices of snow shovels, 82 percent of respondents viewed raising the price of snow shovels to be unfair. And, of the individuals who said it was fair, many would not think it fair for a hardware store to raise the price of generators after a hurricane, even though the logic is the same. Thus, fairness considerations lead to systematic departures from the predictions of economic models.

An interesting reversal of the snow shovel problem emphasizes the importance of thinking about the fairness concerns of others. Assume that you own the hardware store and have 25 remaining shovels. Should you raise the price by $5? Even if you believe that the market is a fair measure of the value of the commodity, the answer may be no. By ignoring concerns for fairness, you might raise the price and collect an additional $125 on the shovels. However, the loss of future business from angry customers might cost you more than $125. It does not matter that you think your customers should understand the nature of the supply and demand relationship. If they think the price increase is unfair, they may react to this perception of unfairness in the future. Thus, someone who acts in an economically rational manner (e.g., increases the price of the shovels) may underperform those who consider norms of fairness, since other parties (e.g., customers) may punish a party for the perceived unfairness of an economically rational action.

Cognitive biases also influence people's perceptions of fairness. For example, fairness judgments are susceptible to the effects of framing (see Chapter 3). Consider Kahneman et al.'s (1986) following two problems:

> **Problem A.** A company is making a small profit. It is located in a community experiencing a recession with substantial unemployment but no inflation. Many workers are anxious to work at the company. The company decides to decrease wages and salaries 7 percent this year.

Sixty-two percent of respondents considered the company's behavior unfair.

> **Problem B.** A company is making a small profit. It is located in a community experiencing a recession with substantial unemployment and 12 percent inflation. Many workers are anxious to work at the company. The company decides to increase wages and salaries 5 percent this year.

In this case, only 22 percent of the participants thought the company's behavior was unfair. Despite the similar changes in real income, judgments of fairness were strikingly different. A wage cut was perceived as an unfair loss, while a nominal gain that does not cover inflation was more acceptable. We seem to carry around with us certain rules of fair behavior, such as the rule that wages should go up and not down. Thus, when economic conditions change for the worse, it is very difficult for employees to regard a pay cut as fair. It is logical to think about money in terms of its real buying power (real dollars), rather than the arbitrary unit of a dollar (nominal dollars), which changes in value as a result of inflation. In contrast, our assessments of fairness are largely built around whether nominal wages follow our intuitive social rules.

Consumers show similar inconsistencies when thinking about discounts and price increases. Consider the following scenarios from Kahneman et al. (1986):

> **Scenario 1:** A shortage has developed for a popular model of automobile, and customers must now wait two months for delivery. A dealer has been selling these cars at list price. Now the dealer prices this model at $200 above list price.

> **Scenario 2:** A shortage has developed for a popular model of automobile, and customers must now wait two months for delivery. A dealer has been selling these cars at a discount of $200 below list price. Now the dealer prices this model at list price.

The majority of individuals view the action in the first scenario to be unfair (71 percent), yet consider the action in the second scenario to be fair (58 percent). Consumers seem to grant special status to the manufacturer's list price, even if they do not expect to pay that amount. The list price acts as a critical anchor for assessments of fairness. It is unacceptable to exceed that amount. Yet, there is no normative basis for the manufacturer's list price having this special value.

The pattern that emerges is that individuals are very concerned with departures from the status quo and that economically justifiable behaviors will often be perceived as unfair. We seem to place special value on list prices, current prices, and so forth, and to develop fairness rules around these numbers. Regardless of whether the reader follows the judgmental patterns just described, it is critical to recognize the existence of such patterns in a world where fairness judgments affect the behavior of others.

THE INFLUENCE OF ULTIMATUMS

Consider the following opportunity:

> You are traveling on an airplane, sitting in an aisle seat next to an eccentric-looking woman in the middle seat (Vivian). Next to her, in the window seat, is a rather formal-looking businessperson (Mark). About 30 minutes into the flight, Vivian interrupts you and Mark, and explains to you that she is quite wealthy, becomes bored easily on flights, and likes to pass the time by playing games. She then pulls fifty $100 bills out of her wallet and makes the following proposition. "I will give the two of you this $5,000 provided that you can agree on how to split the money. In splitting up the money, however, I will impose two rules. First, Mark must decide how the $5,000 is to be split between the two of you. Then, you (the reader) will decide whether to accept the split. If you do accept, then you and Mark will receive the portion of the $5,000 based on Mark's allocation. If you do not accept the split, then you and Mark will each receive nothing." Both you and Mark agree to play the game. Mark thinks for a moment and then says, "I propose that the $5,000 be split as follows: I get $4,900 and you get $100." Now it is up to you: Will you agree to this split?

If you are like most people, you will probably reject this split. Why? Obviously, rejecting such a deal is inconsistent with notions of economic rationality, because each party would be better off (+$4,900 for Mark and +$100 for you) if you were to accept it. However, you might choose to reject this offer for a variety of reasons that lie outside self-interest outcome maximization. Reasons for rejecting the $100 include not wanting to accept an unfair allocation and not wanting Mark to benefit from your acceptance. If you were unaffected by fairness considerations, you would accept the $100. After all, $100 is better than nothing.

This example points out the importance of understanding the role of fairness and equality in decision making. Assume that the roles were reversed: You could determine the allocation, and Mark would have the option of accepting or rejecting it. What would you decide? If you did not factor in fairness considerations, it would be easy to conclude that the other party would accept the $100 or even less. However, this proposal would very likely leave you with $0 because Mark would probably reject your offer. In contrast, a consideration of fairness and emotion would lead you to anticipate the likely response of the other party and consequently improve the expected value that you would receive from this transaction by offering the other party significantly more than $100.

A number of researchers have systematically studied how people respond to ultimatums that are similar to this fictional airplane story (Guth, Schmittberger, and Schwarze, 1982; Roth, 1991). In these studies, Player 1 divides a known, fixed sum of money any way he chooses by filling out a form stating, "I demand X." Player 2 either accepts the offer and receives her portion of the money as allocated by Player 1, or rejects the offer, leaving both parties with nothing. Traditional models of rational actors predict that Player 1 will offer Player 2 only slightly more than zero, and that Player 2 will accept any offer greater than zero. The results, however, show that individuals incorporated fairness considerations into their offers and choices. The average demand by Player 1 was for less than 70 percent of the funds, both for first-time players and for players repeating the game one week later. In addition, individuals in the role of Player 2 rejected profitable but unequal offers.

People often rely on attaining what they consider to be a fair or justifiable result. As a result, they are often willing to pay to punish their opponent if he or she asks for too much. Ochs and Roth (1989) studied a situation in which Player 2 could reject the allocation offer of Player 1, then counterpropose their own allocation. However, the amount of funds available was reduced if Player 2 rejected the first offer. The researchers found that in such ultimatum games, 81 percent of rejected offers were followed by disadvantageous counteroffers in which parties who rejected the initial offer demanded less than they had just been offered. Ochs and Roth argue that players' utilities for fairness may explain the results. However, they also argue that a simple notion of equality does not explain the data, since in most cases Player 1 asks for more than 50 percent of the resources in the first stage. Rather, parties realize that the other side may very well refuse offers perceived as unfair despite the economic rationality of accepting them.

Ochs and Roth's argument is also consistent with Forsythe, Horowitz, Savin, and Sefton's (1988) results. Participants played either an ultimatum game like the one just described, or a "dictator" game in which Player 1 could simply decide how the resources would be split without Player 2's acceptance. They found that while many Player 1s chose a 50:50 split in the ultimatum game, none proposed a 100:0 split. By contrast, under the dictator format, 36 percent of all Player 1s took 100 percent. When acceptance was required, proposals became more equal. However, in the dictator game, when acceptance by the other party was not required, 64 percent still chose to give the other party some portion of the resources. These results demonstrate that both a desire to be fair and the realization that being unfair can generate future costs led to choices that deviated from rational models in systematic and predictable directions.

Murnighan and Pillutla (1995) argue that the psychology behind ultimatum game behaviors is more complicated than a concern for fairness and a concern for future costs associated with being unfair. Specifically, they suggest that Player 1s view these games quite differently than Player 2s. Player 1s tend to analyze the game strategically, while Player 2s tend to define the situation morally and reject profitable offers when they find the behavior of Player 1 to be immoral. This inconsistency in the definition of the situation can lead to unhappiness for both parties, both in terms of the bargaining result and the destruction of the future relationship. We will return to the problems created by inconsistent and self-serving interpretations of competitive situations in Chapter 9.

The discussion of availability in Chapter 2 showed that a vivid example can overwhelm a rational assessment of a decision. Kramer, Shah, and Woerner (1995) found that the vividness of the examples used to explain ultimatum games influences the aggressiveness of study participants. For example, Kramer et al. showed that individuals exposed to President Kennedy's successful ultimatum in the Cuban Missile Crisis (1962) were far more aggressive than individuals exposed to air controllers' unsuccessful ultimatum in their 1981 strike. Blount and Bazerman (1996) and Boles and Messick (1990) also noted inconsistency in how managers respond to the ultimatum game. When individuals are asked for the lowest amount they will accept in an ultimatum game, they specify a higher amount than the minimum they will actually accept when asked to make a choice between accepting or rejecting an ultimatum.

Player 2's expectations in ultimatum games are partially affected by a norm of equality. Messick (1991) identifies many contexts in which individuals expect an even split, even when a rational analysis would not support such a split. The ease with which individuals accept an equal allocation of pleasure and pain probably accounts, in large measure, for the common use of the compromise solutions in decision making. Consider the following situation:

> You visit a car dealer and go on a test drive. You return to the salesperson's cubicle in the showroom. The car has a list price of $18,000. After a short discussion, you offer $15,500. The salesperson counters with $17,600, you counter with $16,000, he counters with $17,200, you counter with $16,400, and he reduces his price to $16,800. You act as if you will not make another move and threaten to visit another dealership. The salesperson then says earnestly, "You look like a nice person, and I can see that you really like the car. My main concern is that you get the car that you want. I assume that you are a reasonable person, and I want to be reasonable. How about if we split the difference—$16,600?"

Many of us would feel like an ogre if we turned down the salesman's offer. After all, a 50:50 split sounds fair. Yet, logic tells us that this 50:50 split, like most 50:50 splits, is quite arbitrary. The final two numbers on the table could have been $16,000 and $16,400, and the 50:50 split would have sounded just as fair, but the resulting price would have been $16,200, or $400 less. The fairness of a 50:50 split depends on the comparative fairness of the two numbers used as anchors for the split. A rational decision maker must be aware of the influence of a seemingly fair 50:50 split, and realize that other 50:50 alternatives are easy to generate.

Again, we see that fairness concerns do affect decisions, and that ignoring these concerns in the decisions of others can be detrimental to your own outcomes. Readers are entitled to their own assessments of fairness. However, we must all realize that others may have very different norms about how to respond to an ultimatum; the goal of maximizing their own outcomes may not fully describe their fairness models.

CONCERN FOR THE OUTCOMES OF OTHERS

People care about what happens to other people. Individuals may suffer intentional losses to harm an adversary, or forego gains to help a loved one. In addition, people are concerned about how their own rewards compare to the rewards of others. Recognizing these concerns, organizations create elaborate job grade systems to specify the compensation available to employees at each level within the organization. Salaries, bonuses, and benefits are carefully calculated within these specified parameters so employees will believe they are being fairly compensated relative to others in comparable positions. In addition, organizations strive to conceal salary data to avoid social comparisons and perceptions of unfairness. Clearly, across a broad variety of situations, individuals exhibit concern for how their own rewards compare to those of relevant others.

Chapter 3 describes a model of individual decision making in which losses and gains are evaluated in comparison to a neutral reference point. The reference point usually represents the status quo; in laboratory studies of choice, it is usually designated as zero. In more natural contexts, the reference point may represent present wealth (Kahneman and Tversky, 1979). Loewenstein, Thompson, and Bazerman (1989) argue that the outcomes of others commonly act as a key reference point in interpersonal decision settings, and that interpersonal comparisons can overwhelm concern for personal outcomes in rating potential resolutions of a dispute. For example, typical individuals rated $500 for self and $500 for another person as a more satisfactory outcome than $600 for self and $800 for the other person. Yet, I would like to believe that I would choose $600 for myself and $800 for another person over $500 for myself and $500 for another person.

Bazerman, Loewenstein, and White (1992) have shown that while individuals care far more about social comparisons when rating a specific outcome, absolute individual outcomes are more important in actual choice behavior. Seventy percent rated the outcome of $400 for self and $400 for the other party as more acceptable than $500 for self and $700 for the other party when asked to evaluate these outcomes separately. However, only 22 percent chose $400 for self and $400 for the other party over $500 for self and $700 for the other party when asked to choose between the two. This basic pattern is consistent across many other comparisons and across a wide variety of contexts. When a series of joint outcomes are evaluated individually, the outcomes of others become the reference point. When choosing between two outcomes for oneself, the outcomes of others are not needed as a reference point, since the two outcomes can be easily compared. In this type of situation, the outcomes of others become less relevant. Instead, the salient attribute in a choice task is outcome to self.

Blount and Bazerman (1996) have extended this result to a real situation involving real payoffs. They agreed to recruit participants for a colleague's experiment. One group of potential participants was offered $7 to participate in a 40-minute experiment, knowing that all participants would be receiving $7. A second group was offered $8 to participate in a 40-minute experiment, knowing that some participants were arbitrarily (based on the last digit of their social security number) being offered $10.

A third group was given an opportunity (1) to participate in a 40-minute experiment in which everyone was being paid $7, (2) to participate in a 40-minute experiment in which some participants, including themselves, would receive $8 and others would receive $10, or (3) not to participate. Although significantly more participants in the first group chose to participate (72 percent) than in the second group (55 percent), the majority of participants in the third group (56 percent) chose to participate in the experiment that gave them $8 while some others were given $10 (16 percent chose the experiment in which everyone received $7; 28 percent chose not to participate in either). Thus, in evaluating whether to participate in one specific experiment, the outcomes of other potential participants were critical. However, when multiple opportunities were available, participants were able to compare what they would receive across the multiple experiments, and the outcomes of others became less important.

In a related set of studies conducted in the fall of 1991, Bazerman, Schroth, Pradhan, Diekmann, and Tenbrunsel (1994) asked second-year MBA students at the Kellogg Graduate School of Management whether they would, under a deadline, accept or reject a hypothetical job offer from a consulting firm. Some participants were presented with one offer at a time, while others were always given two job offers at a time. In both cases, they were told to imagine that it was January 15 of their graduating year, that the job offer(s) expires today, and that they needed to either accept one of the offers or reject the offer(s) and remain on the market. Two of the jobs were described as follows:

Job A: The offer is from Company 4 for $75,000 a year. It is widely known that this firm pays all starting MBAs from top schools $75,000. (Additional descriptive information about the firm is then provided.)

Job B: The offer is from Company 9 for $85,000 a year. It is widely known that this firm is paying some other graduating Kellogg students $95,000 a year. (Additional descriptive information about the firm is then provided.)

The study was interested in how MBA students discriminated between the two jobs; it was not concerned with single-choice participants who accepted neither or both job offers in a pair, or with multiple-choice participants who rejected both offers. Of the 32 participants who accepted one of the two jobs listed above in the single-choice condition, 22 accepted Job A and 10 accepted Job B. In contrast, of the 30 participants who accepted one of the two jobs in the multiple-choice condition, 5 accepted Job A and 25 accepted Job B. Consistent with the earlier Blount and Bazerman (1996) study, this study generalizes the findings to a realistic context with participants who could easily identify with the decision context.

We also explored the question of whether social comparisons are simply one of many possible sources of social information that people use inconsistently. When individuals are assessing any single outcome to self and lack a metric to assess the worth of that outcome, they will search for some social information to make sense of the outcome. However, when they are evaluating more than one option, comparing outcomes to self across multiple options provides evaluative information about each option. Specifically, we examined whether procedural justice information would create effects similar to those caused by social comparison information. The procedural justice literature suggests that individuals value the procedures used to create justice, as well as the justice of the outcomes obtained. However, in past studies, procedural justice research presented participants with one situation at a time, never allowing them a choice between options (Lind and Tyler, 1988). Thus, one interesting question is whether procedural justice information is used only in contexts where decision makers are deprived of the information necessary to assess the worth of their outcomes.

To address this question, we substituted procedural justice information for social comparison information and asked MBA students to assess either six single job offers or three pairs in the same format as described in the previous experiment. As shown in the following pair of offers, the jobs were set up to create a conflict between obtaining procedural justice and maximizing salary:

Job A (lower salary, high procedural justice): The first offer is from Company 1 for $60,000 a year. New associates are given the opportunity to participate in decisions typically made by upper management. New associates are allowed to voice their preferences regarding client and project assignments. The firm encourages all consultants, both junior and senior, to voice their opinions for changes and improvements in the company's policies.

Job B (higher salary, low procedural justice): The second offer is from Company 2 for $75,000 a year. New associates are assigned by senior partners to specific clients, projects, and engagement teams in which a senior partner is in charge and from which they are not allowed to request changes. Decisions involving company policies, including MBA training, job objectives, career advancement, and salary increases, are made by senior management. The new MBAs are not encouraged to voice their opinions or objectives.

It was expected that when individuals assessed jobs individually, procedural justice information would be more important than when individuals assessed pairs of jobs. In the single condition, of the 40 MBA students who accepted one of the two preceding jobs, 29 accepted Job A and 11 accepted Job B. In contrast, in the multiple condition, of the 37 MBA students who accepted one of the two jobs, 14 accepted Job A and 23 accepted Job B.

These findings are consistent with our argument that there are systematic inconsistencies in judgments of fairness. We see that individuals are far more concerned with social comparisons and procedural information when they are evaluating a single outcome than when they are choosing between two outcomes. Thus, fairness considerations play a more dominant role in decision making when individuals need this information to interpret their options. When the value of the outcomes to self are apparent, individuals exhibit significantly less concern for fairness.

SUMMARY

Judgments of fairness permeate organizational life. Comparisons of pay raises, the distribution of scarce budgets, promotions, grades, and prices are just a few of the many situations in which we make fairness judgments that affect our emotions and behavior. Judgments of fairness are based on more than objective reality. This chapter provides an introduction to the cognitive patterns that lead to perceptions of unfairness.

It would be impossible to eliminate concerns for fairness and social comparisons from our decision-making repertoire. Ample evidence supports the argument that people will use fairness and social comparison information to interpret their world. Thus, understanding how you and others judge fairness may help you make better managerial and life decisions. Concerns for fairness will not end with this chapter, but will become a central ingredient in the discussion of negotiation in Chapter 9.

Common Investment Mistakes

*I*magine that you have placed most of your retirement investments in an index fund, a relatively "boring" investment that seeks to match the performance of a large group of stocks (e.g., the entire Standard and Poor's 500 index of large U.S. companies). Your best friend, learning of your investment practices, argues that a bright person like you should be able to outperform that boring index fund. When you counter that you don't enjoy spending time searching for the best investment, he advises you simply to switch your retirement funds to the actively managed mutual fund that he uses. An actively managed fund is run by professional stock-pickers who trade stocks on a regular basis, seeking to own the right ones at the right time. His mutual fund, it turns out, beat your index fund by two percentage points last year.

A year goes by, and your friend brags to you that his fund had another great year, beating the market by 4 percent. He tells you it's time to switch—that you're losing too much money. Still, you decide to stick with your index fund. Another year goes by, and your friend is back to brag about outperforming the market for the third year in a row—this time by 2 percent. Is it time for you to listen to him?

Now consider some more data. In recent years, the Vanguard Index 500 fund, which tracks the S&P 500, has outperformed about 75 percent of the actively managed mutual funds in existence each year. Of course, you do not plan on investing in one of the 75 percent of funds that performs worse than the market; you plan to choose among the top 25 percent like your friend. The only problem is that substantial evidence demonstrates that past stock performance is not predictive of future performance (Bazerman, 1999). While some research suggests minor relationships between past and future performance, these relationships have been small and inconsistent. But, on the other hand, your friend's fund has been consistent!

Now consider that there are a lot of funds—approximately 8000—and that all of them are being managed by people who would like you to believe they can outperform the market, though only an average of 25 percent will succeed in any given year. In other words, each year approximately 2000 of these 8000 funds will outperform the market. Of these, 25 percent, or 500, will outperform the market

[1]This chapter, new to the fifth edition, was improved significantly based on insightful comments on a previous draft from Don Moore, Terry Odean, and Jason Zweig.

again the next year. And among these winners, 25 percent, or 125 funds, will again outperform the market for a third year in a row. The key lesson is that there will always be funds that outperform the market for multiple years in a row, but this trend will happen roughly at random, and past performance will still have little predictive power.

By contrast, index funds are certain to perform at the level of the overall market to which they are indexed, minus a very small operating fee. One reason index funds outperform the majority of mutual funds is simply that their fees are so low—often below .2 percent. Actively managed mutual funds have far higher expenses—often as high as 2 percent annually, or up to 10 times higher than some index funds. What's more, the actively managed funds often trade stocks faster, leading to higher brokerage costs that are subtracted from their returns. By definition, the aggregate of active funds (in which managers choose stocks) is likely to match the market, before fees are subtracted (Sharpe, 1991). In the end, high expenses significantly reduce the returns of these actively managed funds.

But it was your friend who told you to switch from an index fund to actively managed mutual funds three years ago, and you trust your friend. Lots of people rely on others for investment advice. Of course, those friends whose choices underperform the market eventually become too sheepish to make recommendations; we only continue to hear from those who have been lucky. Friends are not the only source of tips on the past performance of mutual funds. Ads in magazines, newspapers, and on television promote mutual funds that have done very well over the last year and try to make investors feel guilty for not having chosen that fund earlier. In fact, in any given time period, any large family of mutual funds (Fidelity has over 150 funds) will always have some funds that have performed well above the market and some that have performed well below the market. The mutual-fund company, of course, will only advertise those funds that performed above the market. If all large mutual-fund companies selected their portfolios by throwing darts at dartboards, companies could still advertise the funds with the luckiest dart throwers. In all likelihood, this system would produce the same numbers of winners and losers as under the current system—but it would be difficult for the dart throwers to justify charging high operating fees for their "expert" opinions.

This may be true, but you, like your friend, are investing for the long term, and you plan to select one of the most successful actively managed mutual funds. This is possible—but not likely! An amazingly small number of funds outperform the S&P 500 index over longer stretches. For the period 1982–1992, for example, 48 of the 205 leading mutual funds underperformed the S&P 500 by at least three percentage points per year, while only three of the 205 funds outperformed the market by at least three percentage points per year (Bogle, 1994). Thus, as the time span lengthens, the performance of actively managed mutual funds looks even worse.

While you might hope to invest in one of the three mutual funds that perform 3 percent or more above the index, don't forget that every other investor who is picking actively managed funds also intends to pick a winner. Of course, you might choose a fund that boasts of having outperformed the market over the last 10 or even 20 years. Be careful, Bogle (1994) warns:

Marketers of mutual funds have a fairly easy time achieving—and then bragging about—returns that mark their fund as '#1.' Here is the strategy: Select a fund that ranks first in any class of funds with similar objectives and asset size . . . over any specified period of time (the past quarter or year or even 25 years). Advertise it as #1. When the ranking subsequently drops (and it will), select another fund . . . and advertise it as #1 . . . These promotions provide simplistic information that is easily manipulated and has absolutely no predictive value . . . Similar rankings published in the financial press lack the fund sponsor's bias . . . However, these rankings are also utterly without predictive value. . . .

Bogle's evidence is very good. For the 20-year span of 1972–1992, he found that the average of the 20 best-performing mutual funds for the first 10 years was ranked 142 out of 309 in the next 10 years. While this performance is marginally better than that of the average fund, it is a far worse deal than buying into an index fund and avoiding expenses. Specifically, while the average total return of these "top" 20 funds during the second decade (+14.3 percent) beat the all-fund average (+13.1 percent), it was far short of the +16.2 percent return of the unmanaged S&P 500 Index (Bogle, 1994).

More recently, the *New York Times* provided performance results for the portfolio selections of five investment pros—Eric Kobren, Sheldon Jacobs, Jack Brill, Russel Kinnel, and Harold Evensky—for a seven-year period ending June 30, 2000 ("A Seven-Year Lesson in Investing," Carole Gould, 7/9/2000, page B18). All five portfolios were invested primarily in stock funds for the seven years, and the decision makers were financial experts regularly featured in the press. The seven-year returns achieved by the five portfolios were 210 percent, 204 percent, 200 percent, 147 percent, and 124 percent, respectively. These numbers sound good, but how did the Vanguard 500 Index do over the same period of time? This unmanaged, low-cost, boring index fund provided a return of 278 *percent* for the same seven-year period. Yet another victory for less management and lower fees.

Why *do* people buy actively managed mutual funds, despite this strong, easily available evidence that they are getting a bad deal? Jason Zweig (2000) warns in *Money Magazine*, "The folks who run mutual funds have always been good at cooking up clever ways to gouge you on fees, confuse you about performance, make you pay unnecessary taxes and goad you into buying funds you don't need." Mutual-fund companies also engage in creative strategies to help them look like they are performing better than an objective assessment would suggest. In addition to advertising their winners, mutual-fund companies can take their losers out of business—and they do! In 1996, 242 of the 4555 stock funds tracked by Lipper Analytical Services were merged or went out of business (Damato, 1997). Note, these funds did not go out of business at random; they were the laggards, and the fund companies were ashamed of their performance. When a fund dissolves, its old track record is erased from history, removed from the databases kept by research organizations like Morningstar and Lipper. Thus, because dropped funds are not part of the analysis, the average performance of a mutual-fund company is often much lower than the company typically reports it to be.

You may argue that some analysts offer good advice, and are capable of identifying the few long-term best funds—after all, they are quoted in financial magazines and newsletters and interviewed on television. Perhaps it is possible to form a fund managed by all-star portfolio analysts selected on the basis of their long-term performance. Bogle (1994) describes a fund that was actually created in this manner. A good idea? Maybe, but in this case it just didn't work. The unmanaged S&P 500 beat the experts by more than one percentage point per year (13.9 percent versus 12.8 percent) between 1986 and 1992.

No individual who buys an active mutual fund expects that it will perform far worse than average. Yet, lots of people buy actively managed funds and continue to hold onto them long after receiving evidence of their failure. The cost of these mistakes adds up to billions of dollars. Why do people make these mistakes? While I believe the answers can be found in the first six chapters of this book, researchers have developed a related field of inquiry: behavioral finance.

Essentially, behavioral finance is an application of what we know about common judgment errors to the world of investment. In the 1980s and early 1990s, behavioral decision research was applied most extensively to the area of negotiation (which we will cover in Chapter 9). In recent years, the most active area for new insights has been in the area of investments. This research gives us a better understanding of an important set of life decisions, and also offers clear evidence that the decision errors described in this book are broad in scope. Behavioral finance focuses both on how biases affect individuals and on how they affect markets. This chapter focuses on the former application; Shleifer (2000) and Shefrin (2000) are good sources on the latter.

In this chapter we will specifically: (1) apply some of the core findings from earlier chapters to investment decisions; (2) explore the growing and scary practice of day-trading; (3) consider the role of investment groups (have you heard of those nice grandmothers from Beardstown?); and (4) close with some clear, common-sense investment advice. As you read, I encourage you to compare these insights to your own beliefs about investing and to your current investment portfolio.

THE PSYCHOLOGY OF POOR INVESTMENT DECISIONS

Investors love new books that promise the market will go up by 300 percent or 1000 percent in the next year. Glassman and Hassett's (1999) *Dow: 36,000*, for example, received enormous media attention. Such titles achieve their success by tapping into the psychological mistakes of investors. This is a great development for the authors who get rich from these books, but this success is unlikely to be passed along to the books' readers. As shown in earlier chapters, even very bright people make poor decisions that cost time, profitability, and in some cases, their financial future.

As you read this chapter, my argument against active investing may sound too strong. However, the evidence is amazing, and it contradicts the massive amount of money and advice changing hands in financial markets. Investors pay high fees to actively managed mutual funds, to brokers to pick stocks, and to electronic trading companies to make frequent trades. These fees are how funds, brokers, and companies make their money. Are all of these investors making mistakes? The great majority of them are! Incorporating the themes of previous chapters with new research on investors, this section will document how investment decisions are affected by: (1) overconfidence; (2) optimism; (3) denying random events and the regression to the mean; (4) anchoring, the status quo, and procrastination; and (5) prospect theory.

Overconfidence

Chapter 2 demonstrated that people are generally overconfident in their decision making. In the area of investing, this overconfidence translates into a tendency to believe that you can pick mutual funds or stocks that will perform better than the market. This overconfidence leads people to engage in more active investing. Why should you be concerned about overconfidence? Because it is likely to lead you to believe that the stocks or actively managed mutual funds that you pick will perform better than they actually will, while also leading you to discount the likelihood of failure. In the investment arena, an additional pattern is vicarious overconfidence. That is, we overestimate the likelihood that our friends or our investment advisor will outperform the market.

Overconfidence is especially pertinent to stock-market investing strategies. The expense associated with owning individual stocks is largely created by the costs of buying and selling them. These expenses, which include transaction costs and differences between buy and sell prices, are dramatically higher for investors who make frequent trades. Collectively, these expenses can add up to a surprisingly large amount of money over time. While I have argued that investing in an index fund is a better strategy than frequent stock trades, it is not your only good option. For an investor with a moderate amount of wealth, a low-cost alternative to an index fund would be to buy a diversified portfolio of stocks and hold them for many years. Thanks to the emergence of a variety of investment vehicles designed to help you build a portfolio cheaply and conveniently, this strategy is becoming easier and more commonplace (Zweig, 2000).

Unfortunately, many stock-market investors fail to recognize the advantages of following this pattern. Barber and Odean (2000a) studied 66,465 households that held an investment account with a large discount broker during the period 1991–1996. In contrast to the buy-and-hold strategy, the average account turned over 75 percent of its portfolio annually. That is, on average, investors with this brokerage house sold 75 percent of their investments in any given year. Similarly, Carhart (1997) reports that the average turnover of mutual funds is 77 percent annually, while the New York Stock Exchange (2000) determined that in 1999, its total turnover rate was 78 percent. These numbers mark a dramatic increase since 1970, when the turnover rate for the New York Stock Exchange was 19 percent, and in 1980, when it was 36 percent. This growing frenzy can be attributed in part to bright people thinking they can predict the moves of the market. Are they right?

The average investor in the Barber and Odean (2000a) database earned a return of 16.4 percent during a booming market, just 1.5 percent lower than the overall market return of 17.9 percent for this same period. Most interesting are the 20 percent of accounts (more than 12,000 accounts) that had the highest turnover rates—those who actively traded stocks. Presumably, these investors believe they can assess the direction stocks will take, and are willing to incur the costs of buying and selling stocks to own the "right" portfolio at the right time. On average, the 20 percent with the highest turnover earned a return of just 11.4 percent. Thus, in comparison to the overall market return, by spending time and money trying to track, buy, and sell stocks, investors *lost* 6.5 percentage points. If active trading is so hazardous to your wealth, why do so many people engage in it? One simple explanation is that they are overconfident in their ability to outperform the market.

Overconfidence does not affect the genders equally. Examining 35,000 investment accounts at a large discount brokerage, Barber and Odean (2000b) sorted the accounts by gender and found that women achieved better results than men. In comparison to the market as a whole, women underperformed the return that they would have obtained by holding the same portfolio for a year by 1.72 annual percentage points, while in a similar comparison, men lost 2.65 percentage points. Does this mean that women pick better stocks than men? No! Actual returns of stocks picked by men and women were not significantly different. Rather, turnover patterns differed; the men had a harder time sitting still. Women had average turnover rates of 53 percent annually, while male turnover rates were 77 percent annually. It was the added costs of these more frequent trades that led men to underperform women; with each trade, the brokers got richer while the investors themselves fell further behind. Barber and Odean conclude that overconfidence among men leads to increased turnover, which in turn leads to lower performance after brokerage costs are carved out of the returns. Before women readers become overly confident about these findings, it is important to note that Barber and Odean are describing men performing worse than women whose results are *already far behind* those of the market. In other words, women did less badly than men—not an achievement worth celebrating.

Optimism

If you have money invested in the stock market, what was the total percentage return of your portfolio last year? Did you beat the market—in other words, did your performance compare favorably to the S&P 500? Now, go check your answers based on the actual data: Look up your account statements or call your brokerage or fund adviser, and don't forget to ask for last year's return on the S&P 500. How did your memory of your performance compare to your actual performance? My guess is that your comparison will be consistent with evidence showing that people tend to be optimistic about a variety of behaviors, such as expected career advancement, driving ability, etc. (see Chapter 4). Once people make an investment, they tend to be overly optimistic about its future profitability, and later maintain optimistic recollections of the investment's past performance. Optimism is closely related to overconfidence, yet distinct from it. When investors make overly confident decisions, they will hold unwarranted optimism regarding future success; retrospectively, they will maintain this optimism, even when the disappointing results of their investments are easily available.

Moore, Kurtzberg, Fox, and Bazerman (1999) created an investment simulation based on the actual performance of the nine largest mutual funds, plus one index fund, over a 10-year period, 1985–1994. MBA students received a computer disk with an investment assignment. Starting with $100,000, for each six-month simulated period, participants were allowed to invest their balance in any of the ten funds, or in a money market account, with the goal of maximizing their ending balance at the end of the simulated 10 years. (The entire task took the typical student 45 minutes to complete.) After making a six-month investment decision, participants received extensive feedback on their return, the return of all funds, and the return on the overall market; they were then prompted to place their next six-month investment. Investing the entire account in the index fund for the entire 10-year period would have led the $100,000 initial portfolio to grow to $380,041. However, the average investor ended up with only $349,620 in his or her account—a return consistent with the evidence from real-world databases presented earlier. The typical investor made too many trades, incurring far too many fees.

False optimism was clearly a factor in the participants' investment strategies. Despite the fact that the market performed very well overall during this 10-year period (1985–1994), participants consistently predicted that their portfolios would grow faster for the next six-month interval than they actually did. Specifically, participants predicted that their portfolios would rise 8.13 percent per six-month period; in fact, they only grew by 5.50 percent. Even more interesting, participants had optimistic illusions about their past performance: At the end of the game, most participants reported that they had matched the market's performance. In fact, participants obtained an average return 8 percent *below* the market. More specifically, Moore et al. (1999) asked participants whether they had performed (1) more than 15 percent below the market, (2) 10–15 percent below the market, (3) 5–10 percent below the market, (4) within 5 percent of the market, (5) 5–10 percent above the market, (6) 10–15 percent above the market, or (7) more than 15 percent above the market. On average, participants overstated their performance by one entire level.

In a parallel study, Goetzmann and Peles (1997) achieved very similar results. Participants remembered obtaining more favorable returns than they actually obtained. Goetzmann and Peles conclude that optimism helps investors justify their past behaviors, allowing them to maintain illusions about the superiority of their investment strategy. I argue that optimism also encourages investors to continue active trading, rather than pursuing wiser, time-saving investments in index funds.

By the way, before reading this chapter, had you ever compared your investment decisions to the market? Most investors have not. Why not? I argue that most investors want to protect their overly optimistic view of their investments—and are willing to pay a high price to maintain their illusions. Similarly, if you use an investment adviser, have you ever instructed this "expert" to provide systematic follow-up on his or her recommendations? It might be instructive for you to ask the adviser to compare the returns on his or her advice to the market's performance during the same period of time. The psychological need to perceive good news may be insulating you—and your hired experts—from the truth about investing, and costing you a great deal of money in the long run.

Plenty of external sources encourage investors' natural optimism. Financial magazines remind us of the wise advice they provided in the past, but generally neglect to mention the advice that was flat-out wrong. These publications also tend to supply anecdotal evidence of past success, rather than risking their reputation by tracking it in a systematic manner. Overall, I have to admit that this is a wise business strategy: If they revealed the true returns on their past advice, they would probably sell fewer magazines.

Denying that Random Events Are Random

As we saw in Chapter 2, people tend to deny that random events are random, and find patterns where none exists—such as having a "hot hand" in basketball. When investors are led to believe that a specific fund is "hot," they will become more willing to pay the fees associated with active investing. In fact, there is a great deal of randomness in the investment arena, and even more denial of this randomness by investors. In their eagerness to outperform the market, most investors are unwilling to accept that performing at the level of the market, while minimizing expenses, may be a level of performance that they should be happy to accept. The most important conclusion? Be wary of any advice that predicts the market's future based on past performance.

Consistent with research by Bogle (1994), Carhart (1997), and Thaler and DeBondt (1992), in the 10-year database used in the Moore et al. (1999) study (1985–1994), the performance of mutual funds tended to regress to the mean. Nevertheless, study participants expected their portfolios' future performance to be highly correlated with past performance. In fact, their expectations were negatively correlated with actual returns. Overall, participants expected "hot" funds to stay hot. This is the same false assumption that leads real-world investors to hold onto expensive funds.

There is some minor evidence that past performance of stocks predicts their future performance. Jegadeesh and Titman (1993) document a momentum effect in which stocks that have done well continue to do well the next year. The only problem is that this pattern then reverses itself in following years (DeBondt and Thaler, 1985). Odean (1999) argues that biased investors who expect past patterns to continue in the future may influence a stock's performance. However, after the last of these momentum traders enter the market and push the value of the stock beyond the underlying value of the company, the price will begin to fall, causing the inevitable reversal.

DeBondt and Thaler (1985) compared the future performance of two groups of stocks: one group of extreme losers from the past three years and one group of extreme winners from the past three years. They found that, over the following five years, the "loser" portfolio dramatically outperformed the "winner" portfolio. DeBondt and Thaler (1985) attribute reversals to the tendency of investors to assume that the past is a good predictor of the future, and thus to their penchant for overbuying winners and overselling losers. The market eventually adjusts, and owners of the underpriced "loser" portfolio will find themselves with a better set of investments than owners of the overpriced "winner" portfolio.

Inspired by Jegadeesh and Titman's (1993) results, you might be tempted to adopt the strategy of buying recent stock-market winners. On the other hand, DeBondt and Thaler's (1985) findings might motivate you to buy recent losers. Unfortunately, it is extremely difficult to predict when the last momentum buyers have entered the market. Once again, the past is not an accurate predictor of the future. Personally, I am more comfortable admitting that I have no way of knowing which stocks will do better in the future, and sticking with index funds.

Anchoring, the Status Quo, and Procrastination

Much of this chapter suggests that many investors think too much about their investments, frantically trading stocks and shifting mutual funds based on the most recent advice of too many experts. However, evidence also exists that most people think too *little* about the type of assets they should hold. Thinking through one's asset allocation and developing a long-term plan makes a great deal of sense. This is where investment advice (e.g., free software program provided by many mutual fund companies) may be helpful. For example, Shefrin (2000), Belsky and Gilovich (1999), and most other sources of good financial advice suggest that most people place too little of their *long-term* investments in stocks. This observation is based on the amazing long-term superior performance of stocks over bonds and other standard investments. Yet, people use fairly naïve strategies for asset allocation, sticking with what they or others have decided in the past; in other words, their investment decisions tend to be fairly mindless.

In a study of scholars who enroll in retirement plans offered by TIAA-CREF, Benartzi and Thaler (1999) found that most professors, facing a choice between investing their retirement funds in either TIAA (bonds) or CREF (stock), commonly allocated their money 50:50 to the two accounts. In addition, the median number of changes that professors made to this allocation over their career was zero. That is, professors (maybe not the smartest of people, but also not the dumbest) made a fairly naïve allocation, and then never adjusted their decision—even as their life circumstances changed over time.

The professors' 50:50 allocation meshes with another of Benartzi and Thaler's (1999) findings: When firms offer a choice of investment options for retirement accounts, the percentage of stock funds offered is an excellent predictor of the percentage of dollars that employees will choose to invest in stocks. That is, if a company offers four funds, three stock funds, and one bond fund, employees put about 75 percent of their money into the stock funds. In contrast, if the company offers one stock fund and three bond funds, then employees hold, on average, 75 percent of their retirement investments in bonds. Thus, people choose their investments the way many diners order food in a Chinese restaurant: one dish from the "Vegetables" column, one from "Chicken," one from "Beef," and so on. That may be a good way to pick a satisfying meal, but it's not the best investment strategy; history shows that if your money will remain invested in a retirement fund for decades, stock funds will offer the best return. The point is that people should think carefully about this allocation, rather than being led naïvely by the choices their employers offer them.

By this point in the chapter, I hope that many of my readers are reconsidering their investment decisions. However, there is a strong force competing against change—the status quo bias. This is the effect that prevented Benartzi and Thaler's (1999) professors from making even one allocation change in a lifetime. Samuelson and Zeckhauser (1988) find that people tend to keep their investments the way that they are. In an experimental study, they presented a thought exercise to a group of individuals with a working knowledge of economics and finance. The participants were asked to imagine that they had inherited a large amount of money from a great uncle, and were asked which of four possible investments they would pick: (1) a stock with moderate risk, (2) a risky stock, (3) U.S. Treasury bills, and (4) municipal bonds. Each investment was described in a bit of detail. Four other randomly selected groups were told that they inherited an investment from their great uncle, and that it consisted of one of the four investments from the preceding list (one group was told that they inherited a stock with moderate risk, a second group was told that they inherited a risky stock, a third group was told that they inherited a U.S. Treasury bill, and a fourth group was told that they inherited a municipal bond). These participants were asked whether they would keep the investment or trade it for one of the three other investments listed above. They chose overwhelmingly to keep the investment that they received, rather than picking the investment best suited to their unbiased preferences. Essentially, the study participants accepted the status quo, rather than switching to the investments that best suited their particular needs.

Finally, the bias against action also leads many people to procrastinate making investments in the first place. It is not uncommon for people to hold a large amount of money in their checking, savings, or money market account, with the intention of investing it soon. Months pass, and they find themselves facing the same decision—but suddenly the market has gone up in value by 6 percent, and they've missed out on a great opportunity. By procrastinating, you may be sacrificing your long-term financial well-being. Somewhat paradoxically, investors procrastinate on making allocation decisions, while being overly active in moving funds within a category (e.g., stocks)—thus putting too much effort into the less important financial decisions and not enough effort into the far more vital ones.

Prospect Theory, Selling Winners, and Keeping Losers

Consistent with Shefrin and Statman (1985), Odean (1998) found that investors have a strong preference to hold on to stocks that are selling below purchase price, so that they will avoid becoming "losers," and to sell stocks that are selling above the purchase price, so that they will come out "winners." Similarly, Barber, Odean, and Zheng (2000) show that investors tend to hold on to losing mutual funds and oversell winning mutual funds. If your goal is to make as much money as you can, then the choice of whether to buy or sell a fund should be based solely on how much you expect its value to increase in the future. Thus, the price at which you bought it is an arbitrary and meaningless reference point, except with regard to taxes. From a tax perspective, when you sell a winner, you must pay taxes on your earnings, and when you sell a loser, your taxes are reduced. Therefore, with respect to taxation, it makes sense to sell more losers than winners. In addition, Odean (1999) finds that the winners that investors sell end up outperforming the losers that they keep. In sum, when investors seek to become winners, stock selection and taxes actually increase their chances of being losers.

Why do investors follow this losing pattern? As we learned from prospect theory in Chapter 3, decision makers tend to compare outcomes to a reference point. For most investors, the most common reference point is the price that they paid. Investors holding stocks valued at a price higher than they paid for them are faced with a sure gain (selling now and becoming a "winner"), or holding the stock and risking the current gain for an unknown return. With gains, we tend to be risk averse; investors tend to sell to guarantee the gain. Investors holding stocks valued lower than their initial purchase price, on the other hand, are faced with a sure loss (selling now), or holding the stock for an unknown return. With losses, we tend to be risk seeking; investors tend to take the risk of holding on to the loser in the hope of becoming a winner. This pattern is also consistent with a regret minimization strategy—an effort to avoid "booking" a loss. As long as you let the loss "ride," you can pretend it doesn't exist; but once you sell the stock, you have to enter it, in your mental accounts, on the loss side of the ledger. However, for three reasons this pattern leads investors to lose money relative to the market's overall performance: high costs associated with making trades, selling the wrong stocks, and paying too much in taxes. Recognition of these errors should encourage investors to adopt wiser and simpler strategies.

DAYTRADING: A DISEASE BASED ON VIVIDNESS

In recent years, online trading has been the dramatic growth area of the investment world. Electronic trading is simply cheaper than going through a stockbroker, and as more people begin trading online, the cost keeps going down. Competition further reduces the costs of trading. From 1996 to 1998, the average online trading commission fell by 75 percent, and the numbers continue to plummet. The full-service brokerage houses have added online services as well. Most people who use online trading services are men (75 percent), and most of them are between 25 and 45 years old.

First, the good news about online trading. If you are planning to invest in stocks, bringing your costs down will be a key to your success. So, for those investors who follow a long-term buy-and-hold strategy, investing online rather than through a full-service broker makes a great deal of sense. However, buy-and-hold is not the strategy of the typical online trader. Rather, online traders tend to be actively engaged in trading stocks. In the worst case, they quit their jobs to be professional traders. Many of them are headed for disaster!

The typical investor who engages in online trading is someone whose trades recently beat the market (most likely because they were lucky). In a 1992–1995 sample of online trading, Barber and Odean (2000b) find that the average new online trader outperformed the market by two percentage points the year before switching to online trading. Note that these investors' confidence was further bolstered by the fact that these were good years for the stock market. Unfortunately, after switching, these traders' average performance regressed to the mean, and was further lowered by the costs of frequent trades. As a result, these online traders lagged the market by three percentage points.

Lagging a very successful market by three percentage points is no disaster, particularly if you engage in online trading in your spare time. However, because online traders tend to be the most overconfident of investors, many of them quit their regular professions to trade full-time, becoming members of a new pseudo-profession called daytrading. The frequency of their trades dooms these full-time traders to underperform the market by even more than three percentage points. When the market goes down, as it is destined to do, big losses will almost certainly follow. In addition, nearly all of a daytrader's profits are short-term capital gains, which are taxed at the highest marginal rate (up to 39.6 percent); a more patient investor would be taxed on long-term gains at a much lower 20 percent. For those who have also given up their regular income, disaster is predictable, and can be tragic—as evidenced by the Atlanta daytrader who went on a shooting spree after a streak of "bad luck."

What causes reasonably smart people to decide to become daytraders? In Chapter 2, I presented evidence that people respond to vivid data. Barber and Odean (2000b) document the recent barrage of ads that made the daytrading success vivid to all Americans. E°TRADE asked its viewers, "If your broker's so great, how come he still has to work?" Ameritrade shows two suburban moms returning from a jog. One goes straight to her computer, and a few clicks later brags, "I think I just made about $1,700." The kids cheer her on, while the other mom is embarrassed to admit, "I have a mutual fund." Finally, Discover Brokerage introduces us to an intrinsically motivated tow-truck driver with a postcard on his dashboard. "Vacation?" his white-collar passenger asks. "That's my home," the driver responds. "Looks more like an island," comments the passenger. The driver explains, "Technically, it's a country." Where did the driver get his wealth? Online trading, of course—it's that easy. While these commercials have doubtless won awards for creativity, their message is dangerous. They will inspire more and more people to trade online, leading in many cases to tragic consequences. Nevertheless, vividness remains an effective advertising strategy.

When I run into a daytrader (they are often also taxi drivers), I like to ask them why they think they know more than the party on the other side of the trade. Most of the daytraders I've met have never considered this question. When they ask me to clarify, I try to explain: When a daytrader is buying a stock, it is because someone has sold it. Similarly, when a daytrader sells a stock, someone else is buying it. Thus, most daytraders are paying fees to make an exchange with someone who has better information about the trade than they do. Overall, I argue, this sounds like a bad bet. But, as I will explain in Chapter 9, people are not very good at considering the other side of a transaction.

THE BEARDSTOWN GANG AND OTHER GROUPS THAT LIMIT INVESTMENT RETURNS

Perhaps, you think, you can get better returns on your investment by pooling your knowledge with others. That's the core concept of investment groups. In fact, a group of nice grandmothers from Beardstown, Indiana, wowed investors with reports of very high returns. Their bestseller, *The Beardstown Ladies' Common-Sense Investment Guide,* claimed that the club's members had outperformed the market and made a 23.4 percent return on their investments over a 10-year period by following the simple, straightforward strategy of investing in well-known companies (such as McDonald's and Wal-Mart). The women appeared as investing experts on many of the most popular talk shows and were profiled by film crews from Great Britain, Germany, and Japan. They produced five books, a video, and a website, and held numerous book signings, seminars, and speaking engagements.

In the midst of the media frenzy, Shane Tritsch, a reporter for *Chicago* magazine, noticed a curious disclaimer on the copyright page of the 1996 edition of the Beardstown Ladies' book. Clarifying a detail not mentioned in previous editions, the disclaimer stated that the members' dues were included in the club's annual return figure. In other words, the Beardstown Ladies calculated their annual returns quite differently than the way mutual funds (and virtually all professionally run investments) calculate theirs. The Ladies set returns equal to the sum of stock appreciation plus dividends plus monthly dues; by contrast, the returns of mutual funds are based only on stock appreciation plus dividends. According to Price Waterhouse, from 1984 to 1993, the decade covered by the Beardstown Ladies' *Investment Guide,* the club's average annual return, as it should have been calculated, was actually *only 9.1 percent*—far below the 23.4 percent return they reported, and also significantly lower than the 15 percent average return of the overall stock market from 1984 to 1993.

When the Beardstown Ladies first heard that their returns were being questioned, a spokesperson sternly told reporters, "You can't get the president of the United States, so you're going after little old ladies now" (Tharp, 1998). Of course, the fact was that these "little old ladies" were promoting themselves to the public as investment experts and urging others to take their advice. While the Beardstown Ladies' investments underperformed the market, the American public's desire to believe in their incredible story turned out to be a cash cow for the retirees, whose book royalties more than made up for returns. Meanwhile, readers shelled out money for the book, and many of them made far poorer investments as a result. Why did the media and the public fall for this story? One possibility is that investors fail to accept the true difficulty of outperforming the market. False optimism allowed the public to believe the story, rather than double-check the amazing record.

Nevertheless, the false claims from Beardstown fueled the growth of investment clubs nationwide; from 1994 to 1998, the number of such groups rose in the United States from 13,000 to 35,000 (Barber and Odean, 2000b). In a study of 166 investment clubs from 1991 to 1997, Barber and Odean found that the groups earned a 14.1 percent annual return, while the S&P index returned 18 percent and individual investors earned 16 percent. All told, 60 percent of the clubs underperformed the index. The investment clubs turned over their investments far too often (65 percent annually), causing them to pay too much in brokerage costs.

There are a variety of reasons to join an investment club. Perhaps your friends are tired of hearing you talk about investments. Perhaps you like the people in the club, or maybe they serve good food. But if you belong to a club to increase your return, it may be time to rethink your investment strategy.

ACTION STEPS

More than any other chapter in this book, the ideas presented in this chapter have action implications for virtually all readers. I have provided an overview of mistakes that many people make, and explained the psychology behind those mistakes. Now that we have observed these mistakes in the investing context, I close with some specific thoughts to consider as you strive to reduce the biases that affect your investments. I begin with the issue of saving for retirement and then close with broader investment advice.

In Chapter 1 of this book, I argued that a key aspect of making more rational decisions is to clearly identify your final goal. Many investors have never put much thought into this issue. Some may have the goal of "accumulating as much money as possible." But, if you are able to take this goal to the extreme—by earning a good income, living frugally, and investing your savings wisely—you could end up dying with mountains of money in your accounts. A different goal is to acquire the funds you need to buy whatever bundle of goods you want to surround yourself with for the rest of your life. This goal is the central theme of the investment bestseller *Die Broke* by Pollan and Levine (1997). I have no objection to a mixed strategy of buying the goods you desire and providing funds for other people and charitable organizations. However, many of us fail to think even this far about our monetary objectives.

The goal of investing to acquire the funds you need for a comfortable retirement seems straightforward. However, a 1997 survey found only 6 percent of U.S. citizens felt they had surpassed their retirement savings goal, while 55 percent felt that they were behind (Laibson, Repetto, and Tobacman, 1998). Laibson et al. (1998) report that the median U.S. household retires with liquid wealth of $10,000 and net worth of $100,000 (including house equity and autos). This finding is consistent with a broad array of evidence that Americans are saving too little for retirement.

Assuming that we are capable of saving more, why do we fail to do so? Perhaps the most critical answer comes from the want/should distinction developed in Chapter 4. People know that they *should* save more for retirement, but they *want* to consume more now (to buy a new TV, eat dinners out, etc.). The evidence in Chapter 4 suggests that our desires typically overcome what we think we should do, particularly when the benefits of listening to our "should self" are decades in the future. This will be particularly true for those who avoid financial planning; the less we plan, the more we allow our desires to gain the upper hand. To assist our want self in defeating our should self, people become overly optimistic that solutions for retirement will suddenly appear. This optimism works out fine for a small minority of citizens—maybe Uncle Edgar will keel over and leave you a fortune in his will, or your numbers will come up in Powerball—but the majority may be in for a rude awakening upon retirement.

With regard to investments, the U.S. government provides support for people who want to make conscientious decisions about their futures by offering tax incentives for retirement investments—IRAs, Keoghs, etc. By investing in these plans, you are not only acting wisely from a long-term perspective, but getting a bonus from the government as well. Quite simply, virtually all readers should be investing as much money as they can to reduce their taxable income. What's more, your own employer probably gives you incentives to save. Many 401(k) retirement plans allow you to contribute a portion of your salary and then have your employer "match," or augment, a portion of that money. Some employers match 25 percent, 50 percent, or more— instantly and automatically turning each dollar you contribute into $1.25, $1.50, or even higher rewards. If you are not contributing the maximum percentage of your salary that your plan allows, then you are missing out on one of the best and safest ways to build your long-term wealth.

Decisions regarding where you place your retirement money should be based on a clear asset allocation plan. Benartzi and Thaler (1995) make a convincing case that most people have far too low a percentage of their retirement funds in stock. The fact that retirement funding is for the distant future means that it should be easier to accept the higher risk of stock in return for the higher returns that stocks achieve over a long period of time. A few bad years are unlikely to lead stocks to underperform bonds between now and the time when most readers will retire. As you approach retirement, it may make more sense to move more money into bonds to reduce risk.

As retirement draws near, for those investors with the goal of buying their desired bundle of life goods, annuities are another good choice. In return for a lump sum of money, the investor gets a guaranteed amount of funds periodically for the rest of their life. If you die ahead of schedule, you lose—but then again, you won't need the money anyway. However, if you outlive expectations, you will get a great return, and you are more likely to need these additional funds. Green (2000) argues that annuities are underused in comparison to the financial benefits that they create. In addition, annuities are now provided by a number of charitable organizations, allowing you to obtain guaranteed income for life and tax benefits, and to provide funds to your preferred charity. These annuities create more total benefit than what you could obtain privately, while making a similarly valued contribution to society. However, while annuities will be logical for many investors, you need to choose them carefully. Some annuities, pushed by the sleaziest outfits in the financial business, come with a slick sales pitch and are wildly overpriced. I recommend sticking with a highly reputable, well-known mutual-fund family that charges low fees, such as T. Rowe Price, Schwab, or Vanguard.

Beyond retirement, the key argument of this chapter is that very bright people are currently paying billions of dollars per year for collectively useless advice. Why? Because they are committing the errors described throughout this book in the area of investing. Now that you understand the psychology behind these mistakes, you must learn to confront them and identify a better plan for the future. This plan should include taking the time to formulate your asset allocation. You should strive to achieve this allocation in a low-cost manner, to avoid paying fees to people and companies who do not truly add value. While many investors now know to avoid "loads" (commissions that are paid when you buy a mutual fund), far too many are still buying funds with very high annual expense ratios (Barber, Odean, and Zheng, 2000). Once you have your plan in place, continue to invest on a regular basis. If you combine these three tasks—appropriate asset allocation, low-cost investing, and adding regular investments—you are well on your way to an excellent investment strategy. Then relax, go back to work on tasks that you enjoy, or play more tennis—there is little reason to think about your investments for more than a few hours per year.

Some final words of caution: Changing your allocation of funds according to the advice in this chapter does require some care on the tax front. Before selling securities that have appreciated in value, you must first seek to understand the taxable consequences of doing so; you may want to check with your accountant. The advice in this chapter is relevant to existing investments, but must be applied to them with care. It should be easiest to follow when you are thinking about making new investments.

CHAPTER EIGHT

Making Rational Decisions in Negotiations

$\mathbf{W}$hen two or more parties need to reach a joint decision but have different preferences, they negotiate. They may not be sitting around a bargaining table; they may not be making explicit offers and counteroffers; they may even be making statements suggesting that they are on the same side. But as long as their preferences concerning the joint decision are not identical, they have to negotiate to reach a mutually agreeable outcome.

Many of our managerial decisions are made in conjunction with other actors who have preferences different from our own. In this respect, negotiation is central to organizational life. Yet, just as our individual decisions are subject to irrationalities, so, too, are negotiated decisions. Negotiation outcomes are affected not only by your decisions, but by the decisions of other parties. Making more rational decisions increases the likelihood of reaching an agreement when it is wise to do so, and increases the quality of negotiated outcomes.

People often believe that the outcomes they reach in a negotiation were inevitable. In fact, in most negotiations, a wide variety of outcomes are possible. When teaching negotiations to MBA students and executives, I typically use simulations in which half of the participants play one role and the other half play another role. All dyads negotiate the same problem and have access to the same data. When the participants reach an agreement or an impasse, they record their results on the chalkboard. The amazing result is that even within fairly homogenous groups, the range of outcomes obtained is enormous. The lesson? The decisions of each negotiator matter!

While the first seven chapters of this book have focused on biases and irrationalities affecting individual decision making, this chapter and the next one examine judgment in multiparty contexts. This chapter outlines a framework for thinking rationally in two-party negotiation contexts. Chapter 9 uses this framework to examine how our individual biases and heuristics are manifested in the negotiation context. It also provides information on cognitive biases created by the competitive environment.

The goals of this chapter are to give you a framework for thinking about two-party negotiations and to introduce prescriptive suggestions for improving decision making within this context. This chapter seeks to improve the quality of your outcomes as the "focal" negotiator. In addition, the chapter will recommend ways to improve the total outcomes for all parties and, hence, increase societal gains. These goals are achieved by learning how to reduce the likelihood of impasse when it is in the interest of all parties to reach a settlement, and by expanding the total range of benefits that both parties can receive.

Economists were the first to provide prescriptive advice to negotiators. The most well-developed component of this economic school of thought is game theory. In game theory, mathematical models are developed to analyze the outcomes that will emerge in multiparty decision-making contexts if all parties act rationally. To analyze a game, specific conditions are outlined that define how decisions are to be made—for example, the order in which players get to choose their moves—and utility measures of outcomes for each player are attached to every possible combination of player moves. The actual analysis focuses on predicting whether or not an agreement will be reached, and if one is reached, what the specific nature of that agreement will be. The advantage of game theory is that, given absolute rationality, it provides the most precise prescriptive advice available to the negotiator. The disadvantages of game theory are twofold. First, it relies on the ability to completely describe all options and associated outcomes for every possible combination of moves in a given situation—a tedious task at its best, infinitely complex at its worst. Second, it requires that all players consistently act in a rational manner. Yet, as we have seen in earlier chapters, individuals often behave irrationally in systematically predictable ways that are not easily captured within rational analyses.

A DECISION-ANALYTIC APPROACH TO NEGOTIATIONS

As an alternative to game-theoretical analyses of negotiations that take place in a world of "impeccably rational, supersmart people," Raiffa (1982; 2001) has developed a decision-analytic approach to negotiations. Such an approach focuses on how "erring folks like you and me actually behave" rather than "how we should behave if we were smarter, thought harder, were more consistent, were all knowing" (1982, p. 21). Raiffa's decision-analytic approach seeks to give the best available advice to negotiators involved in real conflict with real people. His goal is to provide guidance for you as the focal negotiator, given the most likely profile of the other party's expected behavior. Thus, Raiffa's approach is prescriptive from the point of view of the party receiving advice but descriptive from the point of view of the competing party.

Raiffa offers an excellent framework for approaching negotiations. The analytical structure of this approach is based on assessments of three key sets of information:

- Each party's alternative to a negotiated agreement
- Each party's set of interests
- The relative importance of each party's interests

Together, these three sets of information determine the structure of the negotiation game (Lax and Sebenius, 1986; Sebenius, 1989). Negotiation analysis considers how a rational negotiator should think about the structure of the negotiation and the other negotiator (Raiffa, 2001; Lax and Sebenius, 1986), and the common errors that negotiators and their opponents make (Bazerman and Neale, 1992; Thompson, 2001; Bazerman, Curhan, and Moore, 2000; Bazerman, Curhan, Moore, and Valley, 2000).

Alternatives to a Negotiated Agreement

Before we begin any important negotiation, we should consider what we will do if we fail to reach an agreement. That is, we must determine our *Best Alternative to a Negotiated Agreement* (BATNA) (Fisher and Ury, 1981). This is important because the value of a negotiator's BATNA provides a lower bound for determining the minimum outcome we require of a negotiated agreement. We should prefer any negotiated agreement that provides more value to us than our BATNA over impasse; likewise, we should decline any negotiated agreement that provides less than our BATNA. This assessment logically determines the negotiator's *reservation point* (also called an indifference point)—the point at which the negotiator is indifferent between a negotiated agreement and impasse.

Imagine that you believe the other side has made their final offer, and all you have to do is accept or reject it. How do you decide? The BATNA concept makes this a fairly clear decision. If the offer is better than your BATNA, accept it. If not, reject it. Yet many people say "no" to final offers that are better than their BATNA, and say "yes" to offers that are worse than their BATNA. Why? When you have failed to carefully consider your BATNA, it is easy for emotions to hold sway.

Alternatives to agreement take a variety of forms. For example, rather than buy a specific new car, you may decide to continue to use mass transit. Alternatively, your BATNA may be to buy the same car from another dealership at a price that you have been offered in writing. Notice that in the second situation, it is far easier to determine your reservation price. However, whether you have an easy-to-assess reservation price, or whether you seem to be comparing apples and oranges, you should always determine your BATNA and your best estimate of the value of your opponent's BATNA. While this analysis may be difficult, it will provide a better basis for negotiation than your intuitive, unprepared assessments. Often the critical issue will be whether or not to walk out on the negotiation.

The Interests of the Parties

To analyze a negotiation, it is necessary to identify all of the parties' interests—and yet, the fact is that negotiators are not always fully aware of the other side's interests. How can this be? There is a difference between the parties' stated positions and their underlying interests. Positions are the claimed requirements that parties demand from the other side. Interests are ancillary or underlying issues behind these positions that could matter to the negotiators if they were made aware of them. As the following sections highlight, sometimes a focus on deeper interests can identify a more useful set of concerns to the parties and form the basis of a more reasonable bargaining platform.

Recently, the chief purchasing officer for one of my consulting clients (a Fortune 100 organization) participated in negotiating contract terms for the firm's purchase of a new health-care product ingredient from a European company. Both sides agreed to a price of $18 per pound for a million pounds of the product per year. However, conflict arose over exclusivity; the European firm would not agree to sell the ingredient exclusively to my client. My client could not afford to invest in creating a new product based on this ingredient if competitors had access to the same ingredient. When the chief purchasing officer arrived in Europe, the argument over exclusivity continued. Finally, he asked the producer why he would not provide exclusivity to a major corporation that was offering to buy as much of the ingredient as he could produce. The producer explained that exclusivity would require him to violate an agreement with his cousin, who was purchasing 250 pounds per year to make a locally sold product. Once this piece of information emerged, the purchasing officer was able to quickly wrap up an agreement that provided exclusivity, with the exception of a couple hundred pounds annually for the producer's cousin—and the celebration began. The key to this agreement was the chief purchasing officer's decision to ask about the producer's interest (selling a small amount of the ingredient to his cousin), rather than staying focused on the producer's stated goal (not providing exclusivity). Interestingly, the chief purchasing officer is viewed within his corporation as a negotiation genius, and part of his reputation is based on his ability to resolve this dispute. Yet, as he puts it, "All I did was ask them why they didn't want to provide exclusivity."

The Relative Importance of Each Party's Interests

Even when we are aware of our interests, we may not have thought through the relative importance of each issue. To be fully prepared to negotiate, we must become aware of how important each issue is to us. The best agreements are reached by trading off relatively unimportant issues for more important ones. For example, when negotiating a new job offer, you may realize that health benefits are more important to you than an extra three days of personal time, or you may be more interested in postponing your start date in exchange for fewer vacation days during your first year. Whatever your preferences, you must prepare yourself ahead of time to recognize which tradeoffs are more and less attractive to you.

Summary

Together, these three groups of information (each party's alternative to a negotiated agreement, each party's set of interests, and the relative importance of each party's interests) provide the building blocks for thinking analytically about a negotiation. A negotiator should assess all components of this information before entering any important bargaining situation. With this information in hand, the negotiator will be prepared for the two primary tasks of negotiation: creating and claiming value (Lax and Sebenius, 1986). As we develop each of these two themes, it is important to remember that creating and claiming value are processes that occur simultaneously in a negotiation. Many of us are good at one but not the other. My goal is to make you comfortable with both aspects of the negotiation challenge.

CLAIMING VALUE IN NEGOTIATION

Consider the following example:

> An MBA from a very prestigious school who has a number of unique talents is being recruited for a highly specialized position. The organization and the employee have agreed on all issues except salary. The organization has offered $90,000, and the employee has counter-offered $100,000. Both sides believe they have made fair offers, but they both would very much like to reach an agreement. The student, while not verbalizing this information, would be willing to take any offer over $93,000 rather than lose the offer. The organization, while not verbalizing this information, would be willing to pay up to $97,000 rather than lose the candidate.

A simplified view of the bargaining zone concept describes the recruitment problem:

Bargaining zone

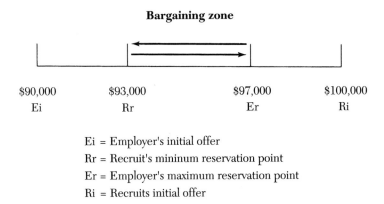

$90,000	$93,000	$97,000	$100,000
Ei	Rr	Er	Ri

Ei = Employer's initial offer
Rr = Recruit's mininum reservation point
Er = Employer's maximum reservation point
Ri = Recruits initial offer

The bargaining zone framework assumes that each party has some reservation point below (or above) which the negotiator would prefer impasse to settlement. Reservation points are set at the negotiator's BATNA. Notice that the two reservation points overlap. Thus, there is a set of resolutions that both parties would prefer over impasse—in this case, all points between $93,000 and $97,000. This area is known as a *positive bargaining zone*. When a positive bargaining zone exists, a rational model of negotiation would dictate that the negotiators should reach a settlement—it is the rational thing to do. When the reservation points of the two parties do not overlap, a negative bargaining zone exists. In such cases, no resolution should occur because there is no settlement that would be acceptable to both parties.

Many people find the notion of a bargaining zone to be counterintuitive. Having participated in a variety of negotiations throughout their lives, they have reached the conclusion that the reservation points of parties never overlap; they simply meet at the point of agreement. This reasoning is incorrect. In fact, at the point of agreement, when both parties choose a settlement rather than impasse, their actual reservation points are overlapping. This settlement point represents only one of what are often many points within the bargaining zone.

Returning to our recruiting example, we can see that the bargaining zone consists of the range between $93,000 and $97,000. If the employer could convince the recruit that an offer of $93,100 was final, we know the recruit would accept the offer, and the firm would minimize its settlement costs. Similarly, if the recruit could convince the employer that $96,900 was the lowest salary she would accept, we know the employer would accept this figure, and the recruit would maximize her settlement benefit. Thus, one of the key skills of negotiation is to determine the other party's reservation point and to aim for a resolution that is barely acceptable to the other party. This is a delicate process. If one or more of the parties were to misjudge the situation, they might rigidly demand a bargain that is beyond the other party's reservation point, leading to impasse. (Such would be the case if, for example, the recruit holds to a demand of $98,000 and the employer holds to the offer of $92,000—both believing that the other side will "cave in.") When this behavior occurs, the parties act in ways that prohibit the rational choice of a solution within the positive bargaining zone. As Ben Franklin (quoted by Raiffa, 1982) observed:

> Trades would not take place unless it were advantageous to the parties concerned. Of course, it is better to strike as good a bargain as one's bargaining position permits. The worst outcome is when, by overreaching greed, no bargain is struck, and a trade that could have been advantageous to both parties does not come off at all.

CREATING VALUE IN NEGOTIATION

The foregoing analysis dealt with negotiation in a situation in which a single issue (salary) was under dispute. Negotiations are often more complex, involving several or more disputed issues. Consider the Camp David talks in 1978 (documented in Pruitt and Rubin, 1985):

> Egypt and Israel tried to negotiate the control of the Sinai Peninsula, a situation in which it appeared that the two sides had directly opposing goals. Egypt wanted the return of the Sinai in its entirety, while Israel, which had occupied the territory since the 1967 war, refused to return this land. Efforts at compromise failed. Neither side found the proposal of splitting the Sinai acceptable.

An initial examination of this conflict suggests that a negative bargaining zone existed and that a negotiated resolution would not be possible. That is, if we mapped the positions of the parties onto a single scale, the reservation points would not overlap, and impasse would be inevitable.

Who gets the Sinai?

100% to Israel   Ir(?)   Er(?)   100% to Egypt

Ir (?) = estimation of Israel's reservation point
Er (?) = estimation of Egypt's reservation point

In contrast to this pessimistic and false prediction, the existence of multiple issues and the development of a creative trade explains the resolution that eventually developed at Camp David.

> As the Camp David negotiations continued, it became clear that while the positions of Egypt and Israel were incompatible, the interests of the two countries were compatible. Israel's underlying interest was security from land or air attack. Egypt was primarily interested in sovereignty over land which was part of Egypt for thousands of years. What emerged was the existence of two real issues, instead of one, with differential importance to the two parties: sovereignty and military protection. The solution that emerged traded off these issues. The agreement called for Israel to return the Sinai in exchange for assurances of a demilitarized zone and new Israeli air bases.

To analyze this agreement, examine the more complex diagram presented in Figure 8.1. The utility of an agreement to Israel is represented on the horizontal axis, and the utility of an agreement to Egypt is represented on the vertical axis.

Figure 8.1   Integrating interests in the Israel–Egypt dispute.

Point A represents the solution of giving the land and total control of it to Egypt. Notice that this solution would be completely acceptable to Egypt and completely unacceptable to Israel. Point B represents the solution of Israel keeping the land and maintaining total control over it. This solution would be completely acceptable to Israel and completely unacceptable to Egypt. Point C represents a straight compromise—giving each party control over half of the land. As illustrated in the bargaining zone diagram, this solution fails to meet the reservation points of either Israel or Egypt. It does not give Egypt sovereignty over the Sinai, and it does not give Israel sufficient security guarantees. Point D (the eventual resolution), however, suggests a redefinition of the bargaining zone. In Figure 8.1, a positive bargaining zone exists to the extent that there are solutions that achieve the reservation points of both parties along the dimensions of sovereignty and security. The upper right-hand segment of the figure beyond the dotted lines represents the reservation points of the two parties.

What occurred in the Camp David accords is that the two parties realized the existence of a positive bargaining zone by considering each other's interests, not just their stated positions. With these interests in hand, it was possible to develop an agreement by trading off the issue that each country cared less about for the issue that each country cared more about.

AN EXTENDED BUSINESS EXAMPLE: THE CASE OF EL-TEK

Virtually all negotiations involve the distribution of outcomes. However, negotiators often overlook the opportunity to create value. In this section we develop an example that involves both the creation and claiming of value (adapted from Bazerman and Brett's "El-Tek" simulation [1991]):

> El-Tek is a large conglomerate in the electrical industry with sales of over $3.1 billion. El-Tek is a decentralized, product-centered organization, in which the various divisions are expected to operate autonomously and are evaluated based on their divisional performance. To preclude competition for sales to external customers, divisions are chartered to sell their products to specific customer groups outside the company.
>
> Recently, the Audio Division (AD) developed a new magnetic material called Z-25. While their corporate charter prevents the division from selling the discovery outside the company, the product is still valuable to AD. They can sell Z-25 within the corporation and also use this magnet to competitively increase the quality of their own audio products. AD has assessed that under this scenario they would earn $5 million from Z-25 over an estimated two years. This figure includes $1.75 million from selling magnets internally to El-Tek and $3.25 million from product improvements to their audio components that would not be available to their competitors.
>
> While this $5 million is attractive to AD and El-Tek, the Magnetic Division (MD) could generate far more income for El-Tek if it sold Z-25. MD has much better manufacturing capabilities and could sell the magnet to a vast outside market. In fact, MD projects that it could earn $14 million over the same two-year period from this magnetic material. Without Z-25, MD would be using their manufacturing and

sales capabilities on an alternative product that is only expected to yield a profit of $4 million.

The parties have agreed to get together to discuss the possibility of AD selling the magnet rights to MD. Both parties already have target prices and reservation points in mind. With this information, the El-Tek situation can be analyzed using the bargaining zone concept diagrammed here:

MD's payment to AD for magnet rights

$2 million	$5 million	$10 million	$12 million
MDt	ADr	MDr	ADt

MDt = MD's target price
ADr = AD's reservation point
MDr = MD's reservation point
ADt = AD's target price

Claiming Value

Most people enter into negotiations with some notion of their target outcomes. However, most negotiators fail to think hard enough about their reservation prices and the reservation prices of other negotiators, which are determined by evaluating both parties' BATNAs. In this example, AD can make $5 million without reaching an agreement with MD. MD can make $4 million without Z-25 and thus is indifferent between this option and paying AD $10 million (of the $14 million) for the rights to the magnet. Note that the two reservation points overlap (at all points between $5 million and $10 million), creating a positive bargaining zone. Note further that any agreement within the bargaining zone will lead to a joint surplus of $5 million. (Without the trade taking place, AD can earn $5 million and MD can earn $4 million, for a total of $9 million. By completing a trade, they have a total of $14 million to divide.) Thus, there is a range of agreements that can be very profitable for both sides.

Creating Value by Identifying Additional Issues

So far, our analysis has been limited to just one issue of the negotiation, namely, the distribution of money. By definition, one-issue negotiations claim but do not create value. Through the process of identifying and adding additional issues, the parties will have the potential to create value, thereby increasing the amount of total benefit available.

Remember that one of AD's benefits of not selling the magnet to MD is that they can obtain a competitive advantage from the product improvement. Before entering into negotiations, it might be useful for AD to assess the value of adding restrictions to outside sales of the magnet by MD. For example, AD could create an information table in the form of Table 8.1, which evaluates the expected value to AD of various agreements. The first two outcomes highlight the possible one-issue results. Outcome 1 shows the $5 million profit obtained if AD were to keep the product. Outcome 2 shows that if AD simply transfers the product to MD, AD's profit will be equal to the negotiated transfer price P. The remaining outcomes incorporate the sales restriction issue on two levels. These include restricting sales to AD's direct competitors and restricting sales to all El-Tek competitors in general. Each outcome is evaluated in monetary terms that include the expected net profit of the specified restrictions, in addition to the negotiated transfer price P. For example, outcome 3 includes the prohibition of sales to AD's competitors for only six months and is expected to yield AD $2 million plus the transfer price. Compare this to outcome 6, wherein sales are restricted to AD's direct competitors for 12 months and all El-Tek competitors for 6 months. This option is estimated to be worth $2.6 million plus the transfer price. In reviewing each of the outcomes, note that AD is more concerned with prohibiting sales to AD's competitors than to El-Tek competitors. (Compare

TABLE 8.1   Audio Division Negotiating Team

Outcome	Lifetime Expected Net Profit to AD
1. AD produces Z-25 and the product is sold only internally.	$5,000,000
2. MD produces and no limitations are put on their distribution efforts.	P
3. MD produces and is prohibited from selling to AD competitors for 6 months.	$2,000,000 + P
4. MD produces and is prohibited from selling to any El-Tek competitors for 6 months.	$2,100,000 + P
5. MD produces and is prohibited from selling to AD competitors for 12 months.	$2,500,000 + P
6. MD produces and is prohibited from selling to AD competitors for 12 months and from selling to other El-Tek competitors for 6 months.	$2,600,000 + P
7. MD produces and is prohibited from selling to any El-Tek competitors for 12 months.	$2,700,000 + P
8. MD produces and is prohibited from selling to AD competitors for 20 months.	$2,900,000 + P
9. MD produces and is prohibited from selling to AD competitors for 20 months and from selling to other El-Tek competitors for 6 months.	$3,000,000 + P
10. MD produces and is prohibited from selling to AD competitors for 20 months and from selling to other El-Tek competitors for 12 months.	$3,100,000 + P
11. MD produces and is prohibited from selling to any El-Tek competitors for 20 months.	$3,200,000 + P

outcomes 5 and 6, wherein the marginal value of adding a six-month restriction to all El-Tek competitors yields only an additional $100,000.) Note also that the value of this protection has diminishing returns due to obtaining product leadership in a relatively short period of time. (Compare outcomes 3 and 5, wherein the first 6 months of protection from AD's direct competitors are worth $2 million, but the next 6 months add only $500,000 in value.)

Conversely, MD can also assess the costs of having their sales restricted in the same manner. These estimates are shown in Table 8.2; please take a moment to review it. Finally, Table 8.3 combines the assessments of AD and MD from Tables 8.1 and 8.2. This combination allows us to look at how three underlying issues—transfer price, AD's competitor protection, and El-Tek competitor protection—collectively affect the joint surplus available to the parties.

Let's look at this table in detail. First, note that all of the outcomes that prevent MD from selling to any of El-Tek's competitors (outcomes 4, 6, 7, 9, 10, and 11)

TABLE 8.2 Magnetic Division Negotiating Team

Outcome	Lifetime Expected Net Profit to MD
1. AD produces Z-25 and the product is sold only internally.	$4,000,000
2. MD produces and no limitations are put on their distribution efforts.	$14,000,000 − P
3. MD produces and is prohibited from selling to AD competitors for 6 months.	$13,100,000 − P
4. MD produces and is prohibited from selling to any El-Tek competitors for 6 months.	$10,400,000 − P
5. MD produces and is prohibited from selling to AD competitors for 12 months.	$12,200,000 − P
6. MD produces and is prohibited from selling to AD competitors for 12 months and from selling to other El-Tek competitors for 6 months.	$9,500,000 − P
7. MD produces and is prohibited from selling to any El-Tek competitors for 12 months.	$6,800,000 − P
8. MD produces and is prohibited from selling to AD competitors for 20 months.	$11,000,000 − P
9. MD produces and is prohibited from selling to AD competitors for 20 months and from selling to other El-Tek competitors for 6 months.	$8,300,000 − P
10. MD produces and is prohibited from selling to AD competitors for 20 months and from selling to other El-Tek competitors for 12 months.	$5,600,000 − P
11. MD produces and is prohibited from selling to any El-Tek competitors for 20 months.	$2,000,000 − P

TABLE 8.3 Joint Profit Resolutions (in millions)

Outcome	AD	MD	AD + MD
1. AD produces and sells only internally.	5.0	4.0	9.0
2. MD produces; AD limit equals 0 months and other limit equals 0 months.	P	14.0 − P	14.0
3. MD produces; AD limit equals 6 months and other limit equals 0 months.	2.0 + P	13.1 − P	15.1
4. MD produces; AD limit equals 6 months and other limit equals 6 months.	2.1 + P	10.4 − P	12.5
5. MD produces; AD limit equals 12 months and other limit equals 0 months.	2.5 + P	12.2 − P	14.7
6. MD produces; AD limit equals 12 months and other limit equals 6 months.	2.6 + P	9.5 − P	12.1
7. MD produces; AD limit equals 12 months and other limit equals 12 months.	2.7 + P	6.8 − P	9.5
8. MD produces; AD limit equals 20 months and other limit equals 0 months.	2.9 + P	11.0 − P	13.9
9. MD produces; AD limit equals 20 months and other limit equals 6 months.	3.0 + P	8.3 − P	11.3
10. MD produces; AD limit equals 20 months and other limit equals 12 months.	3.1 + P	5.6 − P	8.7
11. MD produces; AD limit equals 20 months and other limit equals 20 months.	3.2 + P	2.0 − P	5.2

decrease the joint gain available from this product compared to similar outcomes that prevent MD from selling only to AD's competitors (outcomes 3, 5, and 8). Thus, the two parties are collectively better off not creating restrictions regarding other El-Tek competitors. Furthermore, the highest joint benefit is achieved when the magnet is transferred and MD is restricted from selling to AD's competitors for six months. While this reduces MD's profits (before paying AD) from $14 million to $13.1 million compared to outcome 2, AD's profit increases by $2 million—resulting in an additional $1.1 million of profit to divide. This profit is created by the fact that AD gains more from the six-month restriction than MD loses. However, additional protection beyond six months decreases the joint profit, since additional protection (e.g., outcome 5) costs MD more than it benefits AD.

Opportunities to create and claim value in the El-Tek negotiation are shown in Figure 8.2, which plots AD's profit on the vertical axis and MD's profit on the horizontal axis. Lines A and B are the reservation prices that we discussed earlier. Point X is the no-agreement alternative in which AD keeps the magnet. Forty-five-degree lines can be drawn for the various outcomes (2 through 11) that show the possible agreements on the outcomes after *P* is negotiated. For example, the points on the outcome 2 line (C) yield profit of $14 million, while all the points on the outcome 3 line (D) yield profit of $15.1 million. (Of course, more lines can be drawn for all the possible settlements.)

Clearly, it is in the best interest of both negotiators to reach an agreement on the most northeasterly line. As mentioned earlier, one of the key skills of negotiation is to determine the other party's reservation point and aim for a resolution that is marginally acceptable to the other party based on that value. Thus, AD prefers being as close to MD's reservation price as possible, and MD prefers being as close to AD's reservation price as possible. The task facing the negotiators is to attempt to both create and claim value. Negotiators often make the mistake of focusing on just one dimension, rather than thinking about them simultaneously.

When my students simulate the El-Tek negotiation, a common question from someone who did very well in claiming, but not creating, value (e.g., someone playing the role of AD, who received a payment of $9.5 million out of the $14 million on an

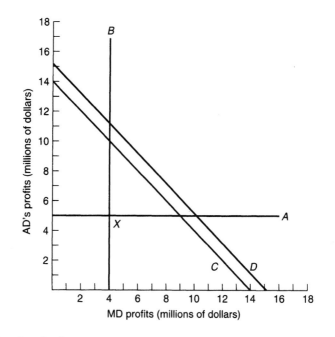

Figure 8.2 The El-Tek negotiation.

outcome 2 agreement) is: "Why shouldn't I be happy with this agreement?" In fact, this agreement is typically one of the better outcomes for someone playing the role of AD. The answer is that although this is a fine agreement for AD, if MD settled for this agreement, MD could also have accepted an agreement that called for six months' protection and a payment of $8.3 million. This would have given MD $4.8 million (rather than $4.5 million) and would have given AD $10.3 million (rather than $9.5 million), making both parties much better off!

An agreement is defined as "Pareto efficient" when there is no other agreement that would render both parties better off or one party better off while keeping the second party at the same level. Anytime you have a Pareto-inefficient agreement, there exists an alternative agreement to which the parties can move that would create greater joint benefit. In the El-Tek case, the set of outcome 3 agreements between the two parties' reservation prices represents the Pareto-efficient frontier.

When negotiators run into differences with other parties, the common response is to see this as a problem. In fact, differences are opportunities. Effective negotiators understand that the easiest way to create value is to trade issues of differential value. By identifying what you care about, and figuring out what the other side cares about, you will be equipped to create value based on these differences.

While trading issues is the most common way to create value in a negotiation, Sebenius (2000; Lax and Sebenius, 1986) has documented a number of ways in which other differences create opportunity. Perhaps the second most important opportunity is created through the development of bets, or contingent contracts.

Creating Value through Bets

When clients seek advice from me regarding stalled negotiations, it often turns out that a surprisingly large percent of them are arguing needlessly with the other side over their conflicting predictions about uncertain future outcomes. The fact is, our society has developed a very effective technique for dealing with differing predictions: bets.

In the El-Tek simulation, MD had a set of assessments concerning the profitability of various outcomes ($14 million with no restrictions, $13.1 million with a six-month restriction on sales to AD's competitors, and so on). Assume that AD also assessed the profits that MD would receive from the product: $40 million with a six-month sales restriction and $40.9 million with no restrictions. On the surface, this difference in perceptions could create a barrier to agreement. AD might expect a payment of around $20 million—an amount MD would never pay. If trust were lacking, there might be little that MD could do to convince AD of the accuracy of its forecast, and impasse would seem inevitable.

Now consider the following proposal: MD is restricted from selling the magnet to AD's competitors for six months, MD receives the first $9 million of the magnet's profit, and AD receives 80 percent of the profits in excess of $9 million. This agreement allows the parties to bet on their predictions of future events. If MD's forecast turns out to be correct, this agreement would be much better for MD than a 50:50 split of the joint profit. If AD's forecast turns out to be correct, this agreement would be better for AD than a 50:50 split of the joint profit. While at least one of them has made an inaccurate prediction, this "contingent contract" allows for a trade in which both parties believe that they will do very well.

You will recall from the discussion of the endowment effect in Chapter 3 that people commonly overvalue what they own. It is important for sellers to recognize their susceptibility to this effect and adjust their expectations. If such adjustments fail to resolve the dispute, parties may be able to use their difference of opinion to craft a contingent contract that allows each side to bet on its opinion. Consider the case of a television production company negotiating the sale of syndication rights to one of its shows, a major sitcom that had just finished its prime-time run, with a major independent television station in one of the three leading television markets in the United States (Bazerman and Gillespie, 1999, based on a case by Tenbrunsel and Bazerman, 1995). The parties differed in their predictions of the ratings the sitcom would obtain in syndication: The seller argued that the show would receive at least a nine share rating (meaning 9 percent of all American households with televisions would tune into the show), while the buyer countered that they expected the show would obtain no more than a seven share. Both parties agreed that each rating point was worth about $1 million in advertising revenue to the television station. After many heated debates about future ratings, the parties reached an impasse. The show was not aired in this market, and the television station bought a less attractive program. This negotiation failure resulted from an honest difference of opinion about how well the show would perform. Bazerman and Gillespie argue that the parties should have made the price that the station would pay the production company contingent on the show's performance. That is, their disagreement about the expected quality of the show could have been resolved by an agreement where the payment price went up as the ratings went up.

Bazerman and Gillespie (1999) describe a number of ways in which contingent contracts can improve the outcomes of negotiations for both sides, four of which are outlined here.

Bets Build on Differences to Create Joint Value. Bets can be extremely useful in short-circuiting debates over the likelihood of future uncertain events. Once parties have agreed to disagree, they will be able to design a contingent contract based on their differing predictions.

Bets Help Manage Biases. In previous chapters, I have documented a number of common decision-making biases, including overconfidence, the endowment effect, and egocentric interpretations of fairness. As we explore further in Chapter 9, these biases form strong barriers to negotiated agreements. Interestingly, contingent contracts allow agreements to be formed despite these biases. Rather than requiring the parties to be debiased, contingent contracts allow parties to bet on their own (biased) beliefs.

Bets Diagnose Disingenuous Parties. Contingent contracts are a powerful tool for identifying bluffs and false claims by one's negotiation opponent. Returning to the El-Tek story, imagine that AD does not actually expect MD's profits to be as high as $40 million, but presents this number as its estimate in order to persuade MD to agree to higher compensation. In this case, when MD offers AD the majority of the profit above $9 million, and AD turns it down, MD will know that AD was bluffing. Interestingly, when you propose a bet, you do not need to know whether the prediction of the other side is sincere. If it is, you have made a nice bet. If it isn't, their rejection of the bet reveals their bluff.

Bets Establish Incentives for Contractual Performance. Contingent contracts are also an excellent technique for increasing the incentive of the parties to perform at or above contractually specified levels. Sales commissions are a prevalent example of a contingent contract designed to establish an incentive for high performance. In 1997, professional basketball player Dennis Rodman and the management of the Chicago Bulls were faced with the joint decision-making task of negotiating a contract for Rodman for the 1997–98 National Basketball Association (NBA) season. Given Rodman's increasingly erratic behavior on and off the court, which caused him to miss 27 games during the 1996–97 season, Bulls' management was nervous about signing him on for another year. Rodman, meanwhile, felt confident that his performance in the upcoming season would meet or exceed that of each of his previous 11 seasons. Using a contingent contract to bridge their differences, Rodman and the Bulls hammered out the most incentive-laden deal in NBA history. Only $4.5 million of Rodman's $10.5 million annual contract was guaranteed; the remaining $6 million was dependent on fulfillment of various performance and behavior clauses. This contingent contract worked very well for both parties. Rodman played in 80 of the 82 games, won his seventh rebounding title, and collected $10.1 million of his potential $10.5 million salary. With Rodman's help, the Bulls went on to win another NBA championship, generating significant income for team owners.

Using Risk, Temporal, and Other Differences to Create Value

Disagreements about future outcomes are just one type of difference that can be used to improve the outcomes of both parties in a negotiation. In Chapter 3, we saw how individuals' differing tolerance for risk affects their decisions. Risk can play a critical role in negotiations as well. Consider the situation in which both parties in El-Tek agree on MD's forecast of future events. Specfically, they both expect MD to earn $13.1 million with a six-month restriction against sales to AD's competitors; however, they concede that the true outcome could be anywhere from $4.1 million to $22.1 million. In addition, AD is unwilling to accept any agreement that would risk ending up below the $5 million it could earn on its own. MD, on the other hand, is willing to take greater risks in the hope of generating high rewards. Thus, because AD is comparatively more risk averse than MD, AD might reject an offer to split the magnet's profits equally, since in the worst case scenario, profits would be below $5 million.

The parties' differential risk preferences create a new opportunity, specifically, the possibility of a tradeoff that guarantees AD more money and MD more of the upside potential. For example, under one possible agreement, AD might receive the six-month sales restriction, the first $4 million of magnet profits, and 15 percent of profits above $4 million. This deal grants AD its guarantee, while giving MD a higher expected return in exchange for its acceptance of high risk. Risk-sharing strategies such as this allow for trades that might not otherwise occur.

Differences in time preference are another source of tradeoffs in negotiations. These differences might arise from individual, cultural, or situational preferences among the parties. The fluctuation of corporate budget cycles is one common real-world difference in time preferences. When a client complains that their negotiating partner is fixated on meeting a certain budget cycle, I encourage them to view this as an opportunity—in all likelihood, the other side will be willing to make important concessions if you help them solve their budget problems! Future consequences can often be rearranged in a way that gives earlier return to the more impatient party in exchange for concessions favored by the more patient party.

Returning to the El-Tek negotiation, imagine that in the midst of a disastrous year, MD is seeking immediate profitability to keep its recent downturn from being made public. In addition, MD is concerned that most of the fixed costs of manufacturing the magnet will be incurred early to set up the manufacturing process. The two sides might work out an agreement whereby MD receives 75 percent of first-year profits and 20 percent of second-year profits, leaving 25 percent of first-year profits and 80 percent of second-year profits for AD. In this agreement, MD gets the immediate return that it desires, and AD gets a slightly higher return for waiting.

A multitude of differences between parties can enhance negotiation outcomes. Northcraft and Neale (1993) have pointed out that skill differences between parties collaborating on a project—such as a CEO and a COO, two researchers writing a book together, or partners in a strategic alliance—often contribute to the partnership's success. Effectively, complementary skills create the opportunity to make trades in work allocation, to the benefit of both parties. In their discussion of "deal-crafting," Lax and Sebenius (1999) cite a joint venture between auctioneer Butterfields and Internet auctioneer eBay as a successful partnership based on value creation. Butterfields' access to upscale commodities combined with eBay's new distribution mechanism to create value for both companies. Lax and Sebenius (1999) note a variety of other trades that can be enhanced by taking advantage of a wide range of differences, including differences in tax status, accounting treatments, and liquidity. By now, the overarching message of this section should be clear: To the well-informed negotiator, differences are not stumbling blocks, but opportunities.

Gathering Information to Create Value in Negotiation

So far, our discussion of value creation has assumed that both parties have full knowledge of information relevant to the negotiation. In fact, negotiators typically have access only to their own preferences. How can negotiators create value when they lack knowledge of the other side's positions and preferences? I will now review five strategies for collecting that information. While no single strategy is guaranteed to work in a specific situation, they collectively increase the likelihood of reaching a Pareto-efficient agreement.

Build Trust and Share Information

The easiest way for parties to create value in the El-Tek simulation is for the two opponents to share information with each other about their preferences—specifically, the values that they place on different issues. Once this information comes to light, determining the outcome that maximizes joint benefit becomes a simple arithmetic task. Unfortunately, information sharing is easier said than done. We often are reluctant to trust the other side in a negotiation because we believe that giving away information could prevent us from claiming value. Consider this dilemma from El-Tek's overall perspective. For the president of El-Tek, creating value guarantees that the divisions will not jeopardize corporate profitability by focusing on the claiming of value. Therefore, creating value should be the negotiation's primary objective. Even between organizations, firms often develop fully trusting relationships based on kinship, a close subculture, or years of working together. In these cases, the parties learn that the long-term joint benefit of creating value more than offsets the one-time gain that a party might achieve through claiming tactics.

One way to approach information sharing is to discuss a distribution rule in advance of sharing information. If AD fears that they will be at a competitive disadvantage if MD finds out that AD can earn only $5 million on their own, the parties could agree on how to divide any surplus before sharing confidential information. For example, they might agree that AD gets 60 percent and MD gets 40 percent of any surplus. With this understanding established, they can then safely share information to create value. When distrust exists regarding the information-sharing process, the parties could also agree to obtain financial assessments from an independent party.

Ask Questions

Full information sharing will not always be to your advantage. You may have some information that will work against you if the other party obtains it; similarly, the other party also may be unwilling to fully disclose confidential information. What can you do? Ask lots of questions! Most people have a tendency to see negotiating primarily as an opportunity to influence the other party. As a result, most of us do more talking than listening. Even when the other side is talking, we concentrate on what we are going to say next rather than listening for new information. This persuasion process is the basis of most sales training and assists the other party in collecting information from you. In negotiations, however, your goal must be to understand the other party's interests as well as possible.

Asking questions and listening actively are the keys to collecting important new information from the other side. AD might ask, "MD, how much would you lose if you didn't sell to our competitors? How much would a six-month restriction cost you? How much would a 12-month restriction cost you?" Before you start the negotiation, assess what information you need from the other side; then ask the questions necessary to collect this information. Some of my students have pointed out that, in the real world, the other side won't always answer your questions. That's true. However, the probability that they will answer is higher if you ask than if you do not!

Strategically Disclose Information

Your negotiation does not have a trusting atmosphere, and the other party is not answering your questions in any useful way. What do you do next? Give away some information of your own. Do not tell the other side your BATNA—this will only anchor your final outcome. Rather, reveal information of comparatively minor importance that focuses on the trades you are willing to make. As AD, for instance, you might inform MD that restricting sales to your competitors is more important in the early months of sales than in later months. In disclosing this, you have not given away any information that MD can use unilaterally against you, and you may open up a dialogue.

One benefit of strategically disclosing information is that it can enable you and the other side to expand the pie of outcomes. An additional benefit is that behaviors in negotiation are often reciprocated. When you scream at people, they tend to scream back. When you apologize for a mistake or offense, they may do the same. And when you give them some information about your position, they may return some information of their own. This strategy can create the information sharing necessary to create mutually beneficial agreements.

Make Multiple Offers Simultaneously

Many negotiators try to put an offer on the table early to anchor the discussion. Unfortunately, this offer is often made before the negotiator has worked hard to create additional value. Because the effect of anchoring is so strong that it may overshadow subsequent discoveries, you should avoid putting an offer on the table before actively collecting information. In some cases, even after actively pursuing information, you may find that you cannot extend a single offer that creates value for both sides. When this happens, consider the possibility of presenting several offers. Most of us put one offer on the table, and when it is turned down, we know little more than we did before we made the offer. If we had presented several alternatives, we might have learned more.

Imagine that as AD, you present MD with three offers: the transfer of the magnet for $9 million with no restrictions on sales to your competitors, for $7 million with a six-month restriction, or for $6.5 million with a 12-month restriction. MD refuses all of these proposals. At this point, you ask which of these proposals is closest to being acceptable. MD evaluates the proposals according to Table 8.2 and sees that they provide a net profit of $5 million, $6.1 million, and $5.7 million, respectively. MD answers that, of these unacceptable proposals, the second one is the least unreasonable. As AD, you now have more information to work with in forming a mutually beneficial agreement. Note that all three proposals by AD were equally valuable to AD, and AD did not give away anything that would not be given away by making only one offer. By making multiple offers, AD appears more flexible and collects valuable information. Making multiple offers that are worth the same amount allows you to identify new opportunities for tradeoffs.

Search for Post-Settlement Settlements

Raiffa (1985) suggests that after negotiators have found a mutually acceptable agreement, they should employ a third party to help them search for a Pareto-superior agreement—one that is potentially even better for both parties than the agreement reached. Under this scenario, each negotiator can reserve the right to veto any new settlement proposed by the third party and revert to the original agreement. With this insurance in hand, Raiffa contends that negotiators may be more willing to allow a third party to create a superior agreement. This new agreement is known as a post-settlement settlement (PSS).

Based on Raiffa's insight, negotiators should look for a PSS as a last step in creating value (Bazerman, Russ, and Yakura, 1987). This process does not necessarily require a third party. After an initial agreement is reached, there is often ample opportunity to improve areas of the contract that may not be completely optimal for either party. If you are not confident that you have achieved a Pareto-efficient outcome, it may be in your best interest to propose to the other side a PSS process whereby both parties agree to be bound by the initial agreement if no better agreement is found. If a better agreement is found, however, the two parties will share the surplus. Thus, if AD and MD reached an agreement to transfer the magnet for $7 million with no limits, they could use a PSS process to share information to locate an agreement that would be worth $550,000 more to both sides (outcome 3—$5.55 million and six-month AD protection). A PSS process offers a last attempt, with limited risk to either party, to ensure that a Pareto-efficient agreement has been found. This process can be initiated after an initial agreement by using any of the four previously defined information-building strategies. As Raiffa (1985, p. 9) writes:

> [W]e must recognize that a lot of disputes are settled by hard-nosed, positional bargaining. Settled, yes. But efficiently settled? Often not . . . they quibble about sharing the pie and often fail to realize that perhaps the pie can be jointly enlarged . . . there may be another carefully crafted settlement that both (parties) might prefer to the settlement they actually achieved.

Summary

These five strategies offer a variety of ideas for creating value. No one strategy will work in all situations. Collectively, however, they increase the potential joint benefit that parties will reach through negotiating. It is important to repeat that no strategy eliminates the need to eventually divide value; any advice is incomplete if it fails to deal explicitly with the claiming dimension. Armed with these strategies for creating and claiming value in negotiations, negotiators should be able to improve their performance on both dimensions.

INTEGRATION AND CRITIQUE

This chapter has introduced a number of methods for increasing the potential for successful negotiations. First, I outlined the decision-analytic approach, which focuses on information collection—namely, the importance of establishing reservation points, exploring the underlying interests of the parties, and weighting the relative importance of these interests. The need to think about the creation and claiming of value was discussed, and I introduced the concept of building on differences (such as estimates of future outcomes, risk preferences, and time preferences) as a strategy for uncovering trades. Five information-collection strategies were outlined for uncovering potential to create value in negotiation situations. These include building trust, asking questions, strategically disclosing information, making multiple offers, and searching for post-settlement settlements. Together, these techniques provide a prescriptive framework for thinking rationally about real-world negotiations.

As a teacher of negotiation, I have noticed that students who fail to thoroughly prepare for a simulation are routinely clobbered by their opponent. The assumption that good intuition will allow you to sail through negotiations is simply wrong; preparation is critical. High-quality preparation requires the negotiator to reflect on a number of simple but important questions. The sample list of questions that follows will not cover every negotiation situation, but is a good place to start:

1. What is your BATNA?
2. What is your reservation price?
3. What are the issues in this negotiation?
4. How important is each issue to you?
5. What do you think the other party's BATNA is?
6. What do you think their reservation price is?
7. How important do you think each issue is to them?
8. Are there viable trades that create value?
9. Are you and the other party in disagreement about future events? If so, is a bet viable?
10. How will you go about identifying the information that you do not currently know?

Although these questions do not guarantee success, they will improve your odds.

As we saw in the first seven chapters, ours is not a fully rational world, particularly when it comes to our own decision-making processes. A central lesson of this book is that even when you are presented with rational advice, like the decision-analytic approach, your ingrained decision biases may limit your ability to follow this advice. In this sense, the decision-analytic approach is only a first step in helping you to become a better decision maker in multiparty contexts. This approach cries out for additional descriptive models that allow you as the focal negotiator to better anticipate your own likely behaviors and those of the other party. If you or your opponent is not acting fully rationally, what systematic departures from rationality can be predicted? How can you better anticipate the actual behavior of your opponent, and how can you identify and overcome barriers that might prevent you from following decision-analytic advice? The decision-analytic approach tells us that we must consider the actual, but not necessarily rational, decisions of the other side. A useful addition to this approach is to identify the specific deviations from rationality that we can anticipate in our own and in other parties' decision making. This is the focus of Chapter 9.

CHAPTER NINE

Negotiator Cognition

*T*he decision-analytic approach to negotiation presented in the previous chapter suggests that it is desirable for two parties to strike an agreement whenever a positive bargaining zone exists. Why, then, do actors in negotiations frequently fail to settle? The decision-analytic approach also provides strategies for reaching agreements of great value to both sides. Why, then, do even negotiators who have access to this advice fail to reach Pareto-efficient outcomes?

This chapter explores the most common cognitive mistakes we make in negotiations. Specifically, we will look at seven key issues that affect negotiator cognition: (1) the mythical fixed pie of negotiation, (2) the framing of negotiator judgment, (3) the nonrational escalation of conflict, (4) negotiator overconfidence, (5) negotiator egocentrism, (6) anchoring, and (7) the tendency to ignore the cognitions of others. Each section illustrates how the decision-making processes of the typical negotiator diverge from a prescriptive model of behavior and discusses how we as negotiators can correct these deviations.

An understanding of these common mistakes will help improve your negotiating skills in two key ways. First, awareness is an essential step toward avoiding these errors in important negotiations. Second, once you have learned to identify these errors in your own behaviors, you will be better able to anticipate them in the decisions of other negotiators.

THE MYTHICAL FIXED PIE OF NEGOTIATIONS

Why do negotiators typically fail to reach agreements that create maximum value for both sides? One reason is the fixed-pie assumption, a fundamental, intuitive bias in human judgment that distorts negotiator behavior. When individuals approach negotiations with a fixed-pie mentality, they assume that their interests necessarily and directly conflict with the interests of the other side. Metaphorically, they believe they are both fighting for the biggest piece of the pie.

Agreements in diplomatic situations, solutions to marital disputes, and the creation of strategic alliances are frequently blocked by the assumption that the parties' interests are diametrically opposed. Creative agreements occur when participants discover tradeoffs across issues—but individuals will not search for these trades if they assume the size of the pie is fixed.

The assumption of a fixed pie is rooted in social norms that lead us to interpret most competitive situations as win–lose. This win–lose orientation is manifested in our society in athletic competition, admission to academic programs, corporate promotion systems, and so on. Generalizing from these objective win–lose situations, individuals create similar expectations for situations that are not necessarily win–lose. When faced with a mixed-motive situation requiring both cooperation and competition, the competitive aspect becomes salient, motivating most negotiators to develop a strategy for obtaining the largest possible share of the perceived fixed pie. Such a focus inhibits the search for creative solutions through mutually beneficial tradeoffs.

The destructiveness of the mythical fixed pie is captured in this Cold War-era declaration by Congressional Representative Floyd Spence, R-South Carolina, regarding a proposed arms reduction treaty: "I have had a philosophy for some time in regard to SALT, and it goes like this: The Russians will not accept a SALT treaty that is not in their best interest, and it seems to me that if it is in their best interests, it can't be in our best interest" (originally cited in Ross and Stillinger, 1991). This kind of dangerously confused reasoning—that anything good for the Soviet Union must have been bad for the United States—defines the mythical fixed pie assumption.

With the benefit of twenty-first-century hindsight, we can easily recognize that treaties like SALT benefited both the United States and the Soviet Union, by reducing wasteful defense spending and the specter of nuclear war. And yet, Thompson (2001) has found that even when two sides want the exact same outcome, such as ending the Cold War, negotiators often settle on a different outcome, or reach an impasse, because they assume they must compromise to get agreement. Imagine that a company wants to increase employee training to improve job flexibility, while employees want to be better trained to solidify their job security. While the two groups may have the same goal, the fixed-pie assumption could lead them to assume that their interests are incompatible. "Maybe my employees are planning to look for work elsewhere once I've given them this extra training," a manager might wrongly infer. The mythical fixed pie can cause parties to fall prey to what Thompson calls the "incompatibility bias"—the assumption that one's own interests are incompatible with the other party's.

The mythical fixed pie also leads us to "reactively devalue" any concession made simply because it is offered by an adversary. Stillinger, Epelbaum, Keltner, and Ross (1990) divided 137 individuals into two groups and asked how favorable a specific arms reduction proposal was to the United States and to the USSR. In one group, the interviewer correctly ascribed the proposal to Communist Party General Secretary Mikhail Gorbachev. In the other group, the interviewer implied that President Ronald Reagan (the study was conducted during his presidency) had made the proposal. Fifty-six percent of those who believed the proposal originated with Gorbachev thought that the provisions dramatically favored the Soviet Union; only 16 percent felt it favored the United States, while the remaining 28 percent thought it favored both sides equally. When participants were led to believe that President Reagan had initiated the proposal, 45 percent thought it benefited both sides equally, 27 percent thought it favored the Soviet Union, and 27 percent thought that it favored the United States. Thus, terms that appear mutually beneficial when advanced by one's own side may seem disadvantageous when proposed by the other party, even if the terms of the proposal are equal. As soon as the other party concedes on an issue, negotiators may devalue the issue's worth: "If they are willing to make this concession, the issue must not be very important."

When individuals make such assumptions about the other party's interests, they inhibit the search for mutually beneficial tradeoffs. The fact is, tradeoffs can be quite easy to find when negotiators actively look for them. But when we ask managerial students why they failed to make a tradeoff in a simulated negotiation, they commonly tell us that they did not know that the tradeoff was possible. Why not? The fixed-pie assumption prevented them from initiating the search.

Executives often ask me, "What issue should we discuss first in a negotiation?" Some believe it is critical to get the most important issue resolved in the beginning, arguing that, "Any other strategy is simply procrastinating." By contrast, in the context of labor relations, many experienced negotiators recommend that it is important to "start with the easy issues first." In my opinion, both perspectives offer bad advice. Leading off with the easy issues may make the initial stages of the negotiation smoother, but it will increase the likelihood of impasse. However, starting with the toughest issue often leads to a breakdown at the beginning of a negotiation. Both strategies eliminate possible tradeoffs that may create joint benefits. Why? Because the mythical fixed pie encourages actors to think about issues one at a time. Unfortunately, once an issue has been "resolved," it is rarely resurrected to create a tradeoff with an issue raised later. Thinking simultaneously about multiple issues is the best way to break the mythical fixed pie and create value in a negotiation.

THE FRAMING OF NEGOTIATOR JUDGMENT

Consider the following scenario:

> You bought your condo in 1998 for $250,000. You have just put it on the market for $299,000, with a real target of $290,000 (your estimation of the condo's true market value). An offer comes in for $280,000. Does this offer represent a $30,000 gain in comparison with the original purchase price, or a $10,000 loss in comparison with your current target?

The answer to this question is "both." From a rational perspective, and based on our intuition, we can easily determine that the difference in the two points of view is irrelevant. However, as described in Chapter 3, Kahneman and Tversky (1982) have demonstrated that important differences arise from individuals' responses to questions framed in terms of losses versus gains. This difference is critical to describing negotiator behavior.

To understand the importance of "framing" in negotiations, consider the following labor–management situation. A trade union insists that management must increase the pay of union members from $12 to $14 an hour and that anything less, given current inflation, represents a loss. Management argues that any raise above $12 an hour imposes an unacceptable loss. What if each side had the choice of settling for $13 an hour (a certain settlement) or going to binding arbitration (a risky settlement)? Since each side views the conflict in terms of what it has to lose, following Tversky and Kahneman's (1981) findings, we can predict that each side will be risk seeking and therefore unwilling to accept the certain settlement. Changing the negotiators' framing from positive to negative, however, results in a very different predicted outcome. If the union views any raise above $12 an hour as a gain, and management views any raise under $14 an hour as a gain, then both sides will be risk averse, and a negotiated settlement will be likely. Neale and Bazerman (1985) found that negotiators with positive frames are significantly more likely to make concessions and to reach mutually beneficial outcomes than their negatively framed counterparts.

The importance of framing is highlighted by a fascinating stock fraud case (Bottom, 1997). In 1989, GAF Corporation and one of its vice presidents, James Sherwin, were charged with illegally manipulating the price of Union Carbide stock. If found guilty, Sherwin faced up to 40 years in prison and $2 million in fines. Prosecutors opened plea bargain negotiations with Sherwin, and approached him with a final settlement offer just as jurors began their deliberations. The government proposed to drop all charges against Sherwin, thereby eliminating the possibility of prison and fines, in exchange for a statement that he had participated in illegal activities on behalf of GAF. The offer also required a guilty plea by GAF, which it had agreed to provide.

By making the small concession of signing the paper, Sherwin could walk away a free man. His reputation would suffer, but that was likely to be true regardless of the outcome. Despite these incentives, Sherwin rejected the offer. A few hours later, the jury returned a verdict of "guilty on all eight counts." Sherwin's sentence? Six months in prison, a year of probation, and a $2 million fine. A related civil suit filed by the Securities and Exchange Commission was then settled out of court for $1.25 million plus interest.

How could a corporate vice president make such an unsuccessful decision? This book has offered a variety of explanations, including overconfidence and egocentrism. However, Sherwin's mistake is likely to be due in part to the finding that individuals tend to be risk seeking in the domain of losses. Framed in terms of the pre-sentencing status quo, even the signing of the paper would appear to be a loss. But if Sherwin had imagined the worst case scenario (prison sentence and a hefty fine), he would have been more likely to frame his options in terms of these serious losses, perhaps leading him to recognize the significant gain offered by his negotiation opponent's plea bargain.

Bazerman, Magliozzi, and Neale (1985) found that the frame of buyers and sellers systematically affects their negotiation behavior. Negotiators were led to view transactions in terms of either (1) net profit (gains) or (2) expenses (losses) away from the gross profit of the transactions. While both frames yielded the same objective profit result, positively (gain) framed negotiators experienced the risk aversion necessary to motivate them to compromise. This incentive to compromise led negotiators with a positive frame to complete a larger number of transactions and obtain greater overall profits than negotiators with a negative frame.

What determines whether a negotiator will have a positive or negative frame? The answer lies in the selection of a perceptual anchor. Consider the anchors available to a union leader negotiating a wage with management: (1) last year's wage, (2) management's initial offer, (3) the union's estimate of management's reservation point, (4) the union's reservation point, or (5) the bargaining position that the union publicly announced to its constituency. As the anchor moves from 1 to 5, a modest gain in comparison to last year's wage becomes a loss when compared to the higher goals touted publicly, thus moving the union negotiator from a positive to a negative frame. Specifically, for workers who are currently making $12 per hour and demanding an increase of $2 per hour, a proposed increase of $1 per hour can be viewed as a $1 per hour gain over last year's wage (anchor 1) or a $1 per hour loss when compared to the goals of the union's constituency (anchor 5).

It is easy to see that the frames of negotiators can result in the difference between an important agreement and impasse. Both sides in negotiations typically talk in terms of a certain wage or price they "must" get—setting a high reference point against which gains and losses are measured. When this happens, any compromise away from the reference point will be viewed as a loss. This perceived loss leads negotiators to adopt a negative frame to all compromise proposals, to exhibit risk-seeking behavior, and to be less likely to reach a settlement. In order to avoid these adverse effects of framing, negotiators should always be aware of their frames and consider the possibility of adopting alternative frames.

Framing has important implications for the tactics used by negotiators. Framing effects suggest that to induce concessionary behavior in an opponent, a negotiator should always create anchors that lead the opposition toward a positive frame. This means you will be negotiating in terms of what the other side has to gain, thereby increasing opportunities for tradeoffs and compromise. In addition, when you recognize that your opposition has a negative frame, you should encourage them to recognize that they have adopted a risky strategy in a situation where a sure gain is possible.

Finally, the impact of framing has important implications for mediators. When the proposed goal is a compromise, the mediator should strive to convince both parties to view the negotiation in a positive frame. This is tricky, however, since the anchor that will lead to a positive frame for one negotiator is likely to lead to a negative frame for the other. This suggests that when mediators meet with each party separately, they need to present different anchors to create risk aversion in each party. Again, to affect the frame, mediators also must emphasize the realistic risk of the situation, thus calling attention to its uncertainty and leading both sides to prefer a sure settlement.

NONRATIONAL ESCALATION OF CONFLICT

Following decades of animosity, on March 18, 1990, baseball team owners and players reached a four-year agreement to avert a strike that threatened to cancel the 1990 baseball season. The agreement expired on December 31, 1993, and the 1994 baseball season began without a new contract in place. The first offer came from the owners on June 14, 1994, but it was well outside the bargaining range. Dysfunctional bargaining ensued, and on August 12, the players went on strike.[1]

The strike effectively ended the 1994 baseball season and destroyed approximately $1 billion worth of financial opportunity for the owners and players. Food vendors, retailers, baseball card companies, and fans also suffered in various ways during the strike. The strike's inefficiency was highlighted when the courts required the team owners to accept the preexisting structure for the 1995 season while negotiations for the future continued.

From 1986 to 1993, Major League Baseball operated at a profit; by 1993, annual profits had risen to $36 million. The strike changed that picture. The owners lost $375 million in 1994, $326 million in 1995, and between $100 million and $200 million in 1996 (Grabiner, 1996). Meanwhile, players lost money, status, and bargaining power. For at least several years, baseball's position as America's national pastime was tarnished. The strike was an extremely costly and vivid example of a conflict that entered an escalatory spiral.

In the midst of the controversy, Sebenius and Wheeler (1994) offered a potentially advantageous strategy for resolving the disagreement: Continue the baseball season, but do not allow the teams to receive revenue or the players to receive their pay. Rather, revenues and foregone pay would go into a pool until a resolution was reached. In the meantime, watching the funds pile up would be an impetus for both sides to agree on a settlement. Sebenius and Wheeler further argued that the parties could set aside a portion of the fund for charity (such as the Special Olympics) if they failed to reach agreement in a timely fashion—again encouraging them to compromise, while creating positive rather than negative public relations. Overall, Sebenius and Wheeler outlined a very wise strategy that would have been far more efficient than the strike.

So, why didn't the parties follow this advice? My answer is that because each party was focused almost exclusively on beating the other side, they were primed to escalate their commitment to their initial course of action. One sign that the parties were absorbed by inappropriate objectives was the team owners' gleeful reaction to the cancellation of the 1994 World Series. Too busy congratulating themselves on sticking together, they failed to notice that they were bonding over their destruction of $1 billion in profits. Just four years later, it became apparent that National Basketball Association team owners had learned nothing from baseball's mistakes. Repeating this escalatory pattern, the NBA entered a 202-day lockout that cost the owners over $1 billion and the players more than $500 million in lost salaries.

Nonrational escalation of commitment unfolds in a wide variety of real-world situations, from custody battles to labor strikes to international disputes over land. Escalation begins when both parties enter a negotiation with extreme demands. The escalation literature predicts that if negotiators become committed to their initial

[1]Many observations about the 1994 baseball strike in this section were prompted by the analysis of Chris Maxcy, Lisa Mroz, Keith Rakow, and Cynthia Safford in a course assignment for the MBA negotiations class at the Kellogg Graduate School of Management of Northwestern University.

public statements, they will nonrationally refuse to even consider concessions. To the extent that negotiators believe they have "too much invested to quit," inappropriate stubbornness is likely. Furthermore, if both sides incur losses as a result of a lack of agreement (such as lost wages and profits in the case of a strike), their commitment to their positions is likely to increase, while their willingness to change to a different course of action (that is, compromise) decreases.

One important finding of the escalation literature is that the public announcement of one's position increases one's tendency to escalate nonrationally (Staw, 1981). Once the general public (or one's constituency) becomes aware of the commitment, it will be much more difficult to retreat from the previously announced position. This suggests that escalation can be reduced if negotiators and third parties avoid setting firm public positions. However, implementation of this recommendation runs contrary to everything known about how negotiators (such as labor leaders, political leaders, and management representatives) behave when they represent constituencies. A firmly set public position is typically perceived as necessary to build constituency support and allegiance. Thus it may be that what is best for the constituency is not necessarily what the constituency rewards.

Diekmann, Tenbrunsel, Shah, Schroth, and Bazerman (1996) explicitly studied escalation in the context of negotiation. They found both sellers and buyers of real estate to be affected by the price that the seller had earlier paid for the property. This "sunk cost" did not affect either party's assessment of the property's value, but it did affect their expectations, reservation prices, and final negotiated outcomes, showing that the seller's sunk costs are transmitted across the negotiation context. An understanding of escalation can be very helpful to a negotiator in anticipating an opponent's behavior. When will the other party really hold out, and when will it give in? The escalation literature predicts that the other side will hold out when it has "too much invested" in its position to quit. Strategically, this suggests that a negotiator should avoid inducing bold, firm statements from an opponent, lest one's adversary later feels trapped in a corner.

NEGOTIATOR OVERCONFIDENCE

Sticking with baseball, consider the following scenario:

> You are an adviser to a major league baseball player who is in the midst of contract negotiations. In baseball, a system exists for resolving compensation conflicts that calls for a player and a team owner who do not agree to submit final offers to an arbitrator. Using final-offer arbitration, the arbitrator must accept one position or the other, not a compromise. Thus, the challenge for each side is to come just a little closer to the arbitrator's perception of the appropriate compensation package than the opposition. In this case, your best intuitive estimate of the final offer that the team owner will submit is a package worth $600,000 per year. You believe that an appropriate wage would be $1,000,000 per year but estimate the arbitrator's opinion to be $800,000 per year. What final offer do you advise your client to propose?

This scenario sets up a common cognitive trap for negotiators. As we learned in Chapter 2, individuals are systematically overconfident that their judgments are correct. Thus, they are likely to be overconfident in estimating the position of a neutral third party and in estimating the likelihood that the third party will accept their position. In the baseball example, the overconfidence bias suggests that you are likely to submit an inappropriately high offer and overestimate the likelihood that the offer will be accepted. For example, if you believe the arbitrator's assessment of the appropriate wage will be $800,000, there is a good chance that it is actually much lower, perhaps $700,000. Consequently, the overconfidence bias is likely to lead you to believe that less compromise is necessary than a more objective analysis would suggest.

Research demonstrates that negotiators tend to be overconfident that their positions will prevail if they do not "give in." Similarly, negotiators in final-offer arbitration consistently overestimate the probability that their final offer will be accepted (Bazerman and Neale, 1982). In laboratory studies where there was, on average, only a 50 percent chance of a final offer being accepted, the average individual nonetheless estimated that there was a much higher probability (68 percent) that his or her offer would be accepted. Overconfidence may inhibit a variety of settlements, despite the existence of a positive bargaining zone. If we consider a final offer as a judgment of how much compromise is necessary to win the arbitration, it is easy to argue that when negotiators are overconfident that a particular position will be accepted, their reservation point becomes more extreme and their incentive to compromise is reduced. If a more accurate assessment is made, the negotiator is likely to be more uncertain and uncomfortable about the probability of success and is more likely to accept a compromise. Based on the biasing impact of this overconfidence, Neale and Bazerman (1985) found "appropriately" confident negotiators to exhibit more concessionary behavior and to be more successful than overly confident negotiators.

Overconfidence is most likely to occur when a party's knowledge is limited. As we learned in Chapter 2, most of us follow the intuitive cognitive rule, "When in doubt, be overconfident." This suggests that negotiators should seek objective value assessments from a neutral party, realizing that this neutral assessment is likely to be closer to the other party's position than the negotiator might have intuitively predicted.

NEGOTIATOR EGOCENTRISM

A concept closely related to negotiator overconfidence is negotiator egocentrism. While negotiator overconfidence refers to the tendency of negotiators to place too much confidence in their own assessments, negotiator egocentrism refers to their tendency to regard these assessments—as well as their overall worldview—as objectively fair. Even when two parties both sincerely claim to want an outcome that is "fair" to both sides, their very different notions of fairness can result in impasse.

Thompson and Loewenstein (1992) found that self-serving, biased attention to available information in a conflict affected the parties' perceptions of what constituted a fair settlement; in a simulated labor dispute, the magnitude of this bias affected the length of a strike. Babcock, Loewenstein, Issacharoff, and Camerer (1995) presented participants with diverse materials (depositions, medical and police reports, etc.) from a lawsuit resulting from a collision between an automobile and a motorcycle. Participants were assigned the role of plaintiff or defendant and were instructed to attempt to negotiate a settlement. If they were unable to do so, they would pay substantial penalties; in addition, they were told that the amount paid by the defendant to the plaintiff would be determined by an impartial judge who had already made his decision based on exactly the same case materials. Before negotiating, the participants were asked to predict the judge's ruling. They were told that this estimate would not be communicated to the other party and would not affect the judge's decision (which had already been made). Nevertheless, plaintiffs' predictions of the judge's award amount were substantially higher than those of defendants, and the degree of discrepancy between plaintiff and defendant was a strong predictor of whether they settled the case (as opposed to relying on the judge's decision). The participants' fairness assessments were egocentrically biased according to their assigned role.

A number of follow-up experiments attempted to reduce the magnitude of the bias. Babcock and Loewenstein (1997) rewarded participants who accurately predicted the judge's ruling with cash and had them write an essay arguing the other side's point of view. Neither of these interventions had a measurable effect; participants consistently believed that the judge's own perception of fair judgments would match their own. Other findings from the same series of experiments point to a likely psychological mechanism underlying negotiator egocentrism. Participants were presented with eight arguments favoring the side to which they had been assigned (plaintiff or defendant) and eight arguments favoring the other side. They were asked to rate the importance of these arguments as perceived "by a neutral third party." There was a strong tendency to view arguments supporting one's own position as more convincing than those supporting the other side, suggesting that the bias operates by distorting one's interpretation of evidence. Consistent with this finding, when the parties were presented with their roles (plaintiff or defendant) only after reading the case materials, the magnitude of the bias was substantially reduced and almost all of the pairs reached rapid agreement on damages.

Egocentrism is just as pervasive and detrimental to negotiated settlements in disputes involving more than two parties. Much of the findings regarding egocentrism and multiparty negotiations concern the decisions of individuals involved in "social dilemmas." In a vivid illustration of a social dilemma, Hardin (1968) offered a parable about a group of herdsmen grazing their cattle in a common pasture. Each herdsman knows that it is to his advantage to increase the size of his herd because each additional animal represents personal profit. However, the cost of grazing, measured by the damage done to the pasture, is shared by all of the herdsmen. If the total number of animals becomes too large, the pasture will be overpopulated and will eventually be destroyed. Thus, the herdsmen have a collective interest in setting individual limits to the number of cattle grazing in the pasture to a degree that matches the rate of pasture replenishment. At the same time, it is in each herdsman's interest to marginally expand his grazing cattle beyond his allotment.

Many of the natural-resource scarcity and pollution issues that we face in contemporary society resemble Hardin's "tragedy of the commons." Wade-Benzoni, Tenbrunsel, and Bazerman (1996) created a social-dilemma simulation in which a group shares a common, scarce resource—in this case, ocean shark—from which individual members can harvest. This simulation is based on the real-life fishery crisis in the northeastern United States, where species of principal groundfish have been depleted, resulting in considerable uncertainty as to when and how they will be brought back to a sustainable level. The two most critical issues facing fishery management are: (1) who will pay the cost of reversing the crisis, and (2) who will receive the subsequent benefits. Thus, the northeastern fishery captures the range of issues inherent in managing any commonly held resource. As in any social dilemma, individuals must choose between personal and group concerns. The group's best interest lies in limited harvesting, but personal interests may induce individual members to harvest excessively.

In our shark simulation, participants were assigned roles as representatives of organizations that relied on shark fishing for income. The representatives were gathering for a conference aimed at finding a solution to their common problem, the depletion of large coastal shark. All participants were told that they had two goals: (1) maximize current profit without depleting the harvest pool to a level that would be too low to provide future harvests, and (2) maximize the net present value of the profit that their associations would receive. This profit would be broken up into two components: profit received from the current harvest and profit expected from future harvests. Participants were told that a given total harvest level was sustainable, enabling the species to reproduce itself at its current population level; if the total harvest rose above the given level, the species would suffer further depletion. Harvesting above the sustainable level decreased opportunities for future harvesting, resulting in a net decrease in total profit.

A characteristic of virtually all real-world social dilemmas is asymmetry in the parties' contribution to the problem and their willingness to cooperate with proposed solutions. When asymmetry exists, negotiators are likely to exhibit egocentrism in their judgments about the fairness of resource distribution. To capture this asymmetry in the simulation, participants were told that their organizations placed different weights on the importance of future shark harvests. Specifically, those participants who represented commercial fishing groups harvested relatively large numbers of shark and had a relatively low interest in the future health of the resource. By contrast, the representatives of recreational fishing groups harvested fewer shark and had a very strong interest in the resource's future. Consistent with the real-world situation, participants were told that the commercial groups were better equipped than recreational groups to switch to a different kind of fish should the shark resource be depleted.

After receiving the information just described, but before their simulated conference, the participants recorded what they personally believed to be a fair solution to the crisis. During the 30-minute conference that followed, participants discussed the issues and potential solutions, but did not make binding commitments. Participants were again asked to make individual fairness judgments following the conference. Egocentric interpretations of fairness were the common pattern in this asymmetric resource dilemma. In addition, we found that the amount of harvesting carried out by each group was positively related to the strength of the level of egocentrism. Discussion of the issues reduced egocentric biases, thereby increasing cooperation. This research strongly suggests that asymmetry is a key driver of egocentrism and overharvesting. Real-world resource dilemmas represent a critical area where ambiguity enables individuals to justify what they want to do (take a larger share of a limited resource) instead of what they should do (practice self-restraint). The source of the problem is not our desire to be unfair, but our difficulty interpreting information in an unbiased manner (Messick and Sentis, 1983). Communication-building strategies, including asking questions, seeking tradeoffs, and making concessions, are key to reducing egocentrism and creating negotiated solutions that benefit not only the interested parties, but society as a whole.

ANCHORING IN NEGOTIATIONS

Should you make the first offer in a negotiation, or wait for the other side to present theirs? Most experienced negotiators have a strong opinion on this question. I do too, and will provide it at the end of this section. First, however, I will develop the logic behind my answer with some research findings. Ritov (1996) finds that even very subtle shifts in how negotiations are anchored can create big differences in final outcomes. In her study, she varies whether buyers and sellers are looking at possible agreements that favor the buyer or those that favor the seller. She finds surprisingly big effects, such that negotiators end up closer to the end of the bargaining zone that corresponds with the starting point (the price listed at the top of the page). As a simplified example, Ritov's research suggests that if possible prices are listed as $1,000, $800, $600, $400, $200, and $0, a higher price will result than if possible prices are listed as $0, $200, $400, $600, $800, and $1,000. In addition, Ritov found that the first offer is positively correlated with the final outcome, a phenomenon that I will explore further below.

From Chapter 2, we know that people tend to be overly affected by an initial anchor, without realizing this effect. Northcraft and Neale (1987) surveyed an association of real estate brokers whose members claimed they could assess the value of a property to within 5 percent of its true or appraised value. Furthermore, they were unanimous in stating that they did not factor the listing price of the property into their personal estimate of its "true" value. Northcraft and Neale then asked four groups of professional real estate brokers and undergraduate students to estimate the value of an actual house. Both brokers and students were randomly assigned to one of four experimental groups. In each group, all participants were given a 10-page information packet about the house being sold, which included considerable information about the house, as well as data on prices and characteristics of recently sold homes in the area. The only difference in the information given to the four groups was the house's listing price, which was listed as +11 percent, +4 percent, −4 percent, or −11 percent of the actual appraised value of the property. After reading the material, all participants toured the house and the surrounding neighborhood. Participants were then asked to estimate the house's true value. The values estimated by both the brokers and the students suggest that both groups were significantly affected by the listing price (the anchor). While the students readily admitted the role that the listing price played in their decision-making process, the brokers flatly denied their use of the listing price as an anchor—despite the evidence to the contrary.

This study shows that even experts are affected by anchors, and fail to recognize their effect. You might assume, therefore, that you should try to anchor your negotiations with early, extreme offers. But this reasoning falls apart when you imagine a situation in which you have put your house on the market for $400,000, and someone quickly puts in the ridiculously low offer of $150,000. Chances are, the offer will offend you, and you will refuse to negotiate further with this potential buyer. Why was their early, extreme anchor ineffective? Because anchors must be reasonable enough to capture the attention of the other side. Following our discussion in Chapter 8, you should strive to anchor within the bargaining zone, but as favorably as possible to your side.

So, should you or should you not make the first offer in a negotiation? When you have a good idea of the bargaining zone, you should make the first offer with the goal of setting an anchor. However, when the bargaining zone is highly ambiguous, you should let the other side make the first offer. Otherwise, you run the risk of either offending the other side with an extreme offer or being too concessionary.

IGNORING THE COGNITIONS OF OTHERS

Imagine that while traveling in a foreign country, you meet a merchant who is selling a very attractive gemstone. Although you have purchased a few gems in your life, you are far from an expert. After some discussion, you make the merchant an offer that you believe, but that you are not certain, is on the low side. He quickly accepts, and the transaction is completed. How do you feel? Following this quick acceptance, most people would feel uneasy about the purchase, sensing that they got a rotten deal. This sensation is known as the "winner's curse." But if you were comfortable with your voluntary offer, why would you suddenly wish it had not been accepted? As we begin to explore this paradox, consider the problem described in Exercise 9.1.

EXERCISE 9.1

ACQUIRING A COMPANY

In this exercise you represent Company A (the acquirer), which is currently considering acquiring Company T (the target) by means of a tender offer. You plan to tender in cash for 100 percent of Company T's shares but are unsure how high a price to offer. The main complication is this: The value of Company T depends directly on the outcome of a major oil exploration project it is currently undertaking. Indeed, the very viability of Company T depends on the exploration outcome. If the project fails, the company under current management will be worth nothing—$0 per share. But if the project succeeds, the value of the company under current management could be as high as $100 per share. All share values between $0 and $100 are considered equally likely. By all estimates, the company will be worth considerably more in the hands of Company A than under current management. In fact, whatever the ultimate value under current management, *the company will be worth 50 percent more under the management of A than under Company T.* If the project fails, the company is worth $0 per share under either management. If the exploration project generates a $50 per share value under current management, the value under Company A is $75 per share. Similarly, a $100 per share value under Company T implies a $150 per share value under Company A, and so on.

The board of directors of Company A has asked you to determine the price they should offer for Company T's shares. This offer must be made now, before the outcome of the drilling project is known. From all indications, Company T would be happy to be acquired by Company A, provided the price is profitable. Moreover, Company T wishes to avoid, at all cost, the potential of a takeover bid by any other firm. You expect Company T to delay a decision on your bid until the results of the project are in, then accept or reject your offer before the news of the drilling results reaches the press. Thus, you (Company A) will not know the results of the exploration project when submitting your price offer, but Company T will know the results when deciding whether or not to accept your offer. In addition, Company T is expected to accept any offer by Company A that is greater than the (per share) value of the company under current management.

As the representative of Company A, you are deliberating over price offers ranging from $0 per share (this is tantamount to making no offer at all) to $150 per share. What price offer per share would you tender for Company T's stock?

My Tender Price is $_____per share.

Source: Samuelson and Bazerman (1985).

The foregoing exercise is conceptually similar to the gem merchant problem. In the "Acquiring a Company" exercise, one firm (the acquirer) is considering making an offer to buy out another firm (the target). However, the acquirer is uncertain about the ultimate value of the target firm. It knows only that its value under current management is between $0 and $100, with all values equally likely. Since the firm is expected to be worth 50 percent more under the acquirer's management than under the current ownership, it appears to make sense for a transaction to take place. While the acquirer does not know the actual value of the firm, the target knows its current worth exactly. What price should the acquirer offer for the target?

The problem is analytically quite simple (as will be demonstrated shortly), yet intuitively perplexing. The responses of 123 MBA students from Boston University are charted in Figure 9.1. This illustration shows that the dominant response was between $50 and $75. How is this $50-to-$75 decision reached? One common, but wrong, explanation is that "on average, the firm will be worth $50 to the target and $75 to the acquirer; consequently, a transaction in this range will, on average, be profitable to both parties." Now consider the logical process that a rational response would generate in deciding whether to make an offer of $60 per share:

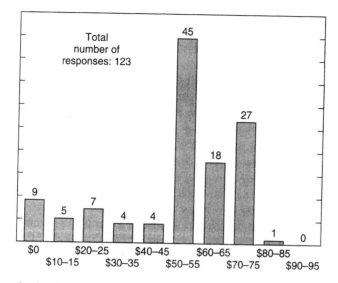

Figure 9.1 The distribution of price offers.

If I offer $60 per share, the offer will be accepted 60 percent of the time—whenever the firm is worth between $0 and $60 to the target. Since all values between $0 and $60 are equally likely, the firm will, on average, be worth $30 per share to the acquirer, resulting in a loss of $15 per share ($45 to $60). Consequently, a $60 per share offer is unwise.

It is easy to see that similar reasoning applies to any positive offer. On the average, the acquirer obtains a company worth 25 percent less than the price it pays when its offer is accepted. If the acquirer offers $X and the target accepts, the current value of the company is worth anywhere between $0 and $X. As the problem is formulated, any value in that range is equally likely, and the expected value of the offer is therefore equal to $X/2. Since the company is worth 50 percent more to the acquirer, the acquirer's expected value is 1.5($X/2) = 0.75($X), only 75 percent of its offer price. Thus, for any value of $X, the best the acquirer can do is not make an offer ($0 per share). The paradox of the situation is that even though in all circumstances the firm is worth more to the acquirer than to the target, any offer above $0 generates a negative expected return to the acquirer. The source of this paradox lies in the high likelihood that the target will accept the acquirer's offer when the firm is least valuable to the acquirer—that is, when it is a "lemon" (Akerlof, 1970).

The answer to this problem is so counterintuitive that only 9 of 123 participants correctly offered $0 per share. Replications with accounting firm partners, CEOs, investment bankers, and many other skilled groups have produced similar results. Finally, even participants who were paid according to their performance exhibited the same pattern of responses depicted in Figure 9.1 (Bazerman and Carroll, 1987).

Most individuals have the analytical ability to follow the logic that the optimal offer is $0 per share. Yet, without assistance, most individuals make a positive offer. Thus, individuals systematically exclude information from their decision-making processes that they have the ability to include. They fail to recognize that their expected return depends on an acceptance by the other party and that an acceptance is most likely to occur when it is least desirable to the negotiator making the offer.

Groucho Marx understood the tendency to ignore the decisions of others when he famously declared that he didn't want to belong to any club that would have him as a member. If a club's standards were so low as to accept *him*, he didn't want any part of it! In the bargaining context, the key feature of the "winner's curse" is that one side often has much better information than the other side; the party with the better information is usually the seller. Although we are all familiar with the slogan "buyer beware," our intuition seems to have difficulty putting this idea into practice when asymmetric information exists. Most people realize that when they buy a commodity they know little about, their uncertainty increases. The evidence presented here indicates that against an informed opponent, our expected return from such a transaction decreases dramatically. Logically, we can conclude that the knowledgeable gem merchant will accept your offer only when the gem is worth less than your estimate. To balance this inequity of information, you need to develop or borrow professional expertise, such as an independent jeweler's appraisal of the coveted gem, a mechanic's unbiased evaluation of a used car, or a professional inspector's assessment of a house. Any negotiator dealing with a better-informed opponent should seek to lessen the strong likelihood that they will fall victim to the winner's curse.

Neale and Bazerman (1983; Bazerman and Neale, 1982, 1983) found that individuals who had a greater tendency to think about the perspective of others were more successful in laboratory negotiations. This focus on the perspective of the other party allowed them to better predict the opponent's goals, expectations, and reservation points. Unfortunately, most individuals do not demonstrate this ability to take the perspective of the other party. Overall, negotiators tend to act as if their opponent is a fairly inactive party in the negotiation; they systematically ignore valuable information about the other side. Consistent with findings on negotiator role reversal, which suggests that having negotiators verbalize each other's viewpoint increases the likelihood of resolution, we can expect that training would increase the perspective-taking ability of negotiators.

A structural inefficiency is built into the Acquiring a Company exercise: A rational buyer will bid $0 despite the fact that the buyer values the company at a price higher than the seller. The problem is that the strategic seller will not provide the buyer with information about the company's true value, especially when the company is of low value. As a result, game theory recommends that buyers not make an offer in order to avoid an expected value loss. Recently, however, in an adapted version of the Acquiring a Company exercise, Valley, Moag, and Bazerman (1998) found that if the parties talk face-to-face, the common result is a trade at a mutually beneficial value. Thus, social interaction creates a mechanism to overcome the inefficient outcomes predicted by game theory and behavioral decision theory. Valley et al. suggest that communication enhances positive utility for benefits gained by the other party, creates trust, and allows for information exchange not expected by game theoretic models.

The winner's curse can also be seen in the context of competitive bidding. Organizations frequently bid against competitors to obtain important resources such as qualified job applicants. In addition, Internet auctions have become an increasingly popular form of transacting. Consider the following auctions:

> Your consulting firm is trying to hire a young, highly regarded MBA student from a prestigious university. Many other organizations are also interested in this apparently talented individual. In fact, your firm seems to be competing against these other firms, motivating you to sweeten the deal with a big signing bonus. Finally, the MBA accepts your offer. As she signs on the dotted line, you wonder if her productivity will exceed the high price of hiring her.

> Your company has placed a bid on a firm that has suggested it will gladly be acquired by the highest bidder. The actual value of the target firm is highly uncertain; even the firm itself does not know its real worth. With at least a half-dozen firms pursuing the target, your bid turns out to be the highest. Your offer is accepted and you obtain the acquisition. Should you break out the champagne?

> You just purchased the most beautiful rug you have ever seen in an Internet auction. There were a lot of bids on the rug, showing that you were not alone in recognizing its value. As you anxiously await delivery of the rug, you start to wonder: Did you get a good deal?

In each scenario, a naive analysis would suggest that you should be glad to have won the competitive situation. However, Bazerman and Samuelson (1983) argue that you may have just become the most recent victim of the "winner's curse" in competitive bidding. In the two-party negotiation setting, the winner's curse usually occurs when the buyer fails to consider the perspective of the seller. In auctions, the winner's curse typically results from the winning bidder's failure to consider the implications of bidding higher than his or her competitors—all of whom are at the same information disadvantage relative to the seller.

Bazerman and Samuelson (1983) argue that, as the highest bidder, you may have significantly overestimated the actual value of the commodity being sold. Figure 9.2 provides a graphic depiction of what may have occurred. Curve E shows the distribution of bidder estimates for the true value of the commodity, and curve B depicts the distribution of bids. The depiction assumes that (1) the mean of the distribution is equal to the true value of the commodity—that is, no aggregate under- or overestimation is expected; and (2) bidders discount their estimates a fixed amount in making bids, which explains the leftward shift of the estimate distribution. The figure suggests that a winning bid—that is, one from the right tail of the distribution—is likely to exceed the actual value of the commodity. The highest bidder is likely to have been one of the highest estimators, and unless they had reason to believe that they had better information than the other bidders, overpayment is likely. In fact, our research found that the winning bidder in auctions of highly uncertain commod-

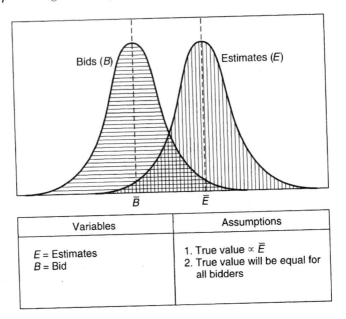

Variables	Assumptions
E = Estimates B = Bid	1. True value $\propto \bar{E}$ 2. True value will be equal for all bidders

Figure 9.2 Graphic illustration of the winner's curse.

Source: M. H. Bazerman and W. F. Samuelson, 1983, "I Won the Auction But Don't Want the Prize." *Journal of Conflict Resolution,* Vol. 27, pp. 618–634. Copyright © by Sage Publications, Inc. Reprinted by permission of Sage Publications, Inc.

ities with a large number of bidders commonly pays more than the commodity is worth.

Why does the winning bidder fall prey to the winner's curse? The answer lies in the failure of bidders to draw a key inference: If a particular bidder or bidding group assumes that their bid will win the auction, their assumption should tell them that they are likely to have overestimated the value of the commodity in comparison to other bidders. Based on this reasoning, bidders on highly uncertain commodities should adjust their estimates of the true value of the commodity downward and lower their bids accordingly. Thus, if they do win, they are less likely to have overbid, or at least not by the same margin.

Corporate takeovers in the 1980s have provided ample evidence that acquiring companies often compete destructively against each other and pay too much for what they get. As many as one-third of all acquisitions proved to be failures, and an additional one-third failed to live up to expectations. In addition, any financial synergy created by mergers usually goes to the target, not the acquirer. On average, any financial benefit achieved by the acquirer goes exclusively to shareholders. Potential acquirers should temper their optimism by recognizing that the winning bidder is likely to acquire a company that is worth far less than the winning bidder's estimate of its value.

As the Internet attracts more and more people to participate in auctions each day, the lessons of the winner's curse become more important. The good news is that eBay and other Web-based auction sites have created an excellent means to create efficient trades between a seller and a buyer who potentially values a particular item more than the seller. The bad news is that among these buyers, there will be lots of suckers. Who will they be? They are most likely to be ill-informed buyers in auctions with lots of bidders; these buyers will have failed to consider the auction from the perspective of the seller or the other bidders. So, the next time you place an online bid on a hot commodity, remember to ask what its popularity might tell you about your valuation.

The tendency to ignore the perspective of others also helps to explain the escalation bias described in Chapter 5. Why do bidders enter into Shubik's dollar-auction exercise? Because they recognize their own potential for profit, but fail to notice that other bidders will be equally optimistic about their chances of success. The central message of this section is obvious: During a negotiation, before you commit to a course of action on behalf of yourself or your organization, consider the decisions of the other party.

INTEGRATION

In Chapter 8, we learned how to think rationally in negotiations. In this chapter we explored situations in which maintaining a rational mindset can be extremely difficult, requiring great vigilance. Drawing on the individual decision-making biases introduced in Chapters 2 through 7, we have seen that many of these biases translate to the negotiation setting. First, we too readily assume a fixed-pie perspective in negotiations and fail to realize opportunities for tradeoffs. Second, our ability to assess possible settlement options is affected by the framing of those options. Framing dramatically affects not only how we view decisions as the focal negotiator, but also whether or not we are able to reach a settlement with the other party. Third, a focus on beating the other side leads us to nonrationally escalate commitment to our initial positions, especially after public statements have been made. Fourth, our tendency toward overconfidence inappropriately interferes with our ability to assess the reasonableness of our positions. Fifth, we tend to be egocentric in assessing "fair" outcomes of a negotiation. Sixth, negotiations are strongly affected by initial anchors, even when they are random. Finally, and perhaps most important, we tend to ignore the cognitions of others when assessing negotiation situations.

All of these biases can lead to foolish behaviors and unwise settlements. To become more successful negotiators, we need to understand the analytical concepts introduced in Chapter 8, while becoming more aware of the cognitive barriers that inhibit us and our opponents from applying these concepts to our own decisions.

CHAPTER TEN

Improving Decision Making

While most of us make decisions that are good enough to get us by in everyday life, we all have plenty of room to improve our judgment. Humans are not "bad" decision makers, but we do fall short of objectively rational behavior, and we do so in specific and systematic ways. The critical question is, What we can do to correct these deficiencies?

Decision researchers have responded to this question with a variety of prescriptive advice that builds on their descriptive work. This concluding chapter outlines five concrete and complementary strategies for making better decisions: (1) acquiring experience and expertise; (2) reducing bias in your judgment; (3) taking an outsider's view; (4) using linear models; and (5) adjusting intuitive predictions.

STRATEGY 1: ACQUIRING EXPERIENCE AND EXPERTISE

Many of the biases examined in this book were identified among student participants who were not rewarded for accurate performance and who were making decisions in task domains unfamiliar to them. Thus, one optimistic possibility is that experts or experienced decision makers facing important real-world decisions might be far less affected by biases than most test subjects. Does this book unfairly distort the prevalence of judgment biases? This is certainly an important question, since experience and expertise might be useful tools for improving decision making.

Some researchers believe that the process of improving judgment will occur naturally as individuals receive feedback about their past decisions. This view is represented by Kagel and Levin (1986, p. 917) in their analysis of the winner's curse in competitive bidding discussed in Chapter 9:

> Given sufficient experience and feedback regarding the outcomes of their decisions, we have no doubt that our experimental participants, as well as most bidders in "real world" settings, would eventually learn to avoid the winner's curse in any particular set of circumstances. The winner's curse is a disequilibrium phenomenon that will correct itself given sufficient time and the right kind of information feedback.

In fact, Kagel and Levin (1986) do show a reduction in the winner's curse in the auction context as the market (but not necessarily specific players) "learns" over time.

However, much of this learning can be attributed to the phenomenon in which the most aggressive bidders go broke and drop out of the market. Additional learning occurs by observing the consistent losses being suffered by "winners" in the auction.

Clearly, life experiences help us to improve numerous skills and abandon many bad habits. Unfortunately, our judgmental distortions might not be among them. Tversky and Kahneman (1986) have argued that basic judgmental biases are unlikely to correct themselves over time. Responsive learning requires accurate and immediate feedback, which is rarely available in the real world because:

> (i) outcomes are commonly delayed and not easily attributable to a particular action; (ii) variability in the environment degrades the reliability of feedback. . . . ; (iii) there is often no information about what the outcome would have been if another decision had been taken; and (iv) most important decisions are unique and therefore provide little opportunity for learning (see Einhorn and Hogarth, 1978) . . . any claim that a particular error will be eliminated by experience must be supported by demonstrating that the conditions for effective learning are satisfied. (pp. s274–s275)

Using the "Acquiring a Company" problem described in Chapter 9, Ball, Bazerman, and Carroll (1991) tested the ability of individuals to learn to avoid the winner's curse by incorporating the decisions of others into their decision making. Participants in this experiment played for real money, played in 20 trials, and were given full feedback immediately after each trial based on a random determination of the value of the firm; in addition, they could observe changes in their asset balance (which virtually always went down). Thus, when compared to the limitations cited by Tversky and Kahneman, ideal conditions existed for learning from past mistakes. The only limitation that was not eliminated, namely, the variability of the environment (ii above), is part of the winner's curse phenomenon. Thus, we were able to look at whether or not the ability to consider the cognitions of the other party in a bilateral negotiation problem can be learned in a highly favorable environment.

Remembering that $0 is the correct answer and that $50 to $75 is the answer typically obtained when decision makers ignore the cognitions of others, examine the mean bids across the 20 trials in Figure 10.1. Across the 20 trials, there is no obvious trend indicating that participants learned the correct response. In fact, only 5 of 72 participants from a leading MBA program learned over the course of the trials. Our general conclusion? Individuals are unlikely to overcome the winner's curse simply by experience or feedback.

This evidence paints a very pessimistic picture of the idea that experience will cure the decision biases identified in this book. This evidence is consistent with the documentation of extensive bias in decision making by actual investors, real estate agents, medical doctors, and numerous other "expert" groups. Neale and Northcraft (1989) proposed that biased decision-making outcomes could be eliminated or ameliorated through the development of expertise. While we often think of experience and expertise as closely related, Neale and Northcraft defined experience simply as repeated feedback. By contrast, they assert that expertise results when individuals develop a "strategic conceptualization" of what constitutes a rational decision-making process and learn to recognize the biases that limit rationality.

Figure 10.1 Mean offers across 20 trials of the "Acquiring a Company" problem.

Neale and Northcraft's experience/expertise distinction is highly relevant to the question of whether or not experienced decision makers can benefit from the study of decision making. Northcraft and Neale's (1987) study of anchoring and adjustment among real estate agents suggests that experienced decision makers can be very biased. In addition, while most "effective decision makers" are successful in a specific domain, experience without expertise can be quite dangerous when it is transferred to a different context or when the environment changes. Evidence from Chapter 2 suggests that as the amount of ignorance increases, individuals become more over-confident regarding their fallible judgment.

Thompson (2001) has found that the lessons of our experience must be in an abstract form in order to generalize to other contexts. In the context of learning to negotiate through simulations, Thompson (2001) discovered that much greater de-biasing (or learning) occurred among students when they took part in two exercises that had the same lesson and were asked how the two simulations were related than when they went through two exercises with different lessons and were asked to ex-plain the lesson of each one. Thompson argues that when people learn from one episode at a time, they too often focus on surface-level characteristics and assume that the message applies only to the specific context of the decision (e.g., buying a house). By contrast, the process of abstracting similar lessons between two episodes (such as learning to overcome the mythical fixed pie of negotiation following a house purchase and a workplace negotiation) creates generalizable insight.

Stressing the drawbacks of relying on experience for knowledge, Dawes (1988) notes that Benjamin Franklin's famous quote "experience is a dear teacher" is often misinterpreted to mean "experience is the best teacher," when in fact Franklin was using "dear" as a synonym for expensive. After all, the quote continues, "yet fools will learn in no other [school]." Dawes writes,

> Learning from an experience of failure . . . is indeed "dear," and it can even be fatal. . . .
> moreover, experiences of success may have negative as well as positive results when

people mindlessly learn from them. . . . People who are extraordinarily successful—or lucky—in general may conclude from their "experience" that they are invulnerable and consequently court disaster by failing to monitor their behavior and its implications.

This view of experience reiterates the comparative value of gaining a conceptual understanding of how to make a rational decision, rather than simply depending upon the relatively mindless, passive learning obtained via experience. Expertise requires much more than the unclear feedback of uncertain, uncontrollable, and often delayed results; it necessitates constant monitoring and awareness of our decision-making processes.

The final benefit of developing a strategic conceptualization of decision-making concerns transferability. If you were to ask experienced decision makers for the secrets of their success, they would probably insist that their skills developed over years of observation and experience and cannot be taught. This obviously reduces their ability to pass their knowledge on to others. Thus, experience without expertise limits the ability to transfer knowledge to future generations.

A key element of developing a strategic conceptualization of decision making is learning to avoid the many biases in individual and group contexts that we have discussed in Chapters 1 through 9. However, awareness is just one step in the process. Another strategy, debiasing, is the topic of the next section.

STRATEGY 2: DEBIASING JUDGMENT

Debiasing refers to a procedure for reducing or eliminating biases from the cognitive strategies of the decision maker. Fischhoff (1982) proposed four steps that decision-making teachers or trainers can follow to encourage their students to make wiser judgments: (1) offer warnings about the possibility of bias; (2) describe the direction of the bias; (3) provide a dose of feedback; and finally, (4) offer an extended program of training with feedback, coaching, and whatever else it takes to improve judgment. Fischhoff also argues that debiasing is an extremely difficult process that must be closely monitored and guided by a psychological framework for change. For example, research on the hindsight bias (Fischhoff, 1977), discussed in Chapter 2, has shown that even when the bias is explicitly described to participants and they are instructed to avoid it, the bias remains. However, research on the overconfidence bias has found that intensive, personalized feedback is moderately effective in improving judgment (Bazerman and Neale, 1983; Lichtenstein and Fischhoff, 1980).

This section offers specific suggestions for debiasing judgment based on Lewin's framework outlined in Chapter 1, Fischhoff's debiasing research, and my own judgment-training programs with MBA and executive students.

Unfreezing

Chapter 1 noted that many behaviors at the individual, group, and organizational levels are ingrained, or part of a standard repertoire, and are therefore quite difficult to change. Factors that inhibit individuals from changing their behavior include satisfaction with the status quo, risk aversion, and a preference for the certain outcomes of known behavior to the uncertain outcomes of innovative behavior. For improved decision to occur and continue over time, an explicit "unfreezing" process of ingrained thinking and behaviors must take place. For at least three key reasons, unfreezing old strategies is crucial to changing the decision-making processes of individuals.

First, individuals will have typically relied on their current intuitive strategy for many years. To want to change would be to admit that past strategies were flawed, and this realization is likely to be psychologically disturbing. Thus, individuals may be motivated to avoid the disconcerting truth about their judgmental deficiencies.

Second, individuals who have achieved a certain level of professional success (such as students in MBA and executive education programs) are likely to have received positive reinforcement for many of their past decisions. According to the basics of reinforcement theory, individuals tend to continue behaviors that are positively rewarded. For example, because many successful executives rise to the top using intuitive strategies, they tend to resist information indicating that their judgment is systematically deficient in some demonstrable manner.

A third, related point has to do with balance theory (Heider, 1958), which suggests that individuals try to manage their cognitions into a consistent order. For successful managers, the cognition that "there is something fundamentally wrong with my decision-making processes" clashes with their awareness of their success. The cognition "I am currently an excellent decision maker" is much more harmonious with the notion of success; therefore, according to balance theory, that cognition is more likely to dominate.

Overall, a pattern emerges of an intelligent manager who has multiple reasons for believing in the high quality of his or her decision-making processes and resisting any change in his or her intuitive strategies. Most successful people will be motivated to view their intuition as a talent rather than a handicap. In fact, this book has provided substantial evidence that there is significant room for improvement in the intuitive strategies of even the brightest, successful managers. Thus, we conclude that improving on intuition is an important activity for successful managers to attempt, but that cognitive resistance to change is a predictable pattern.

This book has sought to create changes in your judgment by exposing you to concrete evidence that leads you to question your current strategies. The quiz–and–feedback format was designed specifically to unfreeze your decision-making processes. Most readers make a substantial number of mistakes on these items and are then ready to learn where they went wrong and how they could have performed better. This format unfreezes the notion that your decision-making processes do not require improvement; as you begin to question your current strategies, you become receptive to alternatives. In other cases (such as the dollar auction), vivid examples were intended to unfreeze your thinking by leading you to identify with individuals who fell victim to judgmental deficiencies.

Change

Once an individual has unfrozen past behaviors, he or she becomes willing to consider alternatives. The next stage consists of making the change itself. However, change is far from guaranteed; internal resistance is likely, causing the individual to continually reassess the desirability of change. There are three critical steps to changing one's decision-making process: (1) clarification of the existence of specific judgmental deficiencies; (2) explanation of the roots of these deficiencies; and (3) reassurance that these deficiencies should not be taken as a threat to the individual's self-esteem.

The first step consists of abstracting from the concrete example that was used for unfreezing to identify the more general bias that exists. In addition, for the bias to have face validity to the individual, an explanation of why the bias exists is necessary; this often consists of clarifying the heuristic or phenomenon that underlies the bias. Finally, this information may be threatening enough to increase the resistance that was partially overcome in the unfreezing stage. Thus, it is critical that the individual understand that virtually everyone is subject to judgment biases and that having them does not imply that one is a poor decision maker, but simply that you are human.

Refreezing

Once the change takes place, it is still easy for the individual to revert back to past practices and bad habits. The old biases still exist and can be easily and even accidentally used. Meanwhile, the new procedures are foreign and must develop into intuitive strategies, a process that takes place with practice over time. As the individual consciously uses new strategies in multiple applications, they will slowly become second nature, taking the place of old patterns. However, frequent application and overviews of past training are necessary if the change is to last.

For refreezing to occur, you must continue to examine your decisions for bias long after you have finished this book. You should schedule routine checkups to evaluate your recent important decisions, those made individually and as a negotiator or group member, while remaining aware of the limits of your judgment.

STRATEGY 3: TAKING AN OUTSIDER'S VIEW

In Chapter 2, I asked you to estimate 10 obscure quantities and to place 98 percent confidence intervals around your estimates. As reported, most people only answer 3–7 of the 10 items correctly, despite being 98 percent confident of their intervals. This study bolsters the widespread finding that people are overconfident in their decisions. Interestingly, after people make these 10 assessments, and are asked to estimate the number of questions for which the correct answer will be within their confidence interval, these more global estimates are fairly accurate (Gigerenzer, Hoffrage, and Kleinbolting, 1991; Kahneman and Lovallo, 1993). That is, participants generally understand that only 3–7 of their 98 percent confidence intervals will actually contain the true estimate!

Kahneman and Lovallo (1993) explain this apparent contradiction by theorizing that we all have two perspectives on decision making: an *insider* view and an *outsider* view. The insider is the biased decision-maker who looks at each situation as unique. The outsider, on the other hand, is more capable of generalizing across situations and identifying similarities. Because these two viewpoints exist simultaneously, a member of a consulting team might be well aware that most projects take longer to complete than initial estimates (outsider view), while also believing that her own estimate of an upcoming project's duration is somehow accurate and unbiased (insider view). Similarly, people who undertake a new home construction or major home renovation know from their friends that such projects typically end up being 20–50 percent over budget and overdue (outsider view). Nevertheless, most people who initiate such a building project believe that theirs will be different—that their home will be completed on time and near the projected costs (insider view).

Kahneman identified a classic situation of insider optimism within a group of colleagues he was working with to define a new curriculum (Kahneman and Lovallo, 1993). The group estimated that the book project would take 18–30 months to complete. Kahneman asked a member of the team, who was a distinguished expert in curriculum design, "We are surely not the only team to have tried to develop a curriculum where none existed before. Please try to recall as many cases as you can. Think of them as they were in a stage comparable to ours at present. How long did it take them, from that point, to complete their project?" The team member answered that 40 percent of the projects were never completed, and none was completed in less than seven years. He also mentioned that he thought their book was "below average, but not by much" in comparison to the other projects he had worked on. As it turned out, the team took *eight years* to finish its book. This pattern resonates well with writers. Most of us understand that books take a long time to write; nonetheless, we are optimistic about meeting our own unrealistic deadlines when we sit down to write the first chapter. We may never complete the book, but we will probably believe that the next project will be different. Similarly, Cooper, Woo, and Dunkelberg (1988) found that over 80 percent of entrepreneurs perceived their chances of success to be 70 percent or better, and one-third of them described their success as certain. In contrast, they estimated the mean success rates of businesses similar to their business to be 59 percent. Meanwhile, the five-year survival rate for new businesses is only about 33 percent (Kahneman and Lovallo, 1993).

Kahneman and Lovallo provide convincing evidence that the outsider makes better estimates and decisions than the insider. The outsider view incorporates more relevant data from previous decisions—yet we tend to believe and act on the insider view. Why? Certainly, optimism and overconfidence are factors. In addition, Kahneman and Lovallo document the human tendency to consider all of a decision's various details into our judgment process and, as a consequence, to view each decision as unique. This focus on the here-and-now leads us to overlook historic data and to let our biases run wild. As a result, we follow the insider view, despite the readily available insights of the outsider view.

The insider–outsider distinction suggests another strategy to reduce bias: When making an important decision, invite an outsider to share his or her insight. This may mean conferring with a trusted friend or colleague who has experience with similar decisions. Interestingly, when a friend is building a house, we often expect that construction will cost more and take longer than expected. Our friend is the only one who doesn't know this! So, for decisions that really matter, ask a friend whom you trust for their estimate of what will happen, and understand that their outsider perspective may be more accurate than your biased insider view. Alternatively, ask yourself what your outsider self thinks of the situation. To assess this, imagine that the decision was a friend's, and ask yourself what advice you would give them. The key is to figure out how to give the outsider a stronger voice in the decision-making process.

STRATEGY 4: USING LINEAR MODELS BASED ON EXPERT JUDGMENT

The three judgment-improvement strategies I have just described respond directly to the biases discussed in this book. Debiasing is the book's central strategy for improving your decisions. However, for a number of reasons, we should examine alternative approaches. First, because we are human, we will never be entirely debiased. Second, even if we could always make the "rational" choice, the amount of time that it would take to perfect our decisions might not be worth the effort. In addition, we are often faced with the problem of creating a decision-making environment under which others, who may not be debiased, will be making decisions. Certain strategies respond to the limitations of human judgment in specific contexts by creating alternative mechanisms for debiasing intuition.

One alternative mechanism for debiasing consists of using the knowledge of an expert to build linear models that will analyze and judge future decisions. Can a computer model adequately replace human judgment? Many experts are not optimistic or even friendly to this possibility. When I asked a well-known arbitrator to make a number of decisions as part of a study on arbitrator decision-making processes, he responded:

> You are on an illusory quest! Other arbitrators may respond to your questionnaire; but in the end you will have nothing but trumpery and a collation of responses which will leave you still asking how arbitrators decide cases. Telling you how I would decide in the scenarios provided would really tell you nothing of any value in respect of what moves arbitrators to decide as they do. As well ask a youth why he is infatuated with that particular girl when her sterling virtues are not that apparent. As well ask my grandmother how and why she picked a particular "mushmelon" from a stall of "mushmelons." Judgment, taste, experience, and a lot of other things too numerous to mention are factors in the decisions (Bazerman, 1985, p. 563).

In contrast with this arbitrator's denial of the value of computer models, research in this area actually shows dramatic success. In repeatable decision-making situations, experts *can* be replaced by models based on their judgments, and these models can make better predictions than the experts! This section examines a strategy that is capable of capturing the arbitrator's decision-making model (or his grandmother's choice of mushmelon).

The statistical technique that is typically used is regression analysis.[1] This ap-

---

[1]Our purpose is not to examine the technical properties of such procedures, but to describe the essence of using a linear model to capture an expert's decision-making processes. Slovic and Lichtenstein (1971), review the technical use of regression analysis to capture decision processes.

proach necessitates that an expert make decisions based on a large number of cases, each of which is defined by the same set of factors. A regression equation that describes the expert's idiosyncratic model for making decisions is then developed.

One compelling example of the success of linear models is provided by Dawes's (1971) work on graduate school admissions decisions. Dawes modeled the average judgment of a four-person committee, using three predictors: (1) Graduate Record Examination scores, (2) undergraduate grade point average, and (3) the quality of the undergraduate school. Dawes used the model to predict the average rating of 384 applicants. He found that the model could be used to reject 55 percent of the applicant pool without ever rejecting an applicant that the selection committee had in fact accepted. In addition, the three predictors of the committee's behavior were better than the committee itself in predicting future ratings of the accepted and matriculated applicants by faculty! In 1971, Dawes estimated that the use of a linear model as a screening device by the nation's graduate schools (not to mention the larger domains of undergraduate admissions, corporate recruiting, and so on) could result in an annual savings of about $18 million in professional time. Adjusted for today's dollars and the current number of graduate-school applications, that number would easily exceed $500 million.

Researchers have found that linear policy-capturing models produce superior predictions across an impressive array of domains. In addition, research has found that more complex models produce only marginal improvements above a simple linear framework. Why do linear models work so well? Dawes (1979) argues that the underlying reason is that people are much better at selecting and coding information (such as what variables to put in the model) than they are at integrating the information (using the data to make a prediction). Einhorn (1972) illustrates this point in a study of physicians who coded biopsies of patients with Hodgkin's disease and then made an overall rating of severity. The individual ratings had no predictive power of the survival time of the patients, all of whom died of the disease. The variables that the physicians selected to code did, however, predict survival time when optimal weights were determined with a multiple regression model. The point is that the doctors knew what information to consider, but they did not know how to integrate this information consistently into valid predictions.

In addition to having difficulty integrating information, we are also unreliable. Given the same data, we will not always make the same decision. Our judgment is affected by mood, subjective interpretations, environment, deadlines, random fluctuations, and many other nonstable characteristics. In contrast, a linear model will always make the same decisions with the same inputs. Thus, the model captures the underlying policy that the expert uses while avoiding the expert's random error. Furthermore, the expert is likely to be affected by certain biases triggered by specific cases. In contrast, the model includes only the actual data that are empirically known to have predictive power, not the salience or representativeness of that or any other available data.

This point was brought home to me by the case of a graduate student, whom I will call Mark Sonet, enrolled in the department of one of my early faculty positions. Sonet was extremely bright, and his acceptance to the department was based on excellent standardized test scores, good grades, and his experience in a number of graduate programs (from which he had not graduated). In our department, Sonet was viewed as a disappointment, never seeming to make much progress toward completing his doctorate and failing to live up to his initial promise. While looking over some recent admissions decisions, I noticed an applicant who had excellent grades, strong test scores, and previous experience in graduate school. The applicant seemed to have identified his real interests, and yet my department had rejected him. It seemed apparent to me that the applicant was well above the standards of the department and would have been easily accepted by a Dawes-type admissions procedure. When I asked the decision committee why the applicant had been rejected, I was told that he reminded them too much of Mark Sonet!

Similar examples of arbitrary bias are common in financial decisions, corporate personnel decisions, bank loan decisions, and routine purchasing decisions. The common aspect of these domains is that each requires the decision maker to make multiple routine decisions based on the same set of variables. These characteristics lend themselves well to the linear policy-capturing methodology, and ample evidence suggests that the linear models of experts will outperform the experts themselves. In addition, such models allow the organization to identify the factors that are important in the decisions of its experts. Thus, independent of their superior predictive powers, the feedback and training opportunities provided by linear models make them a valuable managerial tool.

While evidence amply supports the power of policy-capturing, such models have not been widely used. Why not? Resistance to them is strong. Early in the development of the methodology, some scientists criticized their predictive ability on technical grounds (Dawes, 1979). These arguments have generally been addressed, and the literature continues to provide compelling arguments in favor of the models. Others have raised ethical concerns, such as this one described by Dawes:

> When I was at the Los Angeles Renaissance Fair last summer, I overheard a young woman complain that it was "horribly unfair" that she had been rejected by the Psychology Department at the University of California, Santa Barbara, on the basis of mere numbers, without even an interview. "How could they possibly tell what I'm like?" The answer is they can't. Nor could they with an interview (1979, p. 580).

Dawes argues that decision makers demonstrate unethical conceit in believing that a half-hour interview leads to better predictions than the information contained in a transcript covering three-and-a-half years of work and the carefully devised aptitude assessment of graduate board exams.

The other main argument against the use of linear models is that they have not been used in the past. Change is threatening. What will bank loan officers or college admissions officers do when computers make the decisions? Such concerns are common and express the fear that people are not central to the use of linear models. In fact, people play a crucial role in models. People make the initial decisions that are the ingredients of the model, and people determine the variables to put into the model. People also monitor the model's performance and determine when it needs to be updated. Nevertheless, resistance to change is natural, and resistance to the use of linear decision models is clearly no exception. Overcoming a bias against expert-based, computer-formulated judgments is yet another step you can take toward improving your decision-making abilities.

STRATEGY 5: ADJUSTING INTUITIVE PREDICTIONS

The nature of managerial life requires that one work closely with the decisions of others, reviewing recommendations, transforming recommendations into decisions, and adjusting decisions made by others in the past. The task of evaluating the decisions of others is fundamentally different from the task of auditing one's own decisions. Nonetheless, from reading this book, you have learned that everyone's decisions are influenced to some degree by a shared set of biases. How can you systematically detect bias in your own decisions and those of others? Consider the following managerial situation:

> You are the director of marketing for a retail chain that has 40 stores in 14 cities. Annual sales in these stores average between $2 million and $4 million with mean sales of $3 million. Twenty-five of the stores have opened in the last three years, and the company plans to open 30 new stores in the next four years. Because of this growth, you have hired a site location analyst to predict the sales in each potential site. Unfortunately, predicting sales in new markets is very difficult, and even the best analyst faces a great deal of uncertainty. As the marketing director, you are evaluated in part by the accuracy of the forecasts coming out of your department. The site location analyst has just given you her latest forecast, $3.8 million in annual sales for a potential site. Demographic data back up the analyst's claim that this area should make the store one of the top producers in the chain. What is your reaction to the forecast?

At a naive level, there is reason to have confidence in the analyst's forecast. After all, she knows more than you about the details of the data that underlie the prediction. In addition, your overview of the area also predicts that the store will do well in comparison to existing stores; this evaluation is based on matching the representativeness of this site to other existing sites. The prediction begins to lose force, however, when we consider the prediction in light of a basic but counterintuitive statistical concept: regression to the mean. In Chapter 2, we saw that the extremeness of our predictions should be moderated toward the mean by the degree of uncertainty in the prediction (Kahneman and Tversky, 1982).

With this rule in mind, let's imagine that the site location analyst was known for her extreme accuracy. In fact, there was a perfect (1.0) correlation between her predictions and actual sales. If this were true, it would be appropriate to rely on the $3.8 million prediction. Now let's consider the case in which there is a correlation of zero between the analyst's predictions (based on demographic data) and actual sales. If this is true, her forecast is meaningless, and the only pertinent information is that the average store has sales of $3 million. Therefore, this figure becomes your best estimate. It is most likely, in fact, that the analyst has achieved neither total success nor total failure, but an intermediate level of predictability over the course of her career. The forecast should then fall between sales of the mean store and the analyst's estimate, becoming progressively closer to the analyst's estimate as her ability to predict sales increases (Kahneman and Tversky, 1982). This analysis suggests that, as the director, you will want to reduce the forecast to somewhere between $3 million and $3.8 million, depending on your assessment of the correlation between the analyst's forecasts and actual sales. In essence, the understanding of human judgment taught by this book should help you to systematically adjust the analyst's initial decision.

The preceding analysis offers a rough guide to adjusting the decisions of others. Kahneman and Tversky (1982) have formalized this process into the five-step procedure outlined here, using the site location problem as an example. In reviewing each step, you should think about how you might convert this systematic training into an intuitive, natural response. This will allow you, as a manager, to recognize the existence and direction of a wide range of biases across a wide range of decisions and make adjustments accordingly.

1. **Select a comparison group.** This first step consists of selecting the set of past observations to which the current decision or forecast is to be compared. In the site location problem, comparing the new store to the population of all company stores is an obvious group. However, other comparison groups often exist. For example, you might decide that only stores that have opened in the last three years are appropriate for comparison, particularly if recent stores are closer in description to the future store than established stores. A more inclusive group allows for a larger base for comparison, but its heterogeneity may reduce its comparability to the targeted forecast.

2. **Assess the distribution of the comparison group.** The next step involves assessing the characteristics of the past observations to which the current decision is being compared. If the comparison group consists of all stores, we know the range and mean from the data presented. If we limit the group to recent stores, these data would need to be recalculated. In addition, we might want to get additional data about the shape of the distribution around the mean.

3. **Incorporate intuitive estimation.** This step calls for identification of the decision or forecast of the expert. In this case, the site location analyst's assessment, $3.8 million, is the intuitive estimate that needs to be adjusted. The next two steps attempt to improve this forecast.

4. **Assess the predicted results of the decision.** This is the most difficult step in the corrective procedure, as it requires us to determine the correlation between the decision or forecast and the comparison group data. It may be possible to assess this correlation by comparing past estimates to actual sales. In the absence of these data, you must determine some subjective procedure for this assessment. Kahneman and Tversky (1982) discuss this process in more detail. For our purposes, the key point is that the analyst's estimate assumes a correlation of 1.0 between her prediction and

actual sales. In virtually all cases, we must adjust away from this biased estimate.

5. **Adjust the intuitive estimate.** In this step we must calculate the adjustment that reduces the bias error of the initial decision or forecast. For example, this procedure should produce an estimate of $3.8 million when the correlation in Step 4 is 1.0, an estimate of $3 million when the correlation is zero, and estimates proportionally in-between when the correlation falls between zero and one. This adjustment can be formalized as follows:

adjusted estimate = group mean + correlation (initial estimate − group mean)

In our example it is easy to see that this leads to a prediction of $3.4 million when the correlation is 0.5, $3.6 million when the correlation is 0.75, and so on. The person making the adjustment should fully understand the logic of the procedure and evaluate its relevance to the decision at hand. When arguing for this adjustment, you must recognize that you are likely to face resistance to change.

These five steps provide a clearly delineated process for debiasing an individual's intuition by adjusting for the regression-to-the-mean bias. The formal procedure will typically improve the forecast. More important, a manager who understands the process will become capable of intuitively assessing the degree to which an initial estimate should be regressed to the mean.

We now have a model for adjusting a wide range of biased decisions in both individual and multiparty contexts. Broadly, it involves three phases. First, we need to accurately perceive and analyze the context within which the decision is being made. Next, we need to distinguish the potential bias(es) surrounding the decision and the decision makers. Finally, we need to identify and make the appropriate logical adjustments for that decision. This judgment-improvement technique can be used to evaluate and adjust our own, as well as others', intuitive judgments in a variety of situations.

CONCLUSION

In this final chapter we have introduced five strategies for correcting the deficiencies in our decision-making. The first three strategies seek to create broad change in our intuitive responses to decision-making situations. In general, they strive to heighten our awareness of our cognitive limitations and our susceptibility to bias. The last two strategies, using linear models and adjusting intuitive judgments, provide techniques for improving specific decisions in specific contexts. They offer concrete methods for testing and adjusting actual decisions. Together, these five strategies provide tools for "changing" and "refreezing" your intuitive decision-making processes in the future.

An optimistic, but naïve, view of this book is that its readers are now immediately capable of improving their decision making. Why naïve? Because it is premature to expect readers to have fully integrated the process of changing their judgment for the better. If unfreezing did not take place, then the book failed. If you were not provided with sufficient information for change, the book again failed. However, the responsibility for refreezing new processes and using the decision-improvement strategies suggested in this last chapter lies with you. Refreezing requires a period in which you constantly review your decision-making processes for the errors identified in this book. Refreezing also requires that you be vigilant in your search for biases in the more complex world of decisions that you face. Creating lasting internal improvement in decision making is a complex task that occurs gradually over time through persistent monitoring. It is far easier to identify a bias while you are reading a book about decision making than when you are in the midst of an organizational crisis. Raiffa (1984) has found that his students are likely to use appropriate decision-making strategies in an exam when he is the teacher, but fail to generalize the relevance of these strategies to similar problems in courses taught by other instructors. Thus, making adjustments to your decision-making processes requires constant attention.

In addition to improving your own decisions, the ideas in this book should be very useful for informing you about the decisions of others. We are often faced with situations in which we are suspicious of another party's decision making, but we lack the vocabulary to articulate the flaws in their logic. This book offers systematic clues for understanding and explaining the biases of others. You can practice spotting others' biases while reading the newspaper or watching a sporting event on television. Reporters, sportscasters, politicians, and other information providers and public servants constantly make statements that exemplify the biased decision-making processes outlined in this book.

Finally, I hope that this book has broken some of your assumptions about decision making. Assumptions are the most critical barrier to creative decisions. Too often, individuals make false assumptions about problems in order to fit the problems into their previously established decision-making processes. Inefficient, biased decisions are the inevitable result.

The importance of breaking free from decision-limiting assumptions is illustrated in the final two quiz items of the book. The first is one that many readers have seen before; the second is a less well-known problem that challenges the reader in a similar manner.

Problem 1. Without lifting your pencil (or pen) from the paper, draw four (and only four) straight lines that connect all nine dots shown here:

Problem 2 (Adapted from Winklegren, 1974). You have been given four separate pieces of chain that are each three links in length. It costs $100 to open a link and $150 to close a link. All links are closed at the beginning of the problem. Your goal is to join all 12 links of chain into a single circle. Your total budget for forming the single circle is $750.

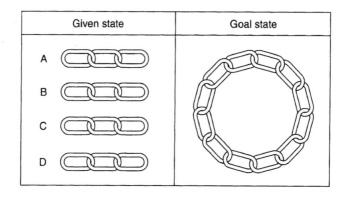

Given state	Goal state

For the first problem, most people come up with unsuccessful attempts that look like one of the following:

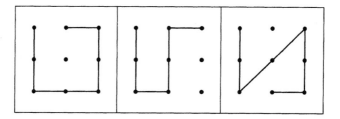

Why are most people unable to solve this problem? Because most people apply their logical decision-making skills to the perceived problem: connecting all nine dots without going outside the boundaries imposed by the nine dots. They make assumptions that frame the problem and constrain them from finding a solution.

Once the assumption that there is a barrier around the nine dots has been broken, the following solution is fairly easy to achieve:

The chain problem is quite similar to the nine-dot problem. Most people fail to connect the chain because they falsely assume that after you open one link you can insert only one closed link into the opened link. For example, they try opening a link at the end of chain A, inserting an end link of chain B, and closing the joining link. They then open one end of the six-link chain and insert one of the other three-link chains, and so on. Unfortunately, this strategy will cost $1,000. A number of strategies similar to this one will also go over budget.

Some people are able to go beyond the assumption that when you open one link, you can insert only one link from another chain into the opening. Breaking this assumption leads to a variety of very similar successful solutions. For example, open all three links in chain A (cost, $300). Use one of them to combine chains B and C ($150), use the second one to combine the free end of chain C to either end of D ($150), and use the final open link to combine the remaining free ends of chains B and D ($150). The total cost is $750.

As you can see, the solution is simple. However, very bright people have studied this problem for hours without seeing the solution. Why? Because they make assumptions about the problem that eliminate the solution. Frequently, we miss the optimal solution to a problem not because we actively chose a different alternative over the optimal choice, but because we never considered the optimal choice as feasible. The reason for this oversight is typically due to the assumptions that we make. My goal in this book is to provide you with tools to break harmful assumptions about the decision-making process.

Overall, the content of this book is meant to raise your awareness of the importance of the decision-making process itself, rather than just the results of this process. I am disturbed by the fact that most managers reward results rather than good decisions. As we have seen, many decisions are made under conditions of uncertainty or for the wrong reasons. Thus, many good decisions turn out badly, and many bad decisions turn out well. To the extent that a manager rewards results, and not sound decision making, the manager is likely to be rewarding behaviors that may not work in the future.

Davis (1971) argues that "interesting" writing leads readers to question issues that they never thought about before. Thus, identifying new issues may be more important than providing new answers to old questions. In this sense, I hope this book has succeeded at being "interesting" by making you aware of aspects of your decision-making process that inspire new questions and problems.

References

AINSLIE, G. (1975). Specious reward: A behavioral theory of impulsiveness and impulse control. *Psychological Bulletin* 82, 463–509.

AKERLOF, G. (1970). The market for lemons. *Quarterly Journal of Economics* 89, 488–500.

ALLISON, S. T., MESSICK, D. M., and GOETHALS, G. R. (1989). On being better but not smarter than others: The Mohammed Ali effect. *Social Cognition* 7, 275–296.

ALPERT, M., and RAIFFA, H. (1969). A progress report on the training of probability assessors. Later published in D. Kahneman, P. Slovic, and A. Tversky (Eds.), *Judgment under uncertainty: Heuristics and biases.* Cambridge: Cambridge University Press, 1982.

ARGOTE, L., SEABRIGHT, M. A., and DYER, L. (1986). Individual versus group: Use of base-rate and individuating information. *Organizational Behavior and Human Decision Processes* 38, 65–75.

BABCOCK, L. and LOEWENSTEIN, G. (1997). Explaining bargaining impasse: The role of self-serving biases. *Journal of Economic Perspectives* 11(1), 109–126.

BABCOCK, L., LOEWENSTEIN, G., ISSACHAROFF, S., and CAMERER, C. (1995). Biased judgments of fairness in bargaining. *American Economic Review* 85 (5), 1337–1343.

BALL, S. B., BAZERMAN, M. H., and CARROLL, J. S. (1991). An evaluation of learning in the bilateral winner's curse. *Organizational Behavior and Human Decision Processes* 48, 1–22.

BARBER, B. M., and ODEAN, T. (2000a). Trading is hazardous to your wealth: The common stock investment performance of individual investors, *Journal of Finance* 55, 773–806.

BARBER, B. M., and ODEAN, T. (2000b). Boys will be boys: Gender, overconfidence, and common stock investment, *Quarterly Journal of Economics*, forthcoming.

BARBER, B. M., ODEAN, T., and ZHENG, L. (2000). Are mutual fund investors rational? Working paper.

BAR-HILLEL, M. (1973). On the subjective probability of compound events. *Organizational Behavior and Human Performance* 9, 396–406.

BAZERMAN, M. H. (1983). Negotiator judgment: A critical look at the rationality assumption. *American Behavioral Scientist* 27, 211–228.

BAZERMAN, M. H. (1984). The relevance of Kahneman and Tversky's concept of framing to organization behavior. *Journal of Management* 10, 333–343.

BAZERMAN, M. H. (1985). Norms of distributive justice in interest arbitration. *Industrial and Labor Relations Review* 38, 558–570.

BAZERMAN, M. H. (1999). *Smart money decisions.* New York: John Wiley & Sons, Inc.

BAZERMAN, M. H., and BRETT, J. M. (1991). El-Tek: A two-party negotiation simulation. Dispute Resolution Research Center, Northwestern University.

BAZERMAN, M. H., and CARROLL, J. S. (1987). Negotiator cognition. In L. L. Cummings and B. M. Staw (Eds.), *Research in Organizational Behavior*, Vol. 9, pp. 247–288. Greenwich, Conn.: JAI Press.

BAZERMAN, M. H., CURHAN, J., and MOORE, D. (2000). The death and rebirth of the social psychology of negotiations. In G. Fletcher and M. Clark (Eds.), *Blackwell Handbook of Social Psychology: Interpersonal Processes*.

BAZERMAN, M. H., CURHAN, J., MOORE, D., and VALLEY, K. (2000). Negotiations. In *Annual Review of Psychology*. Palo Alto, CA: Annual Reviews.

BAZERMAN, M. H., and GILLESPIE, J. J. (1999). Betting on the future: The virtues of contingent contracts. *Harvard Business Review*, September/October.

BAZERMAN, M. H., GIULIANO, T., and APPELMAN, A. (1984). Escalation in individual and group decision making. *Organizational Behavior and Human Performance* 33, 141–152.

BAZERMAN, M. H., and LOEWENSTEIN, G. F. (2001). Taking the bias out of bean counting. *Harvard Business Review*, January.

BAZERMAN, M. H., LOEWENSTEIN, G. F., and WHITE, S. B. (1992). Psychological determinants of utility in competitive contexts: The impact of elicitation procedure. *Administrative Science Quarterly* 37, 220–240.

BAZERMAN, M. H., MORGAN, K., and LOEWENSTEIN, G. F. (1997)). The impossibility of auditor independence. *Sloan Management Review*, Summer.

BAZERMAN, M. H., MAGLIOZZI, T., and NEALE, M. A. (1985). The acquisition of an integrative response in a competitive market. *Organizational Behavior and Human Performance* 34, 294–313.

BAZERMAN, M. H., and NEALE, M. A. (1982). Improving negotiation effectiveness under final offer arbitration: The role of selection and training. *Journal of Applied Psychology* 67, 543–548.

BAZERMAN, M. H., and NEALE, M. A. (1983). Heuristics in negotiation: Limitations to dispute resolution effectiveness. In M. H. Bazerman and R. J. Lewicki (Eds.), *Negotiating in Organizations*. Beverly Hills, Conn.: Sage.

BAZERMAN, M. H., and NEALE, M. A. (1992). *Negotiating rationally*. New York: Free Press.

BAZERMAN, M. H., RUSS, L. E., and YAKURA, E. (1987). Post-settlement settlements in dyadic negotiations: The need for renegotiation in complex environments. *Negotiation Journal* 3, 283–297.

BAZERMAN, M. H., and SAMUELSON, W. F. (1983). I won the auction but don't want the prize. *Journal of Conflict Resolution* 27, 618–634.

BAZERMAN, M. H., SCHROTH, H., PRADHAN, P., DIEKMANN, K., and TENBRUNSEL, A. (1994). The inconsistent role of comparison of others and procedural justice in reactions to hypothetical job descriptions: Implications for job acceptance decisions. *Organizational Behavior and Human Decision Processes* 60 (3), 326–352.

BAZERMAN, M. H., SCHROTH, H., PRADHAN, P., DIEKMANN, K., and TENBRUNSEL, A. (1995). Inconsistent preferences in job acceptance: The role of social comparison processes and procedural justice. Northwestern University, Dispute Resolution Research Center working paper.

BAZERMAN, M. H., TENBRUNSEL, A. E., and WADE-BENZONI, K. (1998). Negotiating with yourself and losing: Understanding and managing competing internal preferences. Working paper.

BELSKY, G., and GILOVICH, T. (1999). *Why smart people make big money mistakes*. New York: Simon and Schuster.

BENARTZI, S., and THALER, R. (1999). Naïve diversification strategies in retirement savings plans, working paper, UCLA.

BLOUNT, S., and BAZERMAN, M. H., (1996). The inconsistent evaluation of comparative payoffs in labor supply and bargaining. *Journal of Economic Behavior and Organizations* 891, 1–14.

BOGLE, J. C. (1994). *Bogle on mutual funds.* New York: Irwin.

BOLES, T. L., and MESSICK, D. M. (1990). Accepting unfairness: Temporal influence on choice. In K. Borcherding, O. Larichev, and D. M. Messick (Eds.), *Contemporary Issues in Decision Making,* pp. 375–390. Amsterdam: North Holland.

BOTTOM, W. P. (1997). The role of negotiator judgment in alliance formation and dispute resolution. Washington University. Working paper.

BREWER, M. B. (1986). Ethnocentrism and its role in intergroup conflict. In S. Worchel and W. G. Austin (Eds.), *Psychology of Intergroup Relations.* Chicago: Nelson-Hall.

BREWER, M. B., and KRAMER, R. M. (1985). The psychology of intergroup attitudes and behaviors. In M. R. Rosenzweig and L. W. Porter (Eds.), *Annual Review of Psychology* (Vol. 36, pp. 219–243). Palo Alto, Calif.: Annual Reviews.

BRINTHAUPT, T. M., MORELAND, R. L., and LEVINE, J. M. (1991). Sources of optimism among prospective group members. *Personality and Social Psychology Bulletin* 17, 36–43.

BROCKNER, J., and RUBIN, J. Z. (1985). *Entrapment in escalating conflicts.* New York: Springer-Verlag.

BRODT, S. E. (1990). Cognitive illusions and personnel management decisions. In C. L. Cooper and I. T. Robertson (Eds.), *International Review of Industrial and Organizational Psychology* (Vol. 5), pp. 229–279. New York: Wiley.

BROWN, J. D. (1986). Evaluations of self and others: Self-enhancement biases in social judgments. *Social Cognition* 4, 353–376.

CALDWELL, D. F., and O'REILLY, C. A. (1982). Responses to failures: The effects of choices and responsibility on impression management. *Academy of Management Journal* 25, 121–136.

CAMBRIDGE, R. M., and SHRECKENGOST, R. C. (1980). Are you sure? The subjective probability assessment test. Unpublished manuscript. Langley, VA.: Office of Training, Central Intelligence Agency.

CAMERER, C. F., LOEWENSTEIN, G. F., and WEBER, M. (1989). The curse of knowledge in economic settings: An experimental analysis. *Journal of Political Economy* 97, 1232–1254.

CAMPBELL, D. T. (1969). Reforms as experiments. *American Psychologist* 24, 409–429.

CARHART, M. M. (1997). On persistence in mutual fund performance. *Journal of Finance* 52, 57–82.

CHAPMAN, L. J., and CHAPMAN, J. P. (1967). Genesis of popular but erroneous diagnostic observations. *Journal of Abnormal Psychology* 72, 193–204.

COOPER, A., WOO, C., and DUNKELBERG, W. (1988). Entrepreneurs' perceived chances for success. *Journal of Business Venturing* 3, 97–108.

COX, A. D., and SUMMERS, J. O. (1987). Heuristics and biases in the intuitive projection of retail sales. *Journal of Marketing Research* 24, 290–297.

CROCKER, J. (1982). Biased questions in judgment of covariation studies. *Personality and Social Psychology Bulletin* 8, 214–220.

DAMATO, K. (1997). Mutual funds quarterly review: Ghosts of dead funds may haunt results, *Wall Street Journal,* R1.

DAVIS, M. S. (1971). That's interesting! *Philosophy of Social Science,* 309–344.

DAWES, R. M. (1971). A case study of graduate admissions: Applications of three principles of human decision making. *American Psychologist* 26, 180–188.

DAWES, R. M. (1979). The robust beauty of improper linear models in decision-making. *American Psychologist* 34, 571–582.

DAWES, R. M. (1988). *Rational choice in an uncertain world*. New York: Harcourt Brace Jovanovich.

DEBONDT, W. F. M., and THALER, R. (1985). Does the stock market overreact? *Journal of Finance* 53, 1839–85.

DIEKMANN, K. A. (1997). 'Implicit justifications' and self-serving group allocations. *Journal of Organizational Behavior* 18 (1), 3–16.

DIEKMANN, K. A., SAMUELS, S. M., ROSS, L., and BAZERMAN, M. H. (1997). Self-interest and fairness in problems of resource allocation. Working paper.

DIEKMANN, K. A., TENBRUNSEL, A. E., SHAH, P. P., SCHROTH, H. A., and BAZERMAN, M. H. (1996). The descriptive and prescriptive use of previous purchase price in negotiation. *Organizational Behavior and Human Decision Processes* 66 (2), 179–191.

EINHORN, H. J. (1972). Expert measurement and mechanical combination. *Organizational Behavior and Human Performance* 7, 86–106.

ELSTER, J. (1979). Ulysses and the Sirens: Studies in rationality and irrationality. Cambridge, UK: Cambridge University Press.

ESTY, B. (1998). The acquisition of consolidated rail corporation. Harvard Business School Case #9-298-095.

FISCHHOFF, B. (1975). Hindsight = foresight: The effect of outcome knowledge on judgment under uncertainty. *Journal of Experimental Psychology: Human Perception and Performance* 1, 288–299.

FISCHHOFF, B. (1977). Cognitive liabilities and product liability. *Journal of Products Liability* 1, 207–220.

FISCHHOFF, B. (1982). Debiasing. In D. Kahneman, P. Slovic, and A. Tversky (Eds.), *Judgment under uncertainty: Heuristics and biases*. Cambridge, Mass.: Cambridge University Press.

FISCHHOFF, B., LICHTENSTEIN, S., SLOVIC, P., DERBY, S., and KEENEY, R. (1981). *Acceptable risk*. New York: Cambridge University Press.

FISCHHOFF, B., SLOVIC, P., and LICHTENSTEIN, S. (1977). Knowing with certainty: The appropriateness of extreme confidence. *Journal of Experimental Psychology: Human Perception and Performance* 3, 552–564.

FISCHHOFF, B., SLOVIC, P., and LICHTENSTEIN, S. (1981). Lay foibles and expert fables in judgments about risk. In T. O'Riordan and R. K. Turner (Eds.), *Progress in resource management and environmental planning* (Vol. 3). Chichester: Wiley.

FISHER, R., and URY, W. (1981). *Getting to yes*. Boston: Houghton Mifflin.

FORSYTHE, R., HOROWITZ, J., SAVIN, N. E., and SEFTON, M. (1988). *Replicability, fairness and pay in experiments with simple bargaining games*. University of Iowa, working paper.

FRIEDMAN, A. (1996, October). High-altitude decision making. Paper presented at the Jeffrey Z. Rubin Memorial Conference, Cambridge, Mass.

GIGERENZER, G., HOFFRAGE, U., and KLEINBOLTING, H. (1991). Probabilistic mental models: A Brunswikian theory of confidence. *Psychological Review* 98, 506–528.

GILOVICH, T., VALLONE, R., and TVERSKY, A. (1985). The hot hand in basketball: On the misperception of random sequences. *Cognitive Psychology* 17, 295–314.

GLASSMAN, J. K., and HASSETT, K. A. (1999). *Dow 36,000: The new strategy for profiting from the coming rise in the stock market*. New York: Times Business.

GOETZMANN, W. N., and PELES, N. (1997). Cognitive dissonance and mutual fund investors. *Journal of Financial Research* 20, 145–158.

GORE, A. (1992). *Earth in the balance: Ecology and the human spirit*. Boston: Houghton Mifflin.

GOULD, C. (2000). A seven year lesson in investing. *New York Times*, July 9, 18.

GRABINER, D. (1996). Frequently asked questions about the baseball strike. [On-line]. Available: ftp://baseball.berkelely.edu/pub/baseball/faq/strike.FAQ.

GREEN, J. (2000). Talk on annuities and retirement planning. Negotiations, Organizations, and Markets seminar, Harvard Business School.

GREENWALD, A. G. (1980). The totalitarian ego: Fabrication and revision of personal history. *American Psychologist* 35, 603–618.

GUTH, W., SCHMITTBERGER, R., and SCHWARZE, B. (1982). An experimental analysis of ultimatum bargaining. *Journal of Economic Behavior and Organization* 3, 367–388.

HAMMOND, J. S., KEENEY, R. L., and RAFFIA, H. (1999). *Smart choices.* Boston, Mass.: Harvard Business School Press.

HARDIN, G. (1968). The tragedy of the commons. *Science* 162, 1243–1248.

HARRIS, S. (1946). *Banting's miracle: The story of the discovery of insulin.* Toronto: J. M. Dent and Sons.

HASTORF, A. H., and CANTRIL, H. (1954). They say a game: A case study. *Journal of Abnormal and Social Psychology* 49, 129–134.

HAZARD, T. H., and PETERSON, C. R. (1973). *Odds versus probabilities for categorical events* (Technical report, 73–2). McLean, Va.: Decisions and Designs.

HEIDER, F. (1958). *The psychology of interpersonal relations.* New York: Wiley.

HERSHEY, J. C., and SCHOEMAKER, P. J. H. (1980). Prospect theory's reflection hypothesis: A critical examination. *Organization Behavior and Human Performance* 3, 395–418.

HOCH, S. J. (1988). Who do we know: Predicting the interests and opinions of the American consumer. *Journal of Consumer Research* 5, 315–324.

HUGHES, E. J. (1978). The presidency versus Jimmy Carter. *Fortune*, December 4, 58.

JANIS, I. L. (1962). Psychological effects of warnings. In G. W. Baker and W. Chapman (Eds.), *Man and Society in Disaster.* New York: Basic Books.

JEGADEESH, N., and TITMAN, S. (1993). Returns to buying winners and selling losers: Implications for stock market efficiency. *Journal of Finance* 48, 65–91.

JOYCE, E. J., and BIDDLE, G. C. (1981). Anchoring and adjustment in probabilistic inference in auditing. *Journal of Accounting Research* 19, 120–145.

KAGEL, J. H., and LEVIN, D. (1986). The winner's curse and public information in common value auctions. *American Economic Review* 76, 894–920.

KAHNEMAN, D., KNETSCH, J. L., and THALER, R. (1986). Fairness as a constraint on profit seeking: Entitlements in the market. *American Economic Review* 76, 728–741.

KAHNEMAN, D., KNETSCH, J. L., and THALER, R. (1990). Experimental tests of the endowment effect and the coarse theorem. *Journal of Political Economy* 98, 1325–1328.

KAHNEMAN, D., and LOVALLO, D. (1993). Timid choices and bold forecasts: A cognitive perspective on risk taking. *Management Science* 39, 17–31.

KAHNEMAN, D., and MILLER, D. T. (1986). Norm theory: Comparing reality to its alternatives. *Psychological Review* 93, 136–153.

KAHNEMAN, D., and RITOV, I. (1994). Determinants of stated willingness to pay for public goods: A study in the headline method. *Journal of Risk and Uncertainty* 9, 5–38.

KAHNEMAN, D., and TVERSKY, A. (1972). Subjective probability: A judgment of representativeness. *Cognitive Psychology* 3, 430–454.

KAHNEMAN, D., and TVERSKY, A. (1973). On the psychology of prediction. *Psychological Review* 80, 237–251.

KAHNEMAN, D., and TVERSKY, A. (1979). Prospect theory: An analysis of decision under risk. *Econometrica* 47, 263–291.

KAHNEMAN, D., and TVERSKY, A. (1982). Psychology of preferences. *Scientific American* 246, 161–173.

KEYSAR, B. (1992). The illusory transparency of intention: Linguistic perspective taking in text. University of Chicago. Working paper.

KORIAT, A., LICHTENSTEIN, S., and FISCHHOFF, B. (1980). Reasons for confidence. *Journal of Experimental Psychology: Human Learning and Memory* 6, 107–118.

KRAMER, R. M. (1991). The more the merrier? Social psychological aspects of multiparty negotiations. In M. H. Bazerman, R. J. Lewicki, and B. H. Sheppard (Eds.), *Handbook of Negotiation Research: Research on Negotiation in Organizations* (Vol. 3), pp. 307–332. Greenwich, Conn.: JAI Press.

KRAMER, R. M. (1994). Self-enhancing cognitions and organizational conflict. Working paper.

KRAMER, R. M., NEWTON, E., and POMMERENKE, P. L. (1991). Self-enhancement biases and negotiator judgment: Effects of self-esteem and mood. *Organizational Behavior and Human Decision Processes.*

KRAMER, R. M., NEWTON, E., and POMMERENKE, P. L. (1993). Self-enhancement biases and negotiator judgment: Effects of self-esteem and mood. *Organizational Behavior and Human Decision Processes* 56, 113–133.

KRAMER, R. M., SHAH, P. P., and WOERNER, S. L. (1995). Why ultimatums fail: Social identity and moralistic aggression in coercive bargaining. In R. M. Kramer and D. M. Messick (Eds.), *Negotiation as a Social Process*. Thousand Oaks, Calif.: Sage Publications.

LAIBSON, D. I., REPETTO, A., TOBACMAN, J. (1998). Self-control and saving for retirement. Brookings paper on economic activity 1, 91–196.

LANGER, E. J. (1975). The illusion of control. *Journal of Personality and Social Psychology* 32, 311–328.

LARRICK, R. P. (1993). Motivational factors in decision theories: The role of self-protection. *Psychological Bulletin* 113, 440–450.

LARRICK, R. P., and BOLES, T. L. (1995). Avoiding regret in decisions with feedback: A negotiation example. *Organizational Behavior and Human Decision Processes* 63, 87–97.

LAX, D. A., and SEBENIUS, J. K. (1986). *The manager as negotiator.* New York: Free Press.

LEWIN, K. (1947). Group decision and social change. In T. M. Newcomb and E. L. Hartley (Eds.), *Readings in Social Psychology*. New York: Holt, Rinehart and Winston.

LICHTENSTEIN, S., and FISCHHOFF, B. (1980). Training for calibration. *Organizational Behavior and Human Performance* 26, 149–171.

LICHTENSTEIN, S., FISCHHOFF, B., and PHILLIPS, L. D. (1982). Calibration of probabilities: State of the art to 1980. In D. Kahneman, P. Slovic, and A. Tversky (Eds.), *Judgment under uncertainty: Heuristics and biases.* New York: Cambridge University Press.

LIND, E. A., and TYLER, T. R. (1988). *The social psychology of procedural justice.* New York: Plenum.

LOEWENSTEIN, G. (1996). Out of control: Visceral influences on behavior. *Organizational Behavior and Human Decision Processes* 65 (3), 272–292.

LOEWENSTEIN, G., THOMPSON, L., and BAZERMAN, M. H. (1989). Social utility and decision making in interpersonal contexts. *Journal of Personality and Social Psychology* 57, 426–441.

MARCH, J. G., and SIMON, H. A. (1958). *Organizations.* New York: Wiley.

MEDVEC, V. H., MADEY, S. F., and GILOVICH, T. (1995). When less is more: Counterfactual thinking and satisfaction among Olympic medalists. *Journal of Personality and Social Psychology* 69, 603–610.

MESSICK, D. M. (1991). Equality as a decision heuristic. In B. Mellers (Ed.), *Psychological Issues in Distributive Justice*. New York: Cambridge University Press.

MESSICK, D. M., BLOOM, S., BOLDIZAR, J. P., and SAMUELSON, C. D. (1985). Why we are fairer than others. *Journal of Experimental Social Psychology* 21, 480–500.

MESSICK, D. M., and SENTIS, K. (1983). Fairness, preference, and fairness biases. In D. M. Messick and S. Cook (Eds.), *Equity Theory: Psychological and Sociological Perspectives*, New York: Praeger, 61–64.

MESSICK, D. M., and SENTIS, K. (1985). Estimating social and nonsocial utility functions from ordinal data. *European Journal of Social Psychology* 15, 389–399.

MILLER, D. T., and ROSS, M. (1975). Self-serving biases in attribution of causality: Fact or fiction? *Psychological Bulletin* 82, 213–225.

MILLER, P. M., and FAGLEY, N. S. (1991). The effects of framing, problem variations, and providing rationale on choice. *Personality and Social Psychology Bulletin.*

MOORE, D. A., KURTZBERG, T. R., FOX, C. R., and BAZERMAN, M. H. (1999). Positive illusions and biases of prediction in mutual fund investment decisions. *Organizational Behavior and Human Decision Processes* 79, 95–114.

MURNIGHAN, J. K., and PILLUTLA, M. M. (1995). Fairness versus self-interest: Asymmetric moral imperatives in ultimatum bargaining. In R. Kramer and D. M. Messick (Eds.), *Negotiation as a social process.* Thousand Oaks, Calif.: Sage Publications.

NEALE, M. A., and BAZERMAN, M. H. (1983). The effect of perspective taking ability under alternate forms of arbitration on the negotiation process. *Industrial and Labor Relations Review* 36, 378–388.

NEALE, M. A., and BAZERMAN, M. H. (1985). Perspectives for understanding negotiation: Viewing negotiation as a judgmental process. *Journal of Conflict Resolution* 29, 33–55.

NEALE, M. A., and NORTHCRAFT, G. B. (1989). Experience, expertise, and decision bias in negotiation: The role of strategic conceptualization. In B. Sheppard, M. Bazerman, and R. Lewicki (Eds.), *Research on Negotiations in Organizations* (Vol. 2). Greenwich, Conn.: JAI Press.

NEW YORK STOCK EXCHANGE (2000). [On-line]. Available: http://www.nyse.com.

NISBETT, R. E., and ROSS, L. (1980). *Human inference: Strategies and shortcomings of social judgment.* Englewood Cliffs, N.J.: Prentice-Hall.

NORTHCRAFT, G. B., and NEALE, M. A. (1987). Experts, amateurs and real estate: An anchoring–and–adjustment perspective on property pricing decisions. *Organizational Behavior and Human Decision Processes* 39, 84–97.

NORTHCRAFT, G. B., and NEALE, M. A. (1993). Negotiating successful research collaboration. In J. K. Murnighan (Ed.), Social psychology in organizations: Advances in theory and research (pp. 204–224). Englewood Cliffs, NJ: Prentice-Hall.

OCHS, J., and ROTH, A. E. (1989). An experimental study of sequential bargaining. *American Economic Review* 79, 335–385.

ODEAN, T. (1998). Are investors reluctant to realize their losses? *Journal of Finance* 53, 1775–1798.

ODEAN, T. (1999). Do investors trade too much? *American Economic Review* 89, 1279–1298.

PERROW, C. (1984). *Normal accidents.* New York: Basic Books.

POLLAN, S. M., and LEVINE, M. (1997). *Die broke.* New York: Harper Business.

PRUITT, D. G., and RUBIN, J. Z. (1985). *Social conflict: Escalation, impasse, and resolution.* Reading, Mass.: Addison-Wesley.

RABIN, M., and THALER, R. H. (In press). Anomalies: Risk aversion. *Journal of Economic Perspectives.*

RAIFFA, H. (1968). Decision analysis: Introductory lectures on choices under uncertainty. Reading, Mass.: Addison Wesley; reissued in 1997, New York: McGraw-Hill.

RAIFFA, H. (1982). *The art and science of negotiation.* Cambridge, Mass.: Harvard University Press.

RAIFFA, H. (1984). Invited address to the Judgment and Decision Making Society (November), San Antonio.

RAIFFA, H. (1985). Post-settlement settlements. *Negotiation Journal* 1, 9–12.

RAIFFA, H. (2001). *Collaborative decision making.* Cambridge, MA: Belknap.

RITOV, I. (1996). Anchoring in simulated competitive market negotiation. *Organizational Behavior and Human Decision Processes* 67, 16–25.

ROSS, J., and STAW, B. M. (1986). Expo 86: An escalation prototype. *Administrative Science Quarterly* 31, 274–297.

ROSS, L., and STILLINGER, C. (1991). Barriers to conflict resolution. *Negotiation Journal* 7 (4), 389–404.

ROSS, M., and SICOLY, F. (1979). Egocentric biases in availability and attribution. *Journal of Personality and Social Psychology* 37, 332–337.

ROTH, A. E. (1991). An economic approach to the study of bargaining. In M. H. Bazerman, R. J. Lewicki, and B. H. Sheppard (Eds.), *Handbook of Negotiation Research: Research in Negotiation in Organizations* (Vol. 3). Greenwich, Conn.: JAI Press.

SALOVEY, P., and RODIN, J. (1984). Some antecedents and consequences of social comparison jealousy. *Journal of Personality and Social Psychology* 47, 780–792.

SAMUELSON, W. F., and BAZERMAN, M. H. (1985). Negotiating under the winner's curse. In V. Smith (Ed.), *Research in Experimental Economics*, Vol. 3. Greenwich, Conn.: JAI Press.

SAMUELSON, W., and ZECKHAUSER, R. (1988) Status quo bias in decision making. *Journal of Risk and Uncertainty* 1, 7–59.

SCHELLING, T. C. (1980). The intimate contest for self-command. *The Public Interest* 60, 94–118.

SCHELLING, T. C. (1984). *Choice and consequence.* Cambridge, Mass.: Harvard University Press.

SCHOEMAKER, P. J. H., and KUNREUTHER, H. (1979). An experimental study of insurance decisions. *Journal of Risk and Insurance* 46, 603–618.

SCHOORMAN, F. D. (1988). Escalation bias in performance appraisals: An unintended consequence of supervisor participation in hiring decisions. *Journal of Applied Psychology* 7(5), 58–62.

SEBENIUS, J. K. (1989). International negotiations: Problems and new approaches. Working paper.

SEBENIUS, J. K. (2000). Dealmaking essentials: Creating and claiming value for the long term. HBS Dealmaking Course Note Series, No. 800–443.

SEBENIUS, J. K., and WHEELER, M. (1994). Let the game continue. *The New York Times*, October 30, Section 3, p. 9.

SELIGMAN, M. E. P. (1991). *Learned optimism.* New York: A. A. Knopf.

SHARPE, W. F. (1991). The arithmetic of active management. *The Financial Analysts' Journal* 47, 7–9.

SHEFRIN, H. (2000). *Beyond greed and fear.* Boston: Harvard Business School Press.

SHEFRIN, H., and STATMAN, M. (1985). The disposition to sell winners too early and ride losers too long: Theory and evidence. *Journal of Finance* 40, 777–790.

SHEFRIN, H., and THALER, R. H. (1988). The behavioral life-cycle hypothesis. *Economic Inquiry* 26, 609–643.

SHLEIFER, A. (2000). *Inefficient markets.* New York: Oxford University Press.

SHUBIK, M. (1971). The dollar auction game: A paradox in noncooperative behavior and escalation. *Journal of Conflict Resolution* 15, 109–111.

SIMON, H. A. (1957). *Models of man.* New York: John Wiley and Sons, Inc.

SIMONSON, I. (1992). The influence of anticipating regret and responsibility on purchase decisions. *Journal of Consumer Research* 19, 105–118.

SLOVIC, P. (1972). Information processing, situation specificity, and the generality of risktaking behavior. *Journal of Personality and Social Psychology* 22, 128–134.

SLOVIC, P., and FISCHHOFF, B. (1977). On the psychology of experimental surprises. *Journal of Experimental Psychology: Human Perception and Performance* 3, 544–551.

SLOVIC, P., and LICHTENSTEIN, S. (1971). Comparison of Bayesian and regression approaches in the study of information processing in judgment. *Organizational Behavior and Human Performance* 6, 649–744.

SLOVIC, P., LICHTENSTEIN, S., and FISCHHOFF, B. (1982). Characterizing perceived risk. In R. W. Kataes and C. Hohenemser (Eds.), *Technological hazard management.* Cambridge, Mass.: Oelgeschlager, Gunn and Hain.

SNIEZEK, J. A., and HENRY, R. A. (1989). Accuracy and confidences in group judgment. *Organizational Behavior and Human Decision Processes* 4(3), 1–28.

SORENSON, T. C. (1965). *Kennedy.* New York: Harper and Row.

SPRANCA, M., MINSK, E., and BARON, J. (1991). Omission and commission in judgment and choice. *Journal of Experimental Social Psychology* 27, 76–105.

STAW, B. M. (1976). Knee-deep in the big muddy: A study of escalating commitment to a chosen course of action. *Organizational Behavior and Human Performance* 16, 27–44.

STAW, B. M. (1980). Rationality and justification in organizational life. In B. M. Staw and L. L. Cummings (Eds.), *Research in Organizational Behavior*, Vol. 2. Greenwich, Conn.: JAI Press.

STAW, B. M. (1981). The escalation of commitment to a course of action. *Academy of Management Review* 6, 577–587.

STAW, B. M., and HOANG, H. (1995). Sunk costs in the NBA: Why draft order affects playing time and survival in professional basketball. *Administrative Science Quarterly* 40, 474–493.

STAW, B. M., and ROSS, J. (1978). Commitment to a policy decision: A multi-theoretical perspective. *Administrative Science Quarterly* 23, 40–64.

STAW, B. M., and ROSS, J. (1980). Commitment in an experimenting society: An experiment on the attribution of leadership from administrative scenarios. *Journal of Applied Psychology* 65, 249–260.

STAW, B. M., and ROSS, J. (1987). Knowing when to pull the plug. *Harvard Business Review* 65, 68–74.

STIGLER, G., and BECKER, G. (1977). De gustibus non est disputandum. *American Economic Review* 67, 76–90.

STILLINGER, C., EPELBAUM, M., KELTNER, D., and ROSS, L. (1990). The reactive devaluation barrier to conflict resolution. Unpublished manuscript, Stanford University.

STROTZ, R. H. (1956). Myopia and inconsistency in dynamic utility maximization. *Review of Economic Studies* 23, 165–180.

SUTTON, R., and KRAMER, R. M. (1990). Transforming failure into success: Impression management, the Reagan Administration, and the Iceland Arms Control Talks. In R. L. Zahn and M. N. Zald (Eds.), *Organizations and Nation-States: New Perspectives on Conflict and Co-operation.* San Francisco: Jossey–Bass.

TAYLOR, S. E. (1989). *Positive illusions.* New York: Basic Books.

TAYLOR, S. E., and BROWN, J. (1988). Illusion and well-being: A social psychological perspective on mental health. *Psychological Bulletin* 103, 193–210.

TEGER, A. I. (1980). *Too much invested to quit: The psychology of the escalation of conflict.* New York: Pergamon Press.

TENBRUNSEL, A. E. (1995). Justifying unethical behavior: The role of expectations of others' behavior and uncertainty. Unpublished doctoral dissertation, Northwestern University.

TENBRUNSEL, A. E., and BAZERMAN, M. H. (1995). Working women: A negotiation simulation. Dispute Resolution Research Center, Northwestern University.

THALER, R. (1980). Toward a positive theory of consumer choice. *Journal of Economic Behavior and Organization* 1, 39–80.

THALER, R. (1985). Using mental accounting in a theory of purchasing behavior. *Marketing Science* 4, 12–13.

THALER, R. (2000). From homo economicus to homo sapiens. University of Chicago. Working paper.

THALER, R. H., and DE BONDT, W. F. M. (1992). A mean reverting walk down Wall Street. In R. H. Thaler (Ed.), *The winner's curse: Paradoxes and anomalies of economic life.* New York: Free Press.

THARP, P. (1998). Ladies who lunch take stock. [Online]. Available: www.nypostonline.com/business/145.htm.

THOMPSON, L. (2001). *The mind and heart of the negotiator* (2nd Ed.). Upper Saddle River, NJ: Prentice Hall.

THOMPSON, L., and LOEWENSTEIN, G. (1992). Egocentric interpretations of fairness and negotiation. *Organization Behavior and Human Decision Processes* 51, 176–197.

TRITSCH, S. (1998). Bull marketing. [Online]. Available: http://www.chicagomag.com/text/features/beards/beards.ttm.

TVERSKY, A., and KAHNEMAN, D. (1971). The belief in the 'law of numbers.' *Psychological Bulletin* 76, 105–110.

TVERSKY, A., and KAHNEMAN, D. (1973). Availability: A heuristic for judging frequency and probability. *Cognitive Psychology* 5, 207–232.

TVERSKY, A., and KAHNEMAN, D. (1974). Judgment under uncertainty: Heuristics and biases. *Science* 185, 1124–1131.

TVERSKY, A., and KAHNEMAN, D. (1981). The framing of decisions and the psychology of choice. *Science* 211, 453–463.

TVERSKY, A., and KAHNEMAN, D. (1983). Extensional versus intuitive reasoning: The conjunction fallacy in probability judgment. *Psychological Review* 90, 293–315.

TVERSKY, A., and KAHNEMAN, D. (1986). Rational choice and the framing of decisions. *Journal of Business* 59, 251–294.

TYLER, T., and HASTIE, R. (1991). The social consequences of cognitive illusions. In M. H. Bazerman, R. J. Lewicki, and B. H. Sheppard (Eds.), *Research in Negotiation in Organizations* (Vol. 3). Greenwich, Conn.: JAI Press.

VALLEY, K. L., MOAG, J. S., and BAZERMAN, M. H. (1998). A matter of trust: Effects of communication on efficiency and distribution of outcomes. *Journal of Economic Behavior and Organization* 35.

WADE-BENZONI, K. A., TENBRUNSEL, A. E., and BAZERMAN, M. H. (1996). Egocentric interpretations of fairness in asymmetric environmental social dilemmas: Explaining harvesting behavior and the role of communication. *Organizational Behavior and Human Decision Processes* 67(2), 111–126.

WADE-BENZONI, K. A., THOMPSON, L. L., and BAZERMAN, M. H. (2001). Positive illusion and environmental sensitivity: Disconfirmability and framing of self-evaulations. Working paper.

WASON, P. C. (1960). On the failure to eliminate hypotheses in a conceptual task. *Quarterly Journal of Experimental Psychology* 12, 129–140.

WINKLEGREN, W. A. (1974). *How to solve problems.* San Francisco: Freeman.

YATES, J. F., and CARLSON, B. W. (1986). Conjunction errors: Evidence for multiple judgment procedures, including 'signed summation.' *Organizational Behavior and Human Decision Processes* 37, 230–253.

ZWEIG, J. (2000). Mutual competition. *Money Magazine*. [Online]. Available: www.money.com/money/depts/investing/fundamentalist/archive/0008/html.

INDEX

Acquisition utility, 56
Adjustment, 7–8, 27–29
AIDS, 15
American Airlines, 81
Anchoring, 7–8
  biases emanating from, 27–33
  and framing, 51–52
  and hindsight bias, 36
  in negotiations, 130, 144–145
  and overconfidence, 32–33
  and perceptions of fairness, 88–89
Arms negotiations, 135–136
Asset allocation, 104, 105, 110
Associations, presumed, 17–18
Attributions, self-serving, 67
Audits, 1–2, 28–29
Availability heuristic, 6–7, 12
  and ease of recall, 14–16
  and presumed associations, 17–18
  and retrievability, 16–17

Bargaining zone, 116–117
Baseball, 138–139
Base rates, insensitivity to, 18–19
BATNA, *see* Best Alternative to a Negotiated Agreement
Beardstown Ladies, 107–108
Bernoulli, Daniel, 46
Best Alternative to a Negotiated Agreement (BATNA), 114, 116, 130
Bets, creating value through, 125–127
Bias(es), 11–40
  from anchoring/adjustment, 27–33
  from availability heuristic, 14–18
  base rates, insensitivity to, 18–19
  chance, misconceptions of, 20–23
  cognitive, 11
  confirmation trap, 34–35
  conjunction fallacy, 25–26
  conjunctive/disjunctive events bias, 29–31
  curse of knowledge, 37
  ease of recall, 14–16
  hindsight, 35–37
  incompatibility, 135

  knowledge of, 2
  motivational, 59–74
  overconfidence, 31–33
  presumed associations, 17–18
  regression to the mean, 23–25
  from representativeness heuristic, 18–27
  retrievability, 16–17
  sample size, insensitivity to, 19–20
  self-serving, 2
Bogle, J. C., 97–99
Boston Celtics, 22
Bounded rationality, 5
Brill, Jack, 98

Camp David negotiations, 117–119
Carter, Jimmy, 84
Certainty effect, 54
Certainty equivalent, 45
Chance, misconceptions of, 20–23
Change, 156–157
Choices, framing of, 49–51
Classroom tracking, 28
Cognitive bias, 11
Cold War, 135
Commitment, nonrational escalation of, 75–85
  and competitive escalation paradigm, 79–82
  and competitive irrationality, 84–85
  and impression management, 83–84
  and judgmental biases, 83
  in negotiations, 138–140
  and perceptual biases, 82
  and unilateral escalation paradigm, 77–79
Companies, acquisition of, 148–150, 153
Comparison groups, 163
Competitive escalation paradigm, 79–82
Competitive irrationality, 84–85
Computer models, 159–162
Confirmation trap, 34–35
Conjunction fallacy, 25–26
Conjunctive events, 29–31
Conrail, 81
Control, illusion of, 67

179